MacArthur's
WAR

MacARTHUR'S WAR

The Flawed Genius Who Challenged the American Political System

BEVIN ALEXANDER

BERKLEY CALIBER, NEW YORK

THE BERKLEY PUBLISHING GROUP
Published by the Penguin Group
Penguin Group (USA) Inc.
375 Hudson Street, New York, New York 10014, USA

USA I Canada I UK I Ireland I Australia I New Zealand I India I South Africa I China

Penguin Books Ltd., Registered Offices: 80 Strand, London WC2R 0RL, England
For more information about the Penguin Group, visit penguin.com.

First Edition: May 2013

Library of Congress Cataloging-in-Publication Data

Alexander, Bevin.
MacArthur's war : the flawed genius who challenged the American political system /
Bevin Alexander.—First edition.
p. cm.
Includes bibliographical references.
ISBN 978-0-425-26120-0
1. MacArthur, Douglas, 1880–1964.   2. Korean War, 1950–1953—United States.
3. Truman, Harry S., 1884–1972.   4. Civil-military relations—United States—
History—20th century.   I. Title.
E745.M3A67 2013
355.0092—dc23
2012048057

PRINTED IN THE UNITED STATES OF AMERICA

10   9   8   7   6   5   4   3   2   1

Jacket design by Jason Gill
Interior maps by Jeffrey L. Ward
Book design by Laura K. Corless

CONTENTS

ACKNOWLEDGMENTS

I want to thank Natalee Rosenstein, vice president and senior executive editor of the Berkley Publishing Group, for the tremendous support, encouragement, and perceptive advice that she gave me from beginning to end of this project. Robin E. Barletta, editorial assistant at Berkley, was splendidly supportive and helpful. She solved all technical problems, answered all questions, and made the task of researching and writing this volume a real pleasure. Rick Willet, copyeditor, corrected numerous errors, smoothed over many awkward passages, and made the text much more orderly and coherent. I am most grateful to all three of these individuals.

A book of this nature is dependent on accurate maps to make the text understandable and comprehensible. I am most fortunate in having Jeffrey L. Ward as my cartographer. His maps of China and Korea in this volume are faultless, clear, extremely easy to read, and truly beautiful. I am deeply appreciative. I wish to give special thanks to picture editor Zachary Bathon, who searched diligently through the National Archives for authentic pictures relating to the Far East in 1950 and 1951.

My agent, Agnes Birnbaum, is a solid rock of wisdom and good advice to which I have clung for a long time. I am tremendously thankful for her support, counsel, and her faith in me.

Finally, I wish to recognize my sons Bevin Jr., Troy, and David, and my daughters-in-law, Mary and Kim, for their sturdy support and unwavering encouragement.

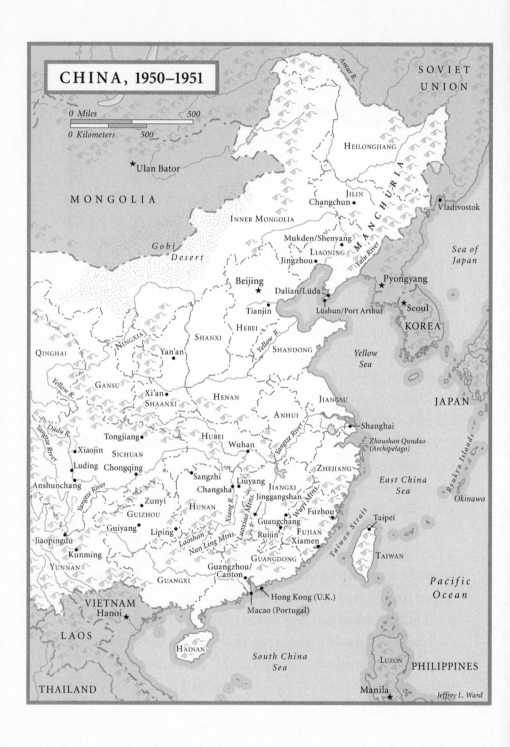

CHINA, 1950–1951

0 Miles 500
0 Kilometers 500

SOVIET UNION

MONGOLIA

Ulan Bator

Gobi Desert

INNER MONGOLIA

HEILONGJIANG

MANCHURIA

JILIN
Changchun

Vladivostok

Mukden/Shenyang
LIAONING
Jingzhou

Yalu River

Sea of Japan

Beijing

Dalian/Lüda

Pyongyang

Tianjin
HEBEI
Lüshun/Port Arthur

Seoul
KOREA

SHANXI

Yellow R.
SHANDONG

Yellow Sea

JAPAN

QINGHAI

NINGXIA
Yan'an

GANSU
Yellow R.

Xi'an
SHAANXI

HENAN

ANHUI

JIANGSU

Shanghai

Dadu R.
Xiaojin
Yangtze River
SICHUAN
Tongjiang
Luding
Chongqing
Anshunchang
Yangtze River

HUBEI
Wuhan

Yangtze River

Zhoushan Qundao (Archipelago)

ZHEJIANG

East China Sea

Ryukyu Islands

Okinawa

Sangzhi
Changsha
Liuyang
JIANGXI
Jinggangshan
Zunyi
GUIZHOU
HUNAN
Xiang R.
Laoshan
Luoxiao Mtns.
Guangchang
Ruijin
FUJIAN
Fuzhou
Wuyi Mtns.

Taipei

Guiyang
Liping
Nan Ling Mtns.
Xiamen

Taiwan Strait

Jiaopingdu
Kunming
YUNNAN
GUANGDONG
GUANGXI
Guangzhou/ Canton

TAIWAN

Pacific Ocean

VIETNAM
Hanoi

Hong Kong (U.K.)
Macao (Portugal)

LAOS

HAINAN

South China Sea

LUZON

PHILIPPINES

THAILAND

Manila

Jeffrey L. Ward

Who Will Rule:
A General or a President?

The confrontation between General Douglas MacArthur and President Harry S. Truman in 1950–51 marked the most spectacular collision between military and civil power ever to occur in the United States. If a military figure had succeeded in dictating national policy, the main premises of the Constitution—the supremacy of popular will and civilian control of the military—would have been perverted. Truman weathered the storm and preserved the American political system. But it was a bitter fight, and he achieved it despite support for MacArthur from many bellicose Republicans in Congress and despite pressure from members of the public who did not understand the principles at stake.

The conflict laid out a clear choice to the American people: was a military or a civilian leader going to control the destiny of the United States? It also laid out a clear choice between total war to eradicate Communism root and branch, and limited war to keep Communism from advancing.

MacArthur, U.S. commander in the Far East, wanted all-out war with Communist China and possibly the Soviet Union. Truman wanted to keep the armed conflict between the Communists and the Free World restricted to the peninsula of Korea.

The quarrel took on added drama because MacArthur was a famous warrior who enjoyed high prestige among the American people, whereas President Truman was not very popular. MacArthur was unquestionably brilliant and impressive, and he spoke in sweeping, grandiloquent phrases. J. Lawton Collins, the army chief of staff, wrote that MacArthur "always gave the impression of addressing not just his immediate listeners, but a large audience unseen."[1] Truman, on the other hand, was colorless, unpretentious, and he talked in matter-of-fact terms. It was not until much later that the American people began to appreciate that Truman's plain speech and down-to-earth ways concealed judgment and insight.

Adding immensely to the intensity of the conflict was a vicious dispute between the minority Republicans and the Democratic Truman administration. The Republicans had been deeply incensed that Truman had won the 1948 presidential election in spite of polls showing that the Republican nominee, Thomas E. Dewey, would win handily. Republicans were searching for any weapon to attack the Democrats. The situation in China offered an opportunity, especially since many Republicans were extremely hawkish and wanted to force a showdown with all Communists everywhere. They selected MacArthur as their champion. His oft-repeated refrain, "there is no substitute for victory," was exactly what they wanted to hear.[2]

In calling for aggressive, offensive action against Communism, the Republicans were summoning up a powerful emotion in the

American people: their vision of war as a crusade.[3] Abraham Lincoln defined the concept in the Gettysburg Address of 1863, which symbolized the conversion of the Civil War into a moral crusade for emancipation.

But in a nuclear-armed world, viewing war as a crusade and demanding unconditional surrender does not make sense. As historian John W. Spanier writes, "All-out war has become an irrational instrument of national policy, for nations do not generally defend their national interest by immolating themselves."[4]

Both sides recognized this fact in the Cuban missile crisis of 1962. When the Soviet Union began building missile sites in Cuba, the survival of the United States was at stake. President John F. Kennedy told the Soviet premier, Nikita Khrushchev, that if he did not remove the missiles, they would be removed by force—whether or not this brought on nuclear war. Khrushchev backed down at once.

The missile crisis proved that total wars are impossible between nuclear powers. Faced with its destruction, a nuclear power will use the bomb. Hence, no leader will risk obliteration of his country in order to defeat another nuclear power.

This was the actual reality in 1950, as well. Top leaders in the Truman administration recognized it, but many belligerent Republicans did not. Yet the possibility of nuclear war was ever-present from August 1949, when the Russians detonated an atomic bomb and began an intense drive to build more.

Americans still remembered with pride that World War II had been a crusade pursued to unconditional surrender. They liked to think that this was how they should fight all their wars. The realization that this no longer was possible in the nuclear age had not fully penetrated the public's consciousness. But it did so in the crisis between MacArthur and Truman in 1950 and 1951. In this collision between opposing concepts of how the nation should be governed, Americans confronted the implications of all-out war. They chose limited war.

A movement to eradicate Communism was not a reasonable objective by 1950. The Democratic Truman administration had adopted a far less combative program. It was seeking to avoid challenging the Communists by following the "containment" policy, outlined by George F. Kennan, attaché at the U.S. embassy in Moscow, in his famous "long telegram" of February 22, 1946.[5]

In this telegram, Kennan recommended that the Western democracies should not attempt to eliminate Communism or to recover territories Communists already possessed. Instead, they should resist all future Communist expansion. The Kremlin, he wrote, would not take unnecessary risks and, if defied, would retreat. Western challenges would force the Soviet Union to concentrate more and more resources on nonproductive military equipment and less on better living standards for the people. The Soviets could not endure this competition indefinitely, Kennan felt, because the industrial power of Communist countries was no match for the vast economic superiority of the West.[6] Kennan believed the Soviet state would ultimately implode, and the Soviet empire in Eastern Europe would break free.[7]

In effect, Kennan and Truman were waiting on the Soviet Union to suffer a slow death. Kennan sketched out the new approach: "Our task is to . . . compel the Soviet government either to accept combat under unfavorable conditions (which it will never do), or withdraw. In this way we can contain Soviet power until the Russians tire of the game."[8]

Kennan saw that containment was in line with the thinking of the renowned nineteenth-century Prussian military theorist Carl von Clausewitz. He wrote: "War is a mere continuation of policy by other means. . . . The political view is the object, war is the means. . . . Does the cessation of diplomatic notes stop the political relations between different nations and governments? Is not war merely another kind of writing and language for political thoughts?"[9] This was also the opinion of Sun Tzu, the ancient Chinese military sage. Both he and Clausewitz held that wars should be pursued only as far as political aims can be perceived and not a step further.[10]

Kennan elaborated on his strategy at Yale on October 1, 1946. The West needed a long-term policy "designed to keep the Russians confronted with superior strength at every juncture where they might otherwise be inclined to encroach," but needed to enact this policy in a friendly and non-provocative manner. On the same day at the Naval War College, Kennan said that the Russians, lacking easily defended borders and unable to count on domestic loyalty, would not willingly engage an adversary stronger than themselves.[11]

This strategy implied a conscious resolve to seek all ways short of war to stop the advance of Communism. In case armed conflict, despite all, did come, the strategy called for limiting its aims and its extent to the narrowest degree possible.

Joseph Stalin in effect declared war on the West in a speech on February 9, 1946. In it, he called for Soviet industrial production three times the prewar level and justified the sacrifices this would require because capitalism had created world conflict in 1914 and 1939, and was certain to do so again. The Soviet Union, Stalin said, would have to be prepared. Stalin basically repudiated his wartime alliance with the West. This speech precipitated Kennan's long tele-gram. It also opened the eyes of Harry Truman and abruptly ended his efforts to reach an accommodation with the Soviet Union.[12]

Winston Churchill launched the containment strategy on March 5, 1946, in a speech orchestrated by Truman at Westminster College, Fulton, Missouri. "From Stettin in the Baltic to Trieste in the Adriatic an iron curtain has descended across the continent," Churchill announced. A year later, on March 12, 1947, Truman asked Congress for massive aid to Greece and Turkey. Since 1945 Greece had been fighting Communist forces infiltrating from Russian satellites to the north, while Joseph Stalin was pressing Turkey to give up the Dardanelles and territory adjacent to the Russian Caucasus. Truman told Congress that "it must be the policy of the United States to support free peoples who are resisting attempted subjugation by armed minorities or by outside pressure." This was the Truman Doctrine.[13]

When the U.S. inaugurated its containment policy, China was still ruled by the right-wing Nationalist regime under Chiang Kai-shek. Thus in theory American policy was to resist Communist encroachment into this ancient land. But the true situation in China made this aim unrealistic. Since 1927, Chinese Communists had been fighting a civil war with the Nationalists. In 1946, they were a huge and growing force, ruling 90 million people in North China. Chiang was incapable of slowing their advance, and the Communists drove him and the Nationalist survivors from the mainland in the fall of 1949. Chiang, with two million of his followers, fled to the island province of Taiwan.

Many people—most especially combative Republicans in Congress—believed incorrectly that the Russians were responsible for the Chinese Communist success, and they thought the United States should drive all Communists out and restore China to Chiang Kai-shek.

The belief that all Communism everywhere was "monolithic"

and ruled from the Kremlin was an article of faith in official Washington. In the *China White Paper* of August 1949, Secretary of State Dean Acheson stated as a fact that the Chinese Communists had "foresworn their Chinese heritage" and "publicly announced their subservience to a foreign power, Russia."[14] But this was completely untrue and perilously wrongheaded.

The Kremlin had long since lost its dominance of the Chinese Communist Party after giving bad advice that had nearly destroyed the movement. In January 1935 at a conference at Zunyi in northern Guizhou province, Mao Zedong seized control of the party. He abandoned orthodox Marxism based on revolt of the urban industrial proletariat or worker, which Moscow had been demanding, and replaced it with a plan to champion the cause of the peasants, who made up 80 percent of China's population.[15]

Although this conference was unknown to the outside world for many years, U.S. Foreign Service officers picked up the Chinese Reds' independent path in 1944 and began reporting it to the State Department. But Washington authorities ignored them, despite the fact that at war's end in 1945, Joseph Stalin recognized the Nationalists as the official rulers of China and rejected the Communists. Few people heeded voices like Edgar Snow, an acquaintance of Mao Zedong and author of *Red Star over China*, who wrote in the April 9, 1949, *Saturday Evening Post* that "China will become the first Communist-run major country independent of Moscow's dictation."[16]

Nevertheless, the Truman administration based its position on China on factors only indirectly related to the Chinese Reds. Chiang Kai-shek was an extreme reactionary autocrat who supported the landowners and industrialists and who had allowed them to exploit the peasants and the few urban workers. Therefore, Truman advisers saw that any "liberation" placing the Nationalists back in control would arouse the violent opposition of the majority of the people. In addition, Chiang had proved himself to be an utterly incompetent military commander, and any campaign in China would require complete American direction and the commitment of an enormous American army, navy, and air force.

Red China did not possess the atomic bomb, but a war of extermination against the Chinese Communists would gravely imperil the Soviet Union, which shared a four-thousand-mile-long boundary with China. It might intervene, or it might strike in Europe while America was tied down in the Far East. And it might use the bomb. The Truman administration saw these dangers clearly. It decided that all-out war with China was emphatically not in American interests. Accordingly, in January 1950, it openly pulled back Kennan's theoretical containment line—or the strategic frontier that the United States would defend—to Japan, the Ryukyus (Okinawa), and the Philippines, omitting all of China, as well as Korea and Taiwan.[17]

This announcement aroused the intense antipathy of pugnacious Republicans. Many of them were quite willing to challenge Red China, despite the risk of nuclear war.[18]

In reality the only possible way to confront the Communists militarily was in limited wars, in which there was no chance of a nuclear confrontation. This was precisely the kind of war the United States got into when the North Koreans invaded South Korea on June 25, 1950. This was a war of containment, a restricted war to keep the Communists from expanding. Except for one profound but brief aberration, it was not an attempt to seize territory the Communists already possessed.

The aberration occurred in the fall of 1950. The Truman administration violated its own resolve to follow the Kennan plan, because it and the American people were mesmerized by the success of the

Inchon invasion on September 15, 1950. This invasion, conceived and carried out by MacArthur, virtually eliminated the North Korean Army without a shot being fired at it. Truman heeded both MacArthur's demands that North Korea be destroyed and prodding from the American people to carry out a crusade. He decided to ignore containment, conquer North Korea, and reunite it with South Korea in a state dependent on the United States. But the Chinese Communists forced this effort to be aborted with a powerful offensive that drove American and other United Nations forces back to the vicinity of the 38th parallel in late 1950.

Truman now saw that a war of annihilation was not a choice for the United States. He immediately gave up the idea of conquering North Korea and reinstated Kennan's containment policy.[19]

In a brilliant political move designed to keep the Americans from attacking China directly, the ruling Communist politburo designated all the forces it sent to Korea as "volunteers."[20] This created the fiction that the war was wholly limited to the peninsula. At the same time, the Chinese were determined to keep North Korea as a buffer in front of the Chinese frontier. Marshal Peng Dehuai wrote on the day, October 4, 1950, that Mao Zedong named him to command Chinese forces in Korea: "The U.S. occupation of Korea, separated from China by only a river [the Yalu], would threaten Northeast China. The U.S. could find a pretext at any time to launch a war of aggression against China."[21]

The deception about "volunteers" suited Truman very well, since he, too, wanted to keep the war restricted to the peninsula. He also wanted to end the war more or less on the basis of status quo antebellum. But this was not the view of MacArthur and it was not the view of many Republicans. It was on this fundamental difference in national policy—not to speak about the question of a nuclear holocaust and the survival of civilization—that the fight between MacArthur and Truman was carried out.

Generals or kings or dictators, with the power of armies behind them, have generally been in charge of nations and of national policies. Indeed, nations and empires historically have been created by military leaders. The Assyrian, Persian, Macedonian, Roman, and other empires of antiquity were founded by military chiefs.[22] The war bands of Germanic tribes that conquered Western Europe on the decline of Rome were commanded by military leaders. These warrior chieftains sought to establish kingdoms in which they were absolute monarchs. They were dictators by another name. The concept reached its zenith in Europe in the seventeenth and eighteenth centuries, when monarchs claimed "the divine right of kings." Under this theory, anyone who crossed the wishes of a king was acting against God himself.[23] The advance of Western civilization can be reduced to the process by which these dictators have been subdued and the people have gained control of their destinies.

But victory has always been tentative. Generals by their nature seek to impose order on undisciplined or disobedient people. Generals believe in superiors and subordinates. They think of themselves as superior and thus uniquely qualified to tell subordinates what to do. This tendency is greatly intensified in some generals who have a deep lust for power. Napoléon Bonaparte was one such general. He stopped a popular march in Paris in 1795 with "a whiff of grapeshot" from his cannons, and he destroyed French democracy in a coup d'état in 1799.

Napoléon's example has been the characteristic pattern of most societies. In 1927, Mao Zedong defined his method of taking over China through a Communist dictatorship with this notorious observation: "We must be aware that political power grows out of the barrel of a gun."[24]

Every country ruled by its military ends up as a dictatorship. Military dictatorships have been the fate of many societies: North Korea, Pakistan, Iran, Burma (Myanmar), Cuba, numerous states of Africa, and all the Arab states of the Middle East. The "Arab spring" of 2011 raised hopes that freedom could spread across the Arab world after Tunisia, Egypt, and Libya ousted dictators. But upheavals in Yemen, Bahrain, and Syria brought bloody reprisals.

The American people have been wary of military dictatorship for a long time. In June 1787 James Madison told the Constitutional Convention that the army had always been the instrument of tyranny and had enslaved the people in Europe.[25] In *The Federalist Papers* (no. 8), Alexander Hamilton wrote that Britain had avoided dictatorship only because of its insular position. If Britain had not been an island, he wrote, it would have been forced to maintain a large standing army to protect itself from other continental powers. In such a circumstance, Britain would have fallen under the absolute power of a single man.[26] To avoid the danger, the Founding Fathers insisted on inserting in the United States Constitution a provision (Article 2, Section 2) making the president, an elected civilian, the commander in chief of all military forces.

Although civilian control of the military is firmly established in American political doctrine, it has not always been accepted by highly ambitious generals.

Both Zachary Taylor and Winfield Scott, the top generals in the Mexican War of 1846–48, engaged in bitter disputes with President James K. Polk.[27] George B. McClellan, the senior Union general in the first two years of the Civil War, wrote his wife that he had received "letter after letter" begging him to assume the presidency or become a dictator. He took to referring to the president as "the original gorilla." On November 13, 1861, he refused to see Lincoln, who had been waiting an hour for him, and went to bed. Another Union officer, Joe Hooker, said publicly that the country needed a dictator to take charge of both the army and the government. Despite this, Lincoln gave him command of the Army of the Potomac. Lincoln wrote Hooker: "Only those soldiers who have gained successes can set up dictators. What I now ask of you is military success, and I will risk the dictatorship."[28] As recently as 2010, General Stanley A. McChrystal, commander in Afghanistan, challenged the American political system by making disrespectful comments about President Barack Obama in *Rolling Stone* magazine. This led to his prompt ouster.

But it was Douglas MacArthur who most overtly defied presidential supremacy and who most clearly tried to limit the authority of the Constitution. In Senate committee hearings on May 3, 1951, he testified: "I think that it is quite impossible to draw a line of differentiation and say this is a political and this is a military situation." When a country commits itself to force, he said, "the minute you reach the killing stage," the military assumes control. "A theater commander is not merely limited to a handling of his troops; he commands that whole area politically, economically, and militarily. You have to trust at this stage of the game, when politics fail, and the military takes over, you must trust the military."[29]

MacArthur tried to backtrack after the *New York Times* wrote in an editorial on May 5, 1951: "General MacArthur advances the thesis that once war has broken out the balance of control must be put in the hands of the military . . . while the administration holds that in peace or war, the civil administration remains supreme." MacArthur said what he meant was "that there should be no non-professional military interference in the handling of troops in a campaign."[30]

His response left in limbo a fundamental question: since the president, a civilian, was almost by definition a "non-professional," how was he to overrule MacArthur, who was manifestly a "professional"? In fact, MacArthur had already answered the question. Less than two months previously he had demonstrated that he wanted to decide whether the United States would or would not have war. On March 24, 1951, he tried to exclude the president by deliberately undermining a vast diplomatic move by Truman to bring about a cease-fire with the Chinese. It was this act of treachery that finally brought the collision of MacArthur and Truman to a head, and that resulted in MacArthur's finally being dismissed.

MacArthur told the Joint Chiefs of Staff (JCS) in July 1950 that the Cold War would be settled in Asia, not Europe, and he accordingly should receive absolute priority in weapons and forces.[31] This was not a rational conclusion. The Soviet Union's military power was infinitely greater than China's, and it was concentrated in Europe. Joseph Stalin not only had seized Eastern Europe, but had directly challenged the West in 1948 with the Berlin blockade. Although Washington had concluded incorrectly that Red China was an obedient satellite of the Kremlin, it was inconceivable that Stalin would fight out the Cold War in the Orient.[32]

MacArthur jumped on the North Korean invasion as evidence that the Soviet Union was using surrogates to make its aggressive conquests. But the facts did not bear this out. Not only did Red China not take part in the war, but the Soviet Union backed away from helping North Korea the moment the United States intervened, thereby confirming George Kennan's conviction that the Kremlin would not risk a direct challenge of the West.[33]

MacArthur revealed his hostile goals on December 30, 1950. He urged the Joint Chiefs to blockade the China coast, bombard China by air and from the sea to destroy its war-making potential, use Chinese Nationalist troops in Korea, and allow Nationalist troops to carry out attacks on the China coast. In an address to the U.S. Congress on April 19, 1951, he called for measures only slightly less aggressive: a blockade of the China coast, air reconnaissance of Manchuria and the China coast, and removal of all restrictions on operations by Nationalist troops against China. "War's very object is victory, not prolonged indecision," he told the Congress. "In war, there can be no substitute for victory."[34] On March 20, 1951, he repeated his proposal to use Nationalist Chinese troops in Korea in a letter to Joseph W. Martin Jr., the Republican leader in the House of Representatives.[35]

Any of these proposals would bring on a full-scale war with China. MacArthur knew this, and this is what he was looking for. But, as JCS Chairman Omar Bradley told the Senate committees on May 15, 1951, "Red China is not the powerful nation seeking to dominate the world. Frankly, in the opinion of the Joint Chiefs of Staff, this strategy would involve us in the wrong war, at the wrong place, at the wrong time, and with the wrong enemy."[36]

MacArthur's intent was proved in his December 30, 1950, message to the Joint Chiefs. In it he said that China had forced a "state of war" on the United States by its intervention in Korea. MacArthur said the actions he recommended "could severely cripple and largely neutralize China's capability to wage aggressive war, and thus save Asia from the engulfment otherwise facing it."[37]

Truman was trying by every means possible to restrict the war to the Korean peninsula. He had rejected recommendations to use Nationalist troops a couple times in the past. Therefore, MacArthur's proposals were a total repudiation of the course of action decided on by the Truman administration. It was MacArthur's refusal to abide by national policy that got him fired on April 11, 1951. The December 30 message and the address to Congress disclosed the scope of MacArthur's naked attempt to dictate national policy.

This defiance had been going on within military channels since June 14, 1950, eleven days before the North Korean attack. On that date MacArthur produced a memorandum stating that Communist occupation of Taiwan would threaten U.S. positions in the Far East and should not be allowed. This implied an American protectorate of Taiwan and direct military assistance to Chiang Kai-shek. Mac-Arthur gave the memorandum to Louis Johnson, secretary of defense, and Omar Bradley during their visit to the Far East, which ended on June 24, a day before the North Korean attack.[38]

MacArthur personified the idea that wars are to be fought to the finish, to total victory. MacArthur did not subscribe to the concept of Clausewitz or Sun Tzu. MacArthur wanted to pursue war to the bitter end. He could only be at odds with national policy in the Korean War and in regard to Red China. In both cases, the United States had only limited goals. Absolute victory was not one of them.

This book tells the story of the titanic collision between two individuals and between two concepts of how people should be led. It is also a story of a historic clash in policy with cataclysmic potential consequences. If Truman had lost and MacArthur had won, the nation, even if it had survived a nuclear holocaust, would have been far different, far less free, than it is today. Truman, in his quiet and unassuming way, saved the United States of America.

CHAPTER 1

Origins of the Far East Dilemma

The Chinese revolution of 1912 ousted the last Qing emperor and turned China into a republic. But the country fell into extreme disorder. The Nationalists or Kuomintang (KMT) formed the recognized government, but they controlled only parts of the country. Warlords ruled many provinces, the Japanese occupied Port Arthur on the southern coast of Manchuria and were encroaching on China proper, and the British and the French dominated Shanghai and numerous other commercial emporiums.[1]

The Nationalist Party itself contained two utterly incompatible factions—an authoritarian right wing under Chiang Kai-shek that supported the landlords, merchants, and industrialists, and the Communists, who were seeking to overthrow the right wing and transform China into a socialist dictatorship.

In April 1927 Chiang Kai-shek turned on the Communists and

killed all of them he could find. In alliance with right-wing groups of industrialists, Chiang slaughtered nearly all the Communists in Shanghai. Zhou Enlai, the leader there, only barely escaped and went into hiding. Chiang's troops spread a white terror to cities in South China where they killed thousands more.

On August 7, 1927, the Communists divorced themselves from the Nationalists or KMT and voted to become a rigidly centralized and secret party. The central committee elected Mao Zedong a member of the ruling politburo and named him to conduct an uprising in Hunan province. Mao (1893–1976), son of a well-to-do Hunanese peasant farmer, told the conference that Communism must become a well-organized military movement in order to succeed. Party members, he said, had not grasped this fact and would continue to fail until they had done so. Here at this conference, Mao enunciated his famous aphorism: "We must be aware that political power grows out of the barrel of a gun."[2]

Mao had come to realize that the regular Communist practice of organizing popular revolts of unorganized and largely unarmed peasants and workers had no chance of success. The masses could not go up against KMT armies firing machine guns and cannons without adequate arms, military training, and strict order. Only reliable, effective Red armies, or at least disciplined guerrilla units, dedicated to the revolution, could fight organized enemy armies and win.

Mao's ideas were borne out in the uprising in Hunan that the party had ordered him to conduct. He had only a few poorly trained groups to assist him. Popular revolts called for in the Hunanese capital of Changsha failed miserably. Mao's forces seized Liuyang, thirty miles east of Changsha, but KMT troops surrounded them and killed or captured most of the members. Nationalist militia caught Mao while he was moving between units, and marched him to within two hundred yards of militia headquarters, where doubtless he was to be shot. At this point he broke free and ran into the fields. He hid in tall grass while soldiers, and peasants forced to help search, came near him several times.

At nightfall, Mao set off across the mountains, finally reaching a point he had designated for survivors to assemble. He persuaded the battered soldiers he found there to retreat to the legendary bandit bastion, Jinggangshan, in the Luoxiao Mountains dividing Hunan and Jiangxi provinces. It was a long and arduous trip, and Mao had only a thousand men when he reached sanctuary in these rugged, heavily forested heights and protected valleys. Another Communist leader, Zhu De, and his six hundred men joined Mao in the spring of 1928. In these forbidding heights, Mao brought together revolutionaries and "floating elements" of Chinese society, including bandits and other disaffected persons. Mao recognized the revolutionary potential of such people, alienated from conventional society because of harsh taxation and exploitation.[3]

In the Jinggangshan Mao worked on his idea of how to win the revolution. With the help of Zhu De, he laid the foundation for a new kind of army with a new kind of soldier. This army over time came to be as democratic as a hierarchical command structure can be. Unlike other armies, there was no distinct officers' corps separated by class and education from the men. There were no ranks, no insignia. Men became leaders by demonstrating their ability. Men addressed commanders by their job titles, like "comrade platoon commander" or "comrade company commander." Officers did not beat or mistreat the men. Everyone lived together, ate the same food, and dressed alike. The Red Army actively proselyted soldiers from opposing forces, and because treatment was better in the Red Army, many men deserted to it. The Red cadres or party leadership groups forbade soldiers seizing food or property from the peasants. They punished rape, robbery, and violence harshly. The Communist soldier came to be seen by the people as a friend, not, as was often the case of warlord or KMT soldiers, as a plague.

In July 1928, Mao Zedong and Zhu De moved to Ruijin, 120 miles southeast in the Wuyi Mountains on the Jiangxi-Fujian border. There they set up a tiny soviet government. Other Reds created smaller rural bases in other out-of-the-way places. Mao and Zhu developed a self-sufficient territory that relied little upon guidance from Moscow or the party leaders, who had moved to secret headquarters in Shanghai.

The forces of Mao and Zhu De withstood several attempts by Chiang Kai-shek to destroy them. But in 1934, the Communist leadership insisted on abandoning the highly effective guerrilla tactics that Mao had developed. These tactics drew Nationalist troops deep into the mountains, where the Reds isolated individual units and destroyed them. This caused the remaining Nationalist forces to withdraw in haste. Instead, the Communist leadership ordered direct attacks against invading KMT forces.[4]

The directive came from Otto Braun, an agent of the Kremlin. He was a German who had served in World War I and had graduated from the Frunze Military Academy in the Soviet Union. Braun fancied himself a military expert, and he poured scorn on Mao's guerrilla methods. The time had come, Braun insisted, for the Red Army to fight a conventional war. This called for direct frontal attacks. Peng Dehuai, one of Mao's principal field commanders, fiercely opposed Braun's orders, but the Communist leadership overruled him.

Braun decided it was crucial to hold Guangchang, at the northern edge of the soviet, about fifty miles north of Ruijin. He moved a large portion of the Red forces to the town and ordered the troops to build field fortifications. Kuomintang aircraft and artillery quickly flattened the fortifications. Peng lost one thousand men the first day, and argued heatedly to withdraw the entire force. Braun again vetoed his proposal, and ordered a direct attack into the heart of KMT artillery and machine gun fire. Peng lost four thousand men dead and twenty thousand wounded. This crippled the Red Army.

There was now nothing to do but abandon the Ruijin soviet. On October 16, 1934, most of the remaining Communists, 72,000 in the Red Army and 14,500 officials, civilians, wives of important leaders, and government workers, broke through a thinly held KMT barricade about seventy-five miles southwest of Ruijin. The "long march" had begun. Moving west, mainly at night along paths and trails, the Reds were able to get past Chiang's forces. By the time he was aware of the escape, Chiang was unable to concentrate any of his four hundred thousand troops in the path of the Communist retreat.

The Reds' original plan was to find refuge in a small soviet in the mountains of northwestern Hunan province, around Sangzhi. Chiang figured out this intention, and concentrated half of his forces to block this northern movement and the other half to press on the rear of the retreating Red Army. Zhu De, the senior Red commander, realized he must get out of this trap, and ordered an all-out flight to the north-flowing Xiang River, some 250 miles west of Ruijin. The Reds had to get across this barrier before turning north toward Sangzhi.

The leading elements of the Red Army reached the Xiang on November 26, 1934. But the civilians who were carrying much of the equipment and records were far slower. This gave Chiang the opportunity to close in on the rear guard of the Red Army and destroy one of its divisions, about twenty-five hundred men. With KMT forces converging on the Xiang crossing site, Zhu De held all combat elements east of the river for three days to allow the non-combatants to get across. Kuomintang cannon and aircraft exacted terrible losses on the defending Communists, including the loss of another entire division of twenty-five hundred men.

The Red Army was now in desperate straits. The Chinese leadership was extremely angry at Otto Braun and other Kremlin advisers, blaming them for the debacle. The army was down to nearly half the force that had broken out of the Ruijin soviet, and the Communists appeared to be in a hopeless situation. To the north a large KMT army blocked movement toward Sangzhi. To the south into Guangxi province lay the certainty of attacks from all sides and a cul-de-sac from which there was no escape. To the west the prospect was almost as bad: the extremely formidable and steep heights of Laoshan ("Old Mountain") and the Five Ridges, a lofty, almost trackless extension of the Nan Ling range in northern Guangxi.

This was the critical moment when Mao Zedong exerted decisive leadership. He saw that the only way the Communist movement could survive was for the remaining people in the Red Army to cast off every nonessential piece of equipment and weapon, to form a lean core of determined partisans, and to climb over Old Mountain and the Five Ridges and to emerge into Guizhou province, where KMT forces were weak and scattered. From Guizhou, the Red Army could march either to Sangzhi in northwest Hunan or to a small Red sanctuary led by Zhang Guotao in northeastern Sichuan province.

The Red leaders realized Mao was right. The remaining army threw away all of their heavy equipment and records, keeping only rifles, machine guns, grenades, and a few mortars that could be broken down and carried on their backs. The leaders merged civilians and soldiers into one force and turned toward Old Mountain. The path in places was no more than two feet wide and was so steep that climbers often could see the soles of the shoes of the person ahead. By the time the Red Army descended to Liping, in the lower country of Guizhou on December 13, 1934, many brave men had fallen along the way, but all the timorous and less courageous had gone as well. What was left was the heart of the Communist movement, about forty thousand men and women.

Now began a dramatic series of marches, first to Zunyi in northern Guizhou province on January 7, 1935. There, on January 15, twenty Red leaders sat down for a three-day conference. Under the direction of Mao Zedong, the Communist Party abandoned its doctrinaire Marxist policies, dictated by the Kremlin, and adopted a purely Chinese policy of championing the cause of the peasants and the few urban industrial workers (1 percent of China's population). Mao seized full control of the movement at Zunyi. But the reason was not the new ideology, which most of the Chinese supported, but his demonstrated brilliance in military matters. The Red leadership realized that it could survive only if directed by Mao.

Now began several attempts to cross the Yangtze River southwest of Chongqing in order to get into Sichuan. But Chiang blocked all these efforts. Mao turned back south and aimed at the Guizhou capital of Guiyang. This drew all the Nationalist forces on a false scent. Once clear of danger, Mao veered the Red Army abruptly west and struck 250 miles into Yunnan province, aiming at the great bend of the upper Yangtze, the Golden Sands at Jiaopingdu, a caravan crossing for a thousand years. Chiang knew of this crossing as well as the Communists did, and concentrated a large force on the north bank to block the way.

But, on Mao's orders, one of his major commanders, Lin Biao, took a strong force and struck directly at the Yunnanese capital of Kunming, pressing noisily within eight miles of the city. This stirred a great panic. Chiang took the bait, removed his forces from the Golden Sands, and went to the rescue of Kunming. Meanwhile the rest of the Red Army made straight for Jiaopingdu. By May 3, 1935, most of the army was safely across the upper Yangtze. Only 5th Corps remained on the south bank, holding open passage for Lin Biao. He and his men were now racing for the Golden Sands, covering a hundred miles in forty-eight hours. By May 9, Lin Biao's men were across the river, and the 5th Corps also slipped over, setting ferryboats adrift and watching them crash on rocks in the river. Fewer than twenty-five thousand men and women remained in the Red Army, but it had survived.

Chiang Kai-shek was furious. He quickly mobilized new forces to block the Reds at one more massive barrier, the Dadu River, two hundred miles north of the Golden Sands. The Dadu rushes fast and deep down an enormous gorge out of the high plateau of Qinghai province. Both the KMT and the Reds aimed for the main crossing of the Dadu at Anshunchang. But the Reds had the most difficult approach, through high, extremely rugged highlands passable only by narrow and steep paths. The country was occupied by the Lolos, a tribe of Yi people, ousted from lower lands by the dominant Han Chinese a thousand years before and still their enemies.

Red forces reached the ferry crossing at Anshunchang on May 24, 1935, and forced back Kuomintang forces there. However, the Communists found only a few ferryboats and learned that large bodies of KMT forces were on the way. Mao Zedong now made a dramatic decision. Upstream fifty miles was the famous bridge of iron chains at Luding, swaying high above the Dadu. Anchored by huge stone buttresses on each bank, the chains stretched for 370 feet across the river. The bridge was built in 1701 and for many years had made it possible for caravans from Tibet and Nepal to reach the emperor's palace at Beijing. Nine huge chains formed the "floor" on which planks were laid, while two chains on either side made "rails" to steady man and cart.

Red elements reached the bridge at Luding on May 29 in advance of major KMT forces. An assault unit of twenty-two men rushed the bridge and secured it before defenders on the east bank could stop them. Within two hours a following regiment secured the town, and stood waiting while the main army crossed in a carnival mood. Though dangers lay ahead, the Red soldiers now knew that their army was going to survive. But it was a pitiful force compared to the army that had marched out of the Ruijin soviet. It was down to about thirteen thousand men and women. Even so, from the moment the Red Army crossed the chain bridge at Luding, the belief in its invincibility was born.

On June 12, 1935, the vanguard of the Red Army bumped into a scouting party of Zhang Guotao's Communist army at Xiaojin, seventy-five miles north of the chain bridge. Zhang had an army six times the force Mao now commanded. He wanted to build a Red soviet deep in the interior of northwestern Sichuan, an inhospitable, largely barren region populated with non-Han Chinese tribes. This plan would lose the party's Han identity and turn it into a tiny protest movement. Mao had no interest in Zhang's proposals. On September 12, 1935, Mao and six thousand men and women from the Ruijin soviet slipped away from Zhang, and struck out for Yan'an in the great loess highlands of northern Shaanxi province.

They arrived on October 21, 1935. It was a tiny force, but it represented the trained cadres that formed the intellectual treasure of the Communist movement. The legend has grown over the years: Communist China was born in the sacrifices, heroism, endurance, determination, and dedication of the few thousand men and women who survived the year-long, incredibly difficult, six-thousand-mile flight of the Communist movement from its base in the south-central provinces to its sanctuary in the harsh landscape of the northwest. There is much truth to this legend. The movement indeed might have been mortally wounded if Mao and his followers had failed. Although the terrible conditions of the peasants and workers formed the reason for the revolution, it could have taken a generation to rebuild leadership and much could have happened in the interim.

However, the enduring appeal of the march to people of all political persuasions lies in the human epic that it depicts. People are still stirred by stories of man's courage in the face of great adversity, like the march to the sea of Xenophon's ten thousand Greeks in 400 B.C. or the Army of Northern Virginia's defiance of impossible odds from the Wilderness to Appomattox in 1864–65. Unlike both of these great retreats, the long march ended ultimately in victory.

Meanwhile Japan had occupied Manchuria in 1931. By 1937 Japan's incursions into North China had led to war and to an insincere truce between the Communists and the Nationalists. When Japan attacked the United States on December 7, 1941, President Franklin D. Roosevelt elected to treat China as a great power and sought to get Chiang's help in pursuing the war. But Chiang was uninterested in making any meaningful effort, though he kept this fact from FDR. His plan was to wait for the United States to win the war for him. However, he demanded large amounts of supplies and money, which he saved to use later against the Communists.

FDR's logic in elevating China to great-power status rested on his conviction that the imperial powers—primarily Britain, France, and the Netherlands—would fade from the Far East after the war. This would create a massive power vacuum, which the Soviet Union would rush to fill. Roosevelt came up with the idea of joining American power to the Kuomintang and creating an effective ally in war and a solid anti-Communist counter to the Soviet Union in peace. He did not understand that he had linked the United States to a hopelessly reactionary regime with no interest in military, political, or economic reforms. Any such change would have destroyed the Nationalist power base and thrown the Middle Kingdom into wild disorder. U.S. aid and money served rather the opposite purpose: permitting Nationalist China to degenerate further into cliques and semi-independent military commands. These trends encouraged the Communist Party to grow stronger, accelerate the internal crisis, and shatter the illusory American policy.[5]

Roosevelt assumed that a friendly and cooperative China depended on its being ruled by the Nationalists. In fact, any unified Chinese government, including a Communist regime, would have followed policies that supported American interests in East Asia. China wanted peace and open trade so it could build a more modern and prosperous economy. It wanted to exclude the Soviet Union and end colonialism. China was not expansionist, having neither the means nor the desire to pursue such aims while the country remained a vast world awaiting development.

When the United States entered the war, FDR also supported Chiang because China was the favorite ally of the United States. Largely on account of laudatory reporting about the Nationalists in the American press (especially *Time* magazine, which idolized Chiang). Americans assumed that China was democratic.[6] Few knew of

Chiang's police-state methods and his suppression of all opponents he could reach.

There was one other misconception about China. It was that it could become a major theater to pursue the war. Secretary of War Henry Stimson believed this. General George C. Marshall, the army chief of staff, was less enthusiastic, but he did see China as the best site for airfields from which to attack Japan. Lieutenant General Joseph W. Stilwell, whom Marshall selected to become the senior American military officer in China and Burma, felt that the United States should deploy a large number of its own troops there.[7] Stilwell also believed he could organize a modern Chinese army and use it to drive the Japanese into retreat. This hope sustained Stilwell, but it was always a mirage. Chiang had no interest in creating a powerful military force, dependent upon American arms and training. Such a force would spawn new leaders who, in traditional Chinese fashion, could count on the loyalty of their soldiers and thereby could build power bases to oust Chiang.

Marshall saw little sense in sending major American military forces to China, although he entertained hopes that the Chinese could build an effective army. Since FDR relied almost wholly on Marshall for military advice, Stimson's and Stilwell's ideas for large American operations in China never had a chance.[8]

Besides, supplying China with more than a few military goods was a virtually impossible task. The only overland route was the 717-mile, ill-maintained Burma Road, hacked out of jungles and mountainsides by the hand labor of two hundred thousand men, women, and children between 1937 and 1939.[9] Beginning at Burma Railways' terminus at Lashio, in east-central Burma, the road crossed a high mountainous rampart and the deep gorges of the Salween, Mekong, and Red rivers to reach Kunming on the Yunnan plateau. Only about ten thousand tons of supplies moved up the Burma Road into China in a month, most of which vanished for private profit with the connivance of Nationalist officials.

The Japanese closed the Burma Road in 1942 when they invaded Burma, and drove British and a few Chinese troops (along with General Stilwell) entirely out of the country. The only means of approaching China was then by air over the "Hump" of the Himalaya Mountains from Sadiya in northeast India to Kunming. The seven-hundred-mile route over the snowcapped and often dangerously turbulent Himalayas, fifteen thousand feet above sea level, twice the normal operating altitude of transports, described the single most difficult and dangerous air route on earth. Though FDR knew about the mountains, he began pulling Douglas two-engine DC-3s off commercial airline routes to get the necessary aircraft. The military version of the DC-3 was the C-47. It and another two-engine transport, the C-46, were virtually the only transports used to fly over the Hump.[10]

With no chance of developing a Chinese Nationalist army that could attack the Japanese, Roosevelt seized on the idea of U.S. Army Air Force Major General Claire L. Chennault. He assured both FDR and Chiang that he could destroy Japan with just a few bombers and fighters operating from bases in eastern China.

Chennault got support directly from Madame Chiang, who arrived in New York on November 27, 1942, for an American visit that lasted until May 1943. Her ostensible reason was treatment for a recurrent skin rash but her real purpose was to promote the Nationalists. Eleanor Roosevelt, FDR's wife, visited her in the hospital and, seeing that she seemed so "small and delicate," invited her to stay in the White House, where she moved in early January 1943. She was a demanding and surly guest, expecting fawning servants everywhere.

Madame Chiang (Soong May-ling), from a prominent Chinese Christian family in Shanghai, married Chiang in 1927 at age thirty. She was the sister of Soong Ching-ling, widow of Sun Yat-sen, the founder of the Nationalist Party. She was a 1917 graduate of Wellesley College in Massachusetts and spoke perfect English with a strong Southern accent because of five years she spent as a girl at Wesleyan College in Macon, Georgia.

Madame Chiang, in FDR's words, immediately set about "vamping" important men in the administration and Congress and often succeeded because of her admitted feminine charm. She "enraptured" members when she spoke before a joint session of Congress February 18, 1943, and promoted China well at citizens' meetings around the country. Before Congress she pushed hard for the defeat of Japan before Germany and brought sustained applause when she said the Chinese were convinced it was better "not to accept failure ignominiously but to risk it gloriously." It was a patent lie, the exact opposite of the way her husband operated, but the members of Congress didn't know this.

Roosevelt quickly realized she was "as hard as steel" and wanted to get her out of the United States (and especially the White House) as soon as possible. Madame Chiang's public relations campaign did not deceive the Nobel Prize laureate and novelist of China Pearl Buck (*The Good Earth*). She wrote Mrs. Roosevelt that the government of the Chiangs and Soongs was a clique with no claim to be representative. "It is a peculiar and interesting situation," she wrote. "It cannot of course last. I fear an outbreak from the people immediately after the war."[11]

To appease Chiang, FDR allowed Chennault's air campaign to receive priority treatment. When Chennault's bombers began to have some effect on Japanese operations along the coast in 1944, however, the Japanese launched a major offensive against the air bases. At Chiang's direction, Nationalist troops retreated swiftly before the Japanese, causing Chennault to lose all of his bases, and ending his air campaign.[12]

Meantime, Chiang was getting increasingly angry at General Stilwell's continued efforts to force him to create an effective army and to cooperate with the Communists at Yan'an to fight the Japanese. He used the opportunity of a visit in June 1944 by U.S. Vice President Henry A. Wallace to get Stilwell replaced by a more tractable representative. This succeeded. Roosevelt removed Stilwell and the U.S. ambassador to China, Clarence E. Gauss, and, on September 6, 1944, sent in Major General Patrick J. Hurley, a political general from Oklahoma who had undertaken several missions for Roosevelt.

By 1944 even a semblance of cooperation between the Nationalists and the Communists had ended. Chiang kept nearly half a million of his best troops blockading the Communists at Yan'an. Meanwhile the Reds had infiltrated into North China, where the Japanese controlled the cities and the main transportation lines but the Communists controlled all the rest. By 1944 the Reds ruled 90 million people in North China and had an army of 470,000 men, though it was very poorly equipped.

Americans had a hard time understanding the confrontation between the Reds and the KMT. Americans could not conceive why the Chinese regarded an internal foe as more dangerous than an external foe. Americans could not see that the Communists represented a force that could destroy the wealth and power of the tiny Nationalist elite, who made up less than 3 percent of China's half a billion people. The Nationalists were like privileged classes everywhere. They were focused on the threat to their wealth and their way of life and were less fearful of the Japanese, who represented a more general and less acute danger. The Communists, likewise, put most of their energy into expanding their movement and spent little effort in fighting the Japanese.

Japan also was stymied. It was incapable of completing the conquest of China. Because of its commitments elsewhere, Japan could keep only about a million troops in China. They were only enough to occupy the coast and North China, leaving the Nationalists in control of southwestern China, from a capital at Chongqing in Sichuan province, and the Communists in control of northwestern China and in the rural areas of North China.

Since Chiang denied access to Yan'an, Americans knew little about the Communists. But they did fear the Russians and assumed that they would use the Chinese Reds to undermine the Nationalists after the war. Accordingly, Roosevelt tried to seal an alliance between the Chinese Reds and the Nationalists in the form of a coalition government. A coalition, FDR figured, would keep the Reds under control and prevent revolt.

This concept was based on the firm belief in Washington that Communists could not be allowed to govern countries freely because they all were under the thumb of the Kremlin. This was true of the Communist parties in Western countries, but it was not true of China. The Kremlin had helped to form the Chinese Communist Party in 1921, and it ruled the party during its early years.[13] But bad directions from Moscow had caused the Communists to lose their sanctuary in southeastern China in 1934. And in January 1935 Mao Zedong seized control of the party at the conference in Zunyi. He focused on assisting the tiny urban industrial working class and the peasants, who had been exploited by landlords, moneylenders, and the government for centuries.[14] From that moment, the Kremlin lost its control of the Chinese Communist Party. Although the Zunyi conference remained unknown in the West for many years, U.S. Foreign Service officers, who were finally able to visit Yan'an in the summer of 1944 (the "Dixie mission"), picked up on the independent course of the Chinese Reds and reported the fact to Washington. But no one was paying attention.

A coalition government was always an illusion, because each party was dedicated to the other's destruction. Even so, the United States pursued it for the next two years. The project began with the arrival of Patrick Hurley. He made a sincere effort to bring the two sides together, but it was a total failure.

Meanwhile the Yalta conference between Joseph Stalin, Roosevelt, and Winston Churchill took place February 4–11, 1945. Both Churchill and FDR had become increasingly suspicious of Soviet intentions. Roosevelt had lost hope that he could save Eastern Europe from Soviet domination, because Russian soldiers already occupied much of the region. Work on the atomic bomb was proceeding, but no one could say whether it would work. Therefore, Roosevelt still wanted the Russians to join in the war against Japan, in order to reduce American casualties. To ensure Stalin's agreement, he was willing to make major concessions. But he wanted one concession from Stalin—his recognition of Chiang Kai-shek's government, not the Communists under Mao Zedong.

The Russians had a more realistic understanding of the situation in China than the Americans. Just prior to his visit to Chiang in June 1944, Henry Wallace rendezvoused with W. Averell Harriman, U.S. ambassador to Moscow, at Tashkent in Soviet Uzebekistan. Harriman passed on to Wallace the views Stalin had just given him. Stalin said Chiang Kai-shek was the best man available under existing circumstances. He maintained that the Chinese Reds were "not real

Communists" but "margarine Communists," that is, fake Communists. Stalin said he had no aggressive intentions toward China, and recent border incidents in Xinjiang province were not significant.[15] Likewise, when Hurley was on the way to China, he met in Moscow with Soviet Foreign Minister Vyacheslav Molotov on August 31. Molotov denied any Russian connection with the Chinese Communists and insisted they "had no relation whatsoever to Communism."[16] It was a blanket repudiation of any affiliation of the Kremlin with the Chinese Reds and, judged by what happened in the months to come, sincere.

It is quite sad that American leaders did not pay attention to what Stalin and Molotov were telling them. It could have greatly influenced U.S. dealings with both sides in China. But they ignored (or disbelieved) the assurances that the Chinese Reds had no attachment to Moscow.

In light of the vast opportunities Roosevelt offered him, Stalin was fully willing to enter the Pacific war. He said he would do so two or three months after the end of the war in Europe. He agreed to recognize Chiang's government and to ignore the Communists. But he got tremendous benefits—joint Soviet-U.S.-British-Chinese trusteeship of Korea, Outer Mongolia to remain a Soviet satellite, the Soviet Union to get southern Sakhalin and the Kuril islands, the Manchurian trunk railways to be operated by a Russian-Chinese company, Dalian (Lüda) to become a free port, and Port Arthur (Lüshun) to be leased as a Soviet naval base.[17]

When the atomic bomb was successfully tested at Alamogordo, New Mexico, on July 16, 1945, the United States no longer needed the Soviet Union in the Pacific war, but by then it was too late. The deal had been struck.

Although Stalin's recognition of Chiang indicated at least a wary handling of the Chinese Communists by the Kremlin, important thinkers like George F. Kennan, a political officer in the Moscow embassy, and John Paton Davies Jr., formerly in China and now in the Moscow embassy, saw large Soviet designs on China in April 1945, and—despite what Stalin and Molotov had said—they viewed the Chinese Communist movement as being substantially under Moscow's control. In June 1945, Davies wrote, "It is clear that Communist China can now operate only in the Soviet orbit," and "Communist China will become a part of the USSR's security cordon, because, if for no other reason, it will scarcely be accepted by any other foreign alignment."[18]

Kennan's and Davies's opinions coincided with the views of other people in the U.S. government, including the ambassador to Moscow, W. Averell Harriman. Consequently, the idea that the Chinese Reds were totally subservient to the Kremlin became official U.S. doctrine, which was accepted by Harry S. Truman, who became president on April 12, 1945, upon Roosevelt's death.

When Patrick Hurley resigned his post in December 1945, President Truman appointed George C. Marshall as his envoy to China. Marshall was a far more prestigious figure than Hurley, and he had the president's ear. But Marshall's one-year effort to bring about a coalition government in China was no more successful than Hurley's. He returned to become secretary of state in January 1947, as China descended into full-scale civil war.

The question facing China was not democracy, but which of the two contending parties most accurately represented the wishes and needs of the people. The Communists had proved that their interpretation of Chinese desires enjoyed far more popular support than the Nationalists' version. This was because the Reds promised a fairer shake than the Nationalists to the exploited peasants and workers in China, who represented the vast majority of the population. The Reds promised to reduce taxes; end mistreatment by landowners, moneylenders, and government officials; divide the nation's farmland equitably; and provide better working conditions for the industrial proletariat. The Nationalists, though advocating ultimate improvements, continued to uphold landlords and industrialists and to extract a tremendously disproportionate share of taxes from the poor. Neither Reds nor Nationalists, despite pious cant directed at the Americans, offered democracy. But the Reds pledged actual relief from economic oppression, while the Nationalists promised only vague future improvements that never came.

The civil war went against the Nationalists almost from the start. Chiang Kai-shek quickly demonstrated that he had no idea how to conduct a successful war. He got little help from his generals, whose major strength was loyalty to Chiang, not military competence. Though the Nationalists held overwhelming superiority in automatic weapons, artillery, tanks, and trucks, these weapons forced the Nationalists onto the roads and into dependence on supplies delivered over roads or railroads, which the Reds often could stop by roadblocks and tearing up tracks.

Nationalist troops were seldom well trained, and many were of doubtful loyalty. Commanders were afraid they would desert in open country. Accordingly, they tended to withdraw behind the fortifications of cities and to wait passively for Communist assaults. Red strategy as a result was quite easy: the Communist soldiers simply surrounded important cities and waited till the Nationalists were starved out. Chiang could think of no way out of this dilemma, and Nationalist forces shrank with every passing month.[19]

In February 1948, the Truman administration proposed giving Nationalist China 570 million dollars for food and industrial materials, but made no recommendation to fight the Communists. Secretary of State Marshall told a joint congressional committee that for the Nationalists to reduce the Reds to a negligible factor would require the United States "virtually to take over the Chinese government and administer its economic, military and governmental affairs." This, Marshall said, "I cannot recommend." Marshall said major American strength had to be directed to meet the principal Communist threat, which was in Western Europe.

The Marshall proposal was recognition that the Nationalists had declined beyond the hope of recovery, but it contained no hint of friendship to the Communists.[20]

The hate campaign against all things Communist reached fever pitch on June 24, 1948, when the Soviet Union imposed the Berlin blockade on American, British, and French zones in the former German capital. The reason was Soviet anger over the decision of the Western Allies to unite their German occupation zones into a single economic unit. From this decision rose a Western-oriented West Germany and a Soviet-oriented East Germany. The Western Allies fought the Berlin land blockade by using guaranteed air corridors to fly in food, fuel, and supplies. Truman moved U.S. long-range bombers to Britain and implied clearly that any attempt to block access to Berlin by air could result in nuclear war. The Russians did not challenge supplying the city by air, and they abandoned the land blockade on May 12, 1949. But the Western Allies kept flying in supplies until September. The Berlin blockade, more than anything else, confirmed in the minds of Americans that Communism was embarked on aggressive expansion throughout the world. The blockade also focused American attention on Europe and diverted interest from China.

The hopeless nature of Chiang's conduct of the war was shown in Manchuria in 1948. Now designated as the People's Liberation Army or PLA, the Reds occupied most of the region. American advisers recommended that Chiang evacuate Manchuria, but Chiang refused, and concentrated all Nationalist troops into two "islands" at Mukden and Changchun. But supplies had to come from the nearest railhead, at Jinzhou, 160 miles southwest of Mukden. On October 19, 1948, the Red commander, Lin Biao, captured Jinzhou after a large part of the garrison defected and the remainder surrendered.

Lin Biao now concentrated on one hundred thousand of Chiang's best troops moving from Mukden to relieve Jinzhou. Most were armed with American weapons, and many of the junior officers had been trained by Americans. But PLA troops surrounded individual elements of the KMT force at Dahushan, sixty miles southwest of Mukden. The vast majority of the troops promptly surrendered. One of the most effective of the Communist approaches was this: "Your rifle is American but your life is Chinese; save them both for the new China."[21]

Chiang now belatedly decided to evacuate Changchun and Mukden, but the opportunity had passed. Changchun surrendered on October 21 when most of the garrison defected. At Mukden, only the most senior KMT officers and officials and their families were flown out. The remaining garrison surrendered on November 1.

In the Manchurian debacle, the Nationalists lost four hundred thousand troops, including many of their best. They also lost vast quantities of military supplies.

In 1949, PLA forces advanced southward on two broad fronts. The KMT generals exhibited the same fatal pattern that had lost them Manchuria: they withdrew into cities, which the PLA quickly surrounded and forced to surrender.

Though the West didn't know of it until much later, Stalin was not at all happy about Red Chinese successes. He told Mao Zedong privately that the Reds should stop at the Yangtze River and accept a divided nation, with the Reds in control of the north and the KMT of the south. It was clear that Stalin hoped to play the two sides against each other. Mao ignored the advice. Soviet interest in continuing to support the Nationalist government emerged in late January 1949 when the Nationalist government began moving its capital to Guangzhou (Canton) in the far south. The Soviet ambassador, N. V. Roschin, was the only foreign chief of mission to follow. He made the move for one reason: to seek agreement from the Nationalist government, before it collapsed, of extensive economic privileges in China's vast Xinjiang province in the northwest, next to the Soviet Union. The Kremlin entertained no hope of getting such concessions from the Chinese Communists, and the Nationalists were their last chance.[22]

On May 24, 1949, PLA forces occupied the great industrial and port city of Shanghai. But prior to this, Chiang Kai-shek had set up an evacuation center on the Zhoushan archipelago south of Shanghai and assembled ships to transport to Taiwan spoils, government personnel, and soldiers and their families. This flight now went on apace, as PLA troops continued to move south to the other great port of Guangzhou. Remaining KMT forces either retreated before them or surrendered.

With KMT collapse on the mainland now certain, Zhou Enlai, the Communist number two man, sent a message to American officials on June 1, 1949, that China needed help from the United States and Britain because the Soviet Union was unable to provide it. Zhou also made approaches to the American ambassador to China, John Leighton Stuart. But Truman was planning to shut down the U.S.

embassy in China, and Secretary of State Acheson forbade Stuart to meet with Zhou and Mao Zedong. Instead, Stuart came home at the end of June.[23]

Having been rebuffed by Truman and Acheson, Mao Zedong announced that a "third world [between imperialism and socialism] does not exist." China, he stated, would lean to the side of the Soviet Union against the exploitative West. Mao had no choice. The snubs by Washington were only confirmations of a decidedly hostile view that had dominated the United States since the end of World War II. American leaders were unable to believe that the Chinese Communists could be operating without direction from the Kremlin. This posture forced Red China into Russia's arms when a policy of recognizing Red China and working with it would have worked to divide China from Russia.[24]

On August 5, 1949, the Truman administration presented its explanation of the Communist victory in China. The *China White Paper* attempted to justify the failure of the United States to intervene militarily in the civil war, while it also sought to exonerate the United States from responsibility for China becoming a Soviet satellite. Secretary of State Dean Acheson stated accurately that the American people "would not have sanctioned" the colossal commitment of American armies and strength that would have been required to keep Chiang Kai-shek in power. He also stated accurately that the Nationalists had lost because of their own inadequacies and failures.

But Acheson claimed incorrectly that the Chinese Communists had "foresworn their Chinese heritage" and "publicly announced their subservience to a foreign power, Russia." In China, Acheson claimed, "the foreign domination has been masked behind the façade of a vast crusading movement which apparently has seemed to many Chinese to be wholly indigenous and national." Acheson wrote piously that he hoped one day the Chinese people would "throw off the foreign yoke." In the interim U.S. policy would be determined "by the degree to which the Chinese people come to recognize that the Communist regime serves not their interests but those of Soviet Russia."

Acheson cleared the United States of all blame. The Nationalist disaster, he said, was "the product of internal Chinese forces" that the United States tried to influence but could not. "Nothing this country did or could have done within the reasonable limits of its capabilities could have changed that result."[25]

The China lobby, which was pushing vociferously for aid to Chiang, accepted Acheson's assertion that China was a new conquest of the Soviet Union, and focused its complaints on why the United States had not done more to save Chiang.

Senator H. Styles Bridges of New Hampshire said the *White Paper* convinced him more than ever "that the Chinese war was lost in Washington, not in China." Senators William F. Knowland of California, Kenneth S. Wherry of Nebraska, and Patrick McCarran of Nevada (a Democrat associated with conservative Republicans) joined with Bridges in declaring that the *White Paper* was "a 1,052-page whitewash of a wishful do-nothing policy which has succeeded only in placing Asia in danger of Soviet conquest."[26]

Acheson built an American foreign policy in the Far East around the assumption of Soviet domination of China without investigating its accuracy. It is likely that Acheson actually believed what he said. In his memoirs published nineteen years afterward, he did not question his judgment.[27] Even if he didn't believe that the Chinese were tools of the Kremlin, he was forced to claim they were. Since policy was based on the "long telegram" of George F. Kennan on February 22, 1946, the United States was bound to resist further advances of Communism everywhere.

However, it soon became clear that—since the administration had no intention of reversing the judgment of the Chinese civil war—the Kennan containment line could not be applied to China. In effect, the United States had already pulled the line east of China. But this was not made plain in the *White Paper*.

The American public saw that the United States was creating a unified barrier against Communist advance in Western Europe under the North Atlantic Treaty Organization (NATO). It was hard for them to see why China was not on the free side of a similar barrier in the Far East. There was an answer, but it was difficult to get it across. The Chinese Communists had been fighting to conquer China since 1927, and they were well on their way when Kennan wrote his long telegram. They completed the task (except for Taiwan) while the containment line was being laid out. The Truman administration was not interested in embarking on a war of conquest in China. So it tried to finesse the inconsistency by accepting a fait accompli in East Asia, but not bringing it to the attention of the American public. This omission was going to make trouble for the administration when, at last, it was obliged to admit it openly a few months hence.

The conclusion in China came swiftly. PLA troops advanced almost unmolested through southern and eastern China. From September 21 to 28, 1949, a Political Consultative Conference (PCC) took place at Beijing. Mao Zedong gave the illusion of a popular mandate by including many minor parties and organizations in the PCC, but full power rested with the Communist Party. The conference created the People's Republic of China and established Beijing as the capital. On October 1, 1949, Mao officially proclaimed the People's Republic with himself as chairman and Zhou Enlai as premier and foreign minister. He declared it to be the sole legal government of China. The Soviet Union quickly recognized the new republic.[28]

Lin Biao's army captured Guangzhou on October 14. A rump Nationalist government meanwhile had moved to Chongqing, where it disintegrated soon after. Most of the remaining Nationalists retreated to Taiwan. Chiang set up the new Nationalist capital at Taipei, Taiwan, on December 9. By this time Taiwan had become the refuge of about 2 million Nationalist supporters, including half a million soldiers.[29]

The last Nationalist military forces on the mainland retreated into Guangxi province or crossed over to the island of Hainan. Resistance was scattered and ineffective, but it took Lin Biao's forces until April 1950 to eliminate the last holdouts.[30]

Communism at last had come to dominate the mainland of China. For the Chinese people, the destruction of the oppressive Nationalist regime signified liberation and a new and equitable society to come. Yet it was a cruel deceit, for the society that emerged was anything but a free realm where men and women could live without authoritarianism governing their every move. Long before, the nineteenth-century anarchist Pyotr Kropotkin had condemned socialism and collectivism as nothing but state capitalism and had prophesied the gruesome reality of the Communist state. If the state became the owner of the land, mines, factories, railways, and other elements of production, and if these powers were added to the powers of taxation and force the state already possessed, "we should create a new tyranny even more terrible than the old one."[31] The Soviet

Union had long since confirmed Kropotkin's premonition, and the new People's Republic of China embarked on the same totalitarian journey.

While China was going through the agonies of a civil war that was forcibly uniting the people, nearby Korea was undergoing a painful process imposed from the outside that was forcibly dividing the people into two antagonistic camps.

Japan surrendered after the United States dropped atomic bombs on Hiroshima and Nagasaki on August 6 and 9, 1945. The Soviet Union immediately entered the war. Russian troops occupied Manchuria. They also moved into Korea, as did American soldiers stationed on Okinawa. Although the Allies had promised Korea ultimate independence, the peninsula was still considered enemy territory, since Japan had annexed it in 1910 after nearly two thousand years of more or less independent existence, most of it under the fairly benign supervision of Imperial China.

The U.S. Army operations chief, Lieutenant General John C. Hull, had already decided that the United States needed the Korean ports of Inchon and Pusan. Accordingly, when officers were drawing up General Order No. 1 on August 11, 1945, to instruct General Douglas MacArthur, the newly named Allied supreme commander in the Far East, they hit upon the 38th parallel as a convenient dividing line between the Russians and the Americans. Inchon, Pusan, and the Korean capital of Seoul lay comfortably south of this line. Japanese soldiers were to surrender to Russians north of the line, to Americans south of the line.[32]

The Soviets accepted the line. It became, with the developing Cold War, the frontier between the two Koreas. The selection of the

38th parallel as a boundary immediately angered Koreans, and they set about to eliminate it and to reunite the country.

But Russia throughout its history had tried to keep territory its troops had occupied, and Joseph Stalin had no intention whatsoever of giving up the northern portion of Korea. The Soviets set about destroying any possibility of a unified country, unless it was dominated by the Communists. They undercut the all-Korea trusteeship (U.S.-Soviet-British-Chinese) agreed to at Yalta, and they sealed the border at the 38th parallel and severely restricted traffic into and out of North Korea. This effectively created two states.

Unable to overcome Soviet intransigence, the United States laid the issue before the United Nations in 1947. The UN voted for an all-Korea election, but Russia banned voting in the north. The UN went ahead with the election in the south. The Korean people were greatly opposed to this admission that the country was partitioned, and just two far-right-wing parties endorsed the election, Syngman Rhee's National Society for the Rapid Realization of Korean Independence, and the Korean Democratic Party. Deeply unhappy, all moderate and leftist parties boycotted the election. Rhee, who had spent forty years in exile outside Korea, was left with no powerful challengers.[33]

Thus the UN election in May 1948 had the effect of dividing the nation into two extreme political factions—a right-wing government in the south under Rhee and a Communist government in the north under a Stalin-appointed leader, Kim Il Sung, a thirty-year-old Communist and former officer in the Soviet Army.

By the accident of history and geography, Korea had become a pawn in a great power struggle between the United States and the Soviet Union. Two hostile Korean governments faced each other across the 38th parallel. Each claimed to represent all of Korea and each was dedicated to the other's destruction.

North Korea, larger in area (46,540 square miles, slightly smaller than England or New York State), possessed most of the few industrial plants, built by the Japanese. It is mostly mountainous and less productive and, in 1950, had only 9 million people. South Korea (38,230 square miles, slightly larger than Portugal and a little smaller than Virginia) had 21 million people, the best agricultural land, most of the light industry, and most of the big cities.

Americans were deeply angered by the course of events in Korea. Russia, which had done practically nothing in the Pacific war, had become a major beneficiary of the defeat of the Japanese. Americans found out quickly that they had been fooled by the Russians, most especially by Russian expressions of solidarity with the West. Americans found that they had eliminated Germany and Japan as counters to the Soviet Union. This left only the United States with the power to challenge totalitarian Russia, which, under Joseph Stalin, was demonstrating a drive toward domination fully equal to that shown by Adolf Hitler and the Third Reich.

It was no wonder, then, that Americans came to despise the Russians and to suspect Communist conspiracies everywhere. The conflicts of the Free World with Communism came to be viewed as something on the order of a cataclysmic Manichean struggle between the beneficent forces of light and the diabolical powers of darkness.

CHAPTER 2

The American Attempt at Stability

By the beginning of 1950, the United States was coming to the end of its occupation of Japan. Under the leadership of Douglas MacArthur, it had achieved a democratic government and assurances of friendship between Japan and the United States. As for Korea, informed Americans were angry at the intransigence of the Russians, but on the whole they felt the situation was reasonably under control. There seemed to be little danger of war, despite threats from north and south, because neither the Soviets nor the Americans had provided their client state with many weapons.

The huge hullabaloo that had erupted in Washington over issuance of the *China White Paper* the previous summer had died down, though claims by belligerent Republicans that the Truman administration had "lost China" were still being muttered. But there was no groundswell for embarking on a crusade to liberate China, and the administration was confident that the whole question of China would recede in the public's mind.

The big uncompleted task was to announce the line in the Far East beyond which the Communists could not trespass. The line had been fully staked out in the West. The new North Atlantic Treaty Organization, or NATO, would resist any Soviet move against Western Europe. Soviet adventures in other parts of the world would be dealt with as they arose, but the same principle applied: resistance to any aggression.

In East Asia, however, where should the containment line be located? The Nationalists occupied the island province of Taiwan. Chiang Kai-shek was authoritarian but reliably anti-Communist. Taiwan was Chinese, however, and the Chinese civil war had not been completed. Should the United States stand aside and let the Chinese Reds take over the island and end Nationalist rule, or should it defend the island? The Truman administration had made it plain that it was not going to liberate mainland China, so why should it protect the last island possession of China? Logically, it made no sense. Nobody argued that Hawaii was not a part of the United States, or that Corsica was not a part of France.[1]

On the other hand, bellicose Republicans *were* calling on the United States to invade the Chinese mainland and restore Chiang to power. So, from their point of view, protecting Taiwan was perfectly logical—and several leading Republicans were clamoring for the United States to do just that.[2]

Acheson failed to get the backing of American allies, especially Britain, in presenting a united front against Red China. Western countries were not impressed with Acheson's intricate arguments. They were pushing the administration to recognize the existing situation, to wash its hands of Chiang, and to support transfer to the

Reds of Nationalist China's seat on the United Nations Security Council (along with the same veto power enjoyed by the United States, Russia, Britain, and France). Britain wanted to protect Hong Kong from a Communist takeover, needed trade with China to aid in recovery from the war, and sought to prove to newly independent India, Pakistan, Ceylon (Sri Lanka), and Burma that it was willing to accept Asian nations on equal terms. France was hesitant as well, especially after Zhou Enlai implied a threat against French Indochina if it granted asylum to fleeing Nationalist troops. France was having great difficulties in Indochina because of a revolt by Communist-led Vietminh under Ho Chi Minh. It wanted no hostile Red China on Indochina's northern frontier.[3]

In this environment, Secretary of State Acheson got President Truman's endorsement of two contradictory policies—he adhered to the implication of the *White Paper* that Chiang Kai-shek should be abandoned, but he refused to recognize Red China or grant its admission to the UN Security Council. He came to the first decision because he did not want the United States to take on defense of the island, which would instantly make Red China an enemy. He came to the second because the anti-Communist mood in the country was far too intense to accept a second Communist state with veto power on the Security Council.

Non-recognition of Red China was safe politically. But the administration was suffering damaging criticism from Republicans about the status of Taiwan. In the *White Paper*, Acheson had deliberately avoided telling Americans in plain language that the administration was going to let events take their course. This would inevitably lead to Red Chinese occupation of the island and the demise of the Nationalist regime. Now Acheson decided to bite the bullet and admit that the administration was abandoning Chiang.

He and Truman arranged for two related pronouncements to set the record straight.

On January 5, 1950, Truman declared that the United States had no desire to acquire special privileges or military bases on Taiwan and no intention of using American military forces to interfere in the Chinese civil war. Truman said the United States would not provide military aid or advice to the Nationalist forces. He also rejected any idea that the United States would dispute China's possession of Taiwan.[4]

On January 12, 1950, Secretary Acheson made a major speech at the National Press Club.[5] In it he drew a strategic line of American defense in the Pacific that expressly omitted Taiwan and South Korea. This strategic line ran from the Aleutians, through Japan and the Ryukyu Islands, and included the Philippines. Acheson thus placed the line well out into the U.S.-dominated seas, far beyond any disturbing continental lands where trouble could erupt with Communists.[6]

Truman's statement and Acheson's speech had a calming effect in Washington, except among Republicans pushing for aid to Chiang. Acheson signaled that the United States possessed an easily defensible line to protect its national interests. The line fitted into the containment strategy conceived by George Kennan in 1946, but it implicitly ignored the Truman Doctrine of March 1947 that promised aid to countries facing Communist aggression. Truman's January 5 statement explained Taiwan's special status, but the exclusion of South Korea rested on two beliefs—that American troops should not be committed to a land war on the Asian continent, and that any disturbances on the Korean peninsula could be dealt with by airpower.

The United States had come to its Korea position quite deliberately. On September 25, 1947, the Joint Chiefs of Staff had concluded that the United States had little strategic interest in keeping its forty-five thousand troops in Korea. In the event of hostilities, the Chiefs said that the troops would have to be reinforced prior to enemy action. The principal danger of an enemy occupation of South Korea would be air and naval bases the enemy could set up that might interfere with U.S. operations in the adjacent seas. The Chiefs concluded: "Neutralization [of these air and naval bases] by air action would be more feasible and less costly than large-scale ground operations."[7] Accordingly, the United States began removing its troops in 1948 and the last elements evacuated on June 29, 1949.[8]

While overall U.S. strategy was designed to resist *any* Communist advance beyond the containment line anywhere in the world, the bewildering speed of the Red Chinese conquest of the mainland had left the policy in tatters in East Asia. Acheson's Press Club pronouncement, therefore, drew a line that recognized existing realities yet did not give away what the Truman administration believed were essential U.S. positions in the Far East. As events were to show, however, not all American leaders were satisfied with this conservative, non-provocative line.

The United States gained a victory in the United Nations. The day after Acheson's speech, the UN Security Council rejected a Soviet proposal to admit Red China to the Security Council and the UN and to expel Nationalist China. The vote came at the end of an intense fight behind closed doors that had begun November 18, 1949, when UN Secretary-General Trygve Lie received a cable from Beijing demanding that the UN deprive Nationalist China of its seat. On January 10, 1950, Jacob A. Malik, the Soviet representative on the Security Council, introduced a resolution to carry out the expulsion.

Acheson was getting heavy pressure from his allies to acquiesce to the admission of Red China. But the situation in Washington made this impossible, and Acheson decided on an underhanded, devious approach. Instead of vetoing the measure, which would have aroused intense international condemnation, Acheson announced that the United States would "accept the decision of the Security Council when made by an affirmative vote of seven members." Acheson had counted noses and was certain Malik couldn't get the votes.[9]

On January 13, six members voted aye and three nay, while Britain and Norway abstained. Although only one vote short, Malik walked out of the Security Council, announcing that the Soviet Union would boycott the United Nations so long as the Nationalist delegate remained. It was an incredibly severe and counterproductive reaction. It eliminated the Soviet Union and its veto from the Security Council—a perverse and detrimental decision that was going to backfire in a few months. It also was not necessary. Twenty-six nations already had recognized Red China (fifteen of them UN members). If Russia had been a little patient, the question could have been settled soon. The United States was not going to press the matter too hard for fear of worldwide criticism. Red China now ruled 98 percent of the Chinese people and 96 percent of Chinese territory. Most nations accordingly were moving toward ousting the discredited Nationalists.

The Soviet Union's real reason for walking out of the UN was quite different from what it was saying publicly. The Kremlin sought to portray to Beijing that it was a firm friend of Red China, but in fact Joseph Stalin wanted to keep China out of the UN Security Council. The Soviet Union had no interest in sharing that world arena with China, considering its enormous potential influence. But the Kremlin tried to obscure its motives by its usual labyrinthine methods. It walked out of the Security Council to show its friendship for Red China, when its true motivation was the opposite. Sir Alexander Cadogan, British delegate to the UN and a wise and experienced observer of the world's political scene, discerned Russia's real aim, and so informed Acheson. Whether Beijing picked up on Moscow's crafty device is unknown.[10]

Red China now made two political errors. On January 14 the Communist government seized American, Dutch, and French diplomatic property in Beijing. The United States immediately announced it was closing down all consular offices in Red China and recalling all its diplomats. The action incensed American officials and the public, and ruled out U.S. recognition of the Beijing government for the present. It also brought a sudden halt to the recognition of Red China by many other countries, though a number had been planning to make the move. Between January 17, when Switzerland recognized Beijing, and June 25, 1950, the Netherlands and Indonesia were the only countries to send envoys to Beijing.[11]

The second error occurred on January 19 when Beijing recognized the Communist Vietminh government under Ho Chi Minh in Vietnam, a government in rebellion and in opposition to a French program to create within the French Union three "independent" countries out of Indochina: Vietnam, Laos, and Cambodia. In fact, the promised independence was illusory and was designed to maintain French control of the region. This move stopped France's plan to recognize Beijing. Red China's decision forced the Soviet Union to follow a few days later in recognizing the Ho Chi Minh regime.[12] These démarches divided the nations involved in East Asia along ideological lines when it was in Beijing's interest to avoid distinctions and to work toward reasonable solutions to disputes. The Beijing errors played into the hands of Americans opposed to any accommodation with Red China.

W hile this drama was playing out in Washington and New York, Mao Zedong and Zhou Enlai were in Moscow negotiating a new treaty and assistance pact with Joseph Stalin. News of the visit aroused the highest suspicions in the United States, for fear that Russia would provide immense economic and military aid to Red China. But the fear was groundless. The Soviet Union had lost more than 25 million people dead in World War II, along with vast portions of its industry and infrastructure. Under the best of circumstances, it was going to take Russia decades to recover, if it ever did. Russia simply did not have the means to give Red China much help. Wise economists recognized this fact, but they were not listened to very carefully.

Although it was not clear to official Washington, the Soviet Union made mainly a business deal with Mao and Zhou, and the advantages largely went to Russia. Red China and the Soviet Union signed a thirty-year treaty on February 4, 1950, but China received only a modest grant of 300 million dollars, which had to be paid back with interest in five years. Any weapons or goods shipped to China had to be paid for. Since most trade by China with the West had been shut off by American pressure, most Chinese exports were going to go to Russia and its satellites, and most imports to come from the same sources. Stalin did agree to provide technicians and technical help to develop Chinese industry. He also promised to restore to China full control of the Manchurian railways, Port Arthur, and Dalian at the end of 1952.[13]

In the midst of all this, a vicious and dishonest Republican demagogue, Senator Joseph McCarthy of Wisconsin, made false claims of Communist infiltration into the State Department. Throughout the winter and spring McCarthy hurled irresponsible and unsubstantiated charges. Despite their falseness, they distracted American leaders and created great anxiety among public officials fearful that McCarthy's witch hunt would single them out. It was terribly unfair and a dark stain on the Congress, which allowed it to happen.

Meantime, the Central Intelligence Agency (CIA) alerted American leaders on April 17 that the Chinese Communists had the capacity to seize Taiwan before the end of 1950 and probably would do so. The unreasoning fear of Communists stirred up by Senator McCarthy's charges motivated Dean Rusk, assistant secretary for Far Eastern affairs, to make a wildly provocative proposal to put Taiwan under a UN trusteeship, with the U.S. Navy assigned to protect the island.[14]

Acheson rejected Rusk's idea, but anxiety about the fate of Taiwan increased greatly. Whether these second thoughts would have brought on a different American policy is doubtful. However, unknown to Washington, events were moving beyond China and the United States to force a radical reappraisal.

At this crucial moment, a new voice entered the argument, and it was destined to affect decisions drastically in the year ahead. The voice was that of General Douglas MacArthur, seventy years old, the U.S. commander in the Far East and America's proconsul ruling occupied Japan. He had been highly successful in guiding this defeated nation onto a new democratic, nonviolent path. MacArthur was a famous soldier who had led the Allied drive across New Guinea to the Philippines in World War II.

But MacArthur was an exceedingly complex man. William Manchester, in his celebrated biography of the general, writes that he was "flamboyant, imperious, and apocalyptic" and "could not acknowledge errors." Yet, Manchester writes, "he was also endowed with great personal charm, a will of iron, and a soaring intellect." Clare Boothe Luce, playwright, member of Congress, and wife of Henry Luce, publisher of *Time* and *Life* magazines, wrote: "MacArthur's temperament was flawed by an egotism that demanded obedience not only to his orders, but to his ideas and his person as well. He plainly relished idolatry." The noted reporter William L. Shirer wrote of MacArthur in 1928: "He was forceful, articulate, thoughtful, even a bit philosophical, and well read. Only his arrogance bothered me." And the historian Walter Millis wrote: "He was prepared to use his prestige as a soldier to influence civil policy decisions, and the arguments of military necessity overrode the diplomatic or political objectives of his civilian superiors."[15]

Up to now MacArthur had not made his views about Taiwan known officially, but now he did so in a most determined way.[16] General Omar N. Bradley, chairman of the Joint Chiefs of Staff, and Secretary of Defense Louis A. Johnson were in the Far East on an inspection tour. While in Tokyo on June 22, 1950, en route home, Johnson and Bradley received from General MacArthur a June 14 memo of his which concluded that "the domination of Formosa [Taiwan] by an unfriendly power would be a disaster of utmost importance to the U.S. and I am convinced that time is of the essence." MacArthur advocated that he be authorized to make an immediate survey of the requirements to prevent Red seizure of the island and that the results "be acted upon as a basis for U.S. national policy with respect to Formosa."[17]

The memo made a huge impression on Johnson, who had been strongly influenced by Republicans demanding the same thing. It made less of an impression on Bradley, who was in agreement with Truman's and Acheson's decision to abandon Chiang Kai-shek.

But MacArthur could not be ignored, and neither could his memorandum, although it called for the immediate and total reversal of the policy established by the Truman administration. It implied that the United States should go to war with Red China, and thus was a complete repudiation of American strategy.

MacArthur's claims, if taken at face value, were terrifying. "Formosa in the hands of the Communists can be compared to an unsinkable aircraft carrier and submarine tender located to accomplish Soviet offensive strategy and at the same time checkmate counteroffensive operations by United States forces based on Okinawa and the Philippines," he wrote. "Pending the actual outbreak of hostilities, United States military forces will be unable to prevent stockpiling of essential military supplies on Formosa. . . . It is apparent to me that the United States should initiate measures to prevent the domination of Formosa by a Communist power."[18]

MacArthur's memo frightened numerous civilians in Washington, but experienced soldiers, like Omar Bradley, recognized that MacArthur's claims didn't add up strategically. Likening Taiwan to an "unsinkable aircraft carrier and submarine tender" was nonsense. A carrier and tender anchored in the midst of an American-controlled sea would have been virtually impossible to supply if possessed by the Soviet Union or Red China and used for offensive operations. Anyway, both were land powers with insignificant naval forces. Neither was going to launch a naval offensive into the Pacific against the world's greatest navy, especially not from an easily blockaded island. China and the Soviet Union already possessed continental-sized hinterlands which would serve as bases far better than Taiwan, given modern aircraft and submarine ranges.

Soviet or Chinese possession of Taiwan was only dangerous as a shield or base to protect against an *American* invasion of mainland

China. In that case, aircraft based on the island could damage or inhibit an amphibious U.S. landing on the coast of China. Although MacArthur did not propose invasion in his memo, its implication was glaringly apparent to experienced soldiers. It was the only strategic reason why the United States should occupy the island. In other words, MacArthur proposed a preemptive strike to safeguard a future American assault on the mainland. His purpose was entirely offensive and signified war, not passive defense.

However, events elsewhere were about to overtake the debate over Taiwan. Soon everything was going to change.

CHAPTER 3

War and the Quarantine of Taiwan

Sometime in late 1949, the North Korean dictator, Kim Il Sung, visited Joseph Stalin and tried to get Soviet agreement to a plan he had developed to conquer South Korea. According to the memoirs of Nikita Khrushchev, later to become the Soviet premier, "the North Koreans wanted to prod South Korea with the point of a bayonet. Kim Il Sung said the first poke would touch off an internal explosion in South Korea" that would lead to the overthrow of Syngman Rhee. The idea appealed to Stalin, Khrushchev wrote, but he told Kim to come back with a definite plan. Kim did so, but now Stalin feared that the United States might intervene and refused to go along.[1]

But Secretary of State Acheson's statement of January 12, 1950, placing Korea beyond the line the United States was going to defend almost certainly played a crucial role in changing Stalin's mind. In early

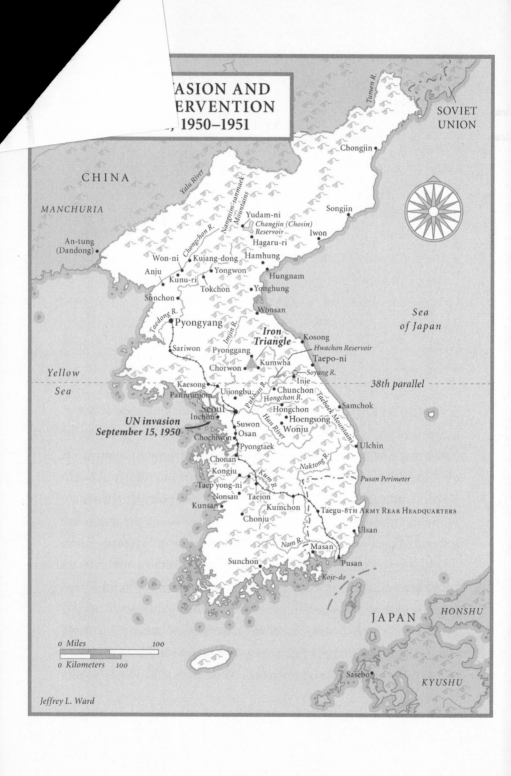

ASION AND
ERVENTION
_, 1950–1951_

SOVIET
UNION

CHINA

MANCHURIA

Chongjin

Tumen R.

Yalu River

Nangnim-sanmaek Mountains

Chongchon R.

Songjin

Yudam-ni
Changjin (Chosin)
Reservoir
Hagaru-ri

Iwon

An-tung
(Dandong)

Won-ni Kujang-dong
Anju
Kunu-ri
Sunchon Tokchon

Hamhung

Yongwon

Hungnam

Yonghung

Taedong R.

Pyongyang

Imjin R.

Wonsan

Sea
of Japan

Sariwon Pyonggang

**_Iron
Triangle_**

Kosong

Hwachon Reservoir

Chorwon
Kumwha

Taepo-ni

Soyang R.

38th parallel

Yellow
Sea

Kaesong
Panmunjom Uijongbu

Pukhan R.

Chunchon

Hongchon R.

Inje

Samchok

Seoul
**_UN invasion
September 15, 1950_** Inchon

Hongchon

Hoengsong
Wonju

Taebaek Mountains

Suwon
Osan
Chochiwon Pyongtaek

Han River

Ulchin

Chonan
Kongju

Kum R.

Naktong R.

Pusan Perimeter

Taep'yong-ni
Nonsan Taejon
Kunsan
Chonju Kumchon

Taegu–8ᴛʜ Aʀᴍʏ Rᴇᴀʀ HᴇᴀᴅQᴜᴀʀᴛᴇʀs

Ulsan

Chonju

Nam R.

Masan
Sunchon
Pusan

Koje-do

JAPAN HONSHU

0 _Miles_ 100

0 _Kilometers_ 100

Sasebo

KYUSHU

Jeffrey L. Ward

1950, he began sending Kim Il Sung modest amounts of offensive equipment, including artillery, automatic weapons, 60 propeller-driven warplanes, and 154 T-34 tanks, heavily armored twenty-nine-ton monsters armed with a high-velocity eighty-five-millimeter gun. The T-34s were the best tanks to come out of World War II and were a decidedly superior weapon, because the Americans had given the South Koreans no tanks and only obsolescent bazookas, whose rockets bounced off the sides of heavy tanks.

To the astonishment of the world, in the early hours of Sunday, June 25, 1950, a ninety-thousand-man North Korean Army led by Russian T-34 tanks crossed the 38th parallel in three main columns and invaded South Korea. The North Koreans achieved total tactical and strategic surprise. The thirty-eight thousand South Korean troops facing them were unprepared. Not all units were on the line, and many soldiers were absent on weekend passes.

The North Koreans clearly knew the South Koreans had nothing to stop a tank, because they lined up their T-34s in columns, one tank behind the other, on the narrow eighteen-foot-wide gravel roads and headed south, their infantry strung out behind them. Even a few antitank mines placed in roadbeds could have stopped the columns. Armor-piercing shells from the eighty-nine short-range 105-millimeter light M-3 howitzers that the Americans had given the South Koreans could have destroyed stalled columns of tanks, as also could have jellied gasoline napalm from attack aircraft. But the South Koreans had no antitank mines, no armor-piercing shells, no aircraft, and no napalm. The North Koreans ran the tanks down the roads not only because the South Koreans couldn't stop them, but also because three-fourths of Korea was mountainous terrain that was difficult or deadly for tanks, while most of the flatland was covered with tiny, wet rice paddies divided by narrow raised walk-ways and embankments. In many of these paddies armor would have mired, and in nearly all it would have faced hard going.

The South Koreans fell back in complete chaos on the capital, Seoul, only twenty-five miles below the 38th.

The attack came as an utter shock to official Washington. No one had predicted it. No one could explain how an army of ninety thousand men had been able to assemble on the border of a friendly state with no American intelligence apparatus detecting it. For weeks the various military, diplomatic, and intelligence services of the United States collected argument after argument to prove that they were not responsible. But in fact they had all failed. North Korea had pulled off a completely unanticipated offensive.[2]

As American officials hurriedly gathered in Washington, the first reaction was that the Russians—possibly with the help of the Red Chinese—had planned the invasion, had egged on Kim Il Sung to undertake it, and were directing the operation. There were numerous Russian advisers with the North Korean Army, and in October 1950 Americans discovered two attack orders in *Russian*, dated June 22, 1950, issued by North Korean military officials to a North Korean division.[3] To U.S. leaders, it made no sense for the North Koreans to risk such a dangerous move without assurance that the Soviet Union would come to their assistance if they ran into trouble.

It took Americans a long time to figure out that actually Kim Il Sung had planned the attack, and Joseph Stalin had only gone along with it. Stalin almost certainly concluded that the United States would do nothing but protest, because Secretary Acheson had announced only six months previously that Korea lay outside the American strategic defensive line.

It therefore was a comparable shock to the Kremlin and to Kim

Il Sung to realize that they had made a grave mistake believing official American pronouncements. For the United States decided almost
at once that it was going to defend South Korea.

When Washington got the news of the attack, Secretary of State
Acheson immediately called President Truman, spending the weekend at his home in Independence, Missouri, and got his permission
to call an emergency meeting of the UN Security Council—still
missing the Soviet delegate who'd walked out in January. Acheson
and Dean Rusk spent the rest of the day drawing up a proposed
resolution.

On Sunday afternoon (Washington time is fourteen hours earlier
than Seoul and Tokyo time) Truman flew back from Independence
and called a dinner conference of all top military and diplomatic
officers that night at Blair House, since the White House was undergoing renovation.

As he was flying to Washington, Truman's thoughts were already
turning toward intervention. He wrote later: "If the Communists were
permitted to force their way into the Republic of Korea without opposition from the free world, no small nation would have the courage to
resist threats and aggression by stronger Communist neighbors."[4]

Acheson also was moving away from the containment line he
had marked out on January 12. The attack, he said, was "an open,
undisguised challenge to our internationally accepted position as the
protector of South Korea. . . . It looked as though we must steel
ourselves for the use of force."[5]

At the emergency meeting of the UN Security Council, Acheson
was able to get a 9–0 vote calling on the North Koreans to withdraw
at once, though no one thought they would obey.

The Blair House conference, attended by the Joint Chiefs, all the
Defense Department secretaries, and Acheson, dealt less with Korea

than with Taiwan, indicating that concern over the island was far greater than anxiety over Korea. Louis Johnson, the secretary of defense, asked Omar Bradley to read aloud the memorandum about protecting Taiwan that General MacArthur had given to them three days previously in Tokyo. Truman approved MacArthur's request that a survey team be sent to Taiwan to determine its defense needs. Acheson proposed that the U.S. 7th Fleet, stationed in the Philippines, be moved northward at once to prevent an attack on Taiwan from the Chinese mainland, and vice versa. Truman authorized the 7th Fleet to move to Sasebo, on the southern Japanese island of Kyushu, but he was not ready to order a blockade of the China coast.[6]

This first meeting of American leaders treated defense of Korea and protection of Taiwan as completely interrelated, despite the fact that Red China had made no aggressive move and there was not a shred of evidence that Red China had any role in the North Korean attack. But American leaders *saw* Red China as a satellite of Russia and accepted without further thought that it *must* be a party to the attack.

Illogical as this was militarily, it made tremendous sense politically. Not only had MacArthur raised his demand to protect Taiwan, but a noisy group of Republicans in Washington was demanding the same thing. Truman and Acheson saw that it would be political suicide for the administration to send U.S. forces to protect South Korea and not send U.S. forces to protect Taiwan. Unrelated or not, they were identical perils in the eyes of many Americans. This meeting, therefore, foreshadowed an abrupt reversal of national policy in regard to Taiwan. The meeting also implied that the Red Chinese somehow were involved in the North Korean invasion.

The next day, Monday, June 26, 1950 (Tuesday, June 27 in Seoul), it became clear that North Korea was ignoring the Security

Council resolution and that Communist troops were about to occupy Seoul. That evening, Acheson telephoned Truman and persuaded him to call another meeting at Blair House that night. Most of the men who had attended the meeting the evening before returned. This time, Truman made positive decisions.

Truman authorized American air and naval forces to attack North Korean troops, armor, and artillery at will. He approved a recommendation from Acheson for a Security Council resolution the next day to call for open military intervention. Truman also agreed to another Acheson proposal that the 7th Fleet be moved at once to prevent hostilities between Taiwan and the Chinese Communists.[7]

The next morning, June 27, 1950, President Truman announced his decisions to the nation. Korea got one sentence: "I have ordered United States air and sea forces to give the Korean government troops cover and support." He was much more detailed about Taiwan: "The attack upon Korea makes it plain beyond all doubt that Communism has passed beyond the use of subversion to conquer independent nations and will now use armed invasion and war. It [the "it" being Communism as a whole, not merely North Korea alone] has defied the orders of the Security Council of the United Nations issued to preserve international peace and security. In these circumstances the occupation of Formosa [Taiwan] by Communist forces would be a direct threat to the security of the Pacific area and to the United States forces performing their lawful and necessary functions in that area.

"Accordingly, I have ordered the 7th Fleet to prevent any attack on Formosa. As a corollary of this action I am calling upon the Chinese government on Formosa to cease all air and sea operations against the mainland. The 7th Fleet will see that this is done. The determination of the future status of Formosa must await the restoration of security in the Pacific, a peace settlement with Japan, or consideration by the United Nations."[8]

So, as the United States was going to war in Korea, Taiwan was drawn into the net. Politically, the Truman administration could not have withstood the furor if Red Chinese troops, while American forces were engaged in Korea, had moved to occupy Taiwan. Truman had stepped ahead of this possibility by placing the 7th Fleet between the mainland and the island. In so doing, he accomplished much of what MacArthur had demanded in his June 14 memorandum, and he instantly made Red China an enemy.

Within twenty-four hours the Red Chinese premier, Zhou Enlai, denounced Truman's move as "armed aggression against Chinese territory and a total violation of the United Nations Charter." A few days later Mao Zedong said the United States had broken its promises not to interfere in China's internal affairs and called on the Chinese to "defeat every provocation of American imperialism."[9]

Truman had tried to assure the Red Chinese on January 5, 1950, that the United States had no designs on Taiwan. He tried to do the same thing in a message to Congress on July 19 in which he said the United States had no territorial ambitions concerning Taiwan and the neutralization was "without prejudice to political questions affecting that island."[10] But to Beijing, facts spoke louder than words.

Truman got overwhelming support from the American people. Congress quickly extended the draft for a year and authorized the president to call up reservists in all the services.

In the UN Security Council, the United States was set to deliver the Russians a crushing propaganda defeat on June 27. The United States had prepared a resolution calling on all UN states "to repel the armed attack and to restore international peace and security" to Korea. The only way the resolution could be stopped was if the Soviet

Union rushed back and reoccupied the seat on the Security Council that it had vacated on January 13, when it failed to oust Nationalist China from the council. But if the Soviet delegate, Jacob Malik, vetoed the measure, he would instantly label the Soviet Union as a co-conspirator. Failure to do so would brand North Korea as an aggressor. The Kremlin weighed its options—and the Soviet Union's seat on the Security Council remained vacant that day. The resolution passed with seven aye votes, one nay vote (Yugoslavia), while India and Egypt abstained.[11]

There could be no doubt that the vote against North Korea was also a vote against the Soviet Union. Still it was a step removed from directly charging Russia with aggression. And the Soviet Union had already signaled by its silence that it was not going to intervene in the conflict.[12] The Soviets thereby confirmed George Kennan's conviction that they would not take unnecessary risks and, if defied, would retreat. They were not prepared to hazard a global conflict to help North Korea. So, because the United States stepped in to defend South Korea, Russia quickly abandoned the North Korean Army, sending very few additional supplies and weapons, and withdrawing all of its military advisers. Joseph Stalin in effect told Kim Il Sung that he had to win the battle on his own.[13]

Truman so far had committed only U.S. air and sea forces. But the virtual disintegration of the South Korean Army guaranteed swift North Korean occupation of the entire peninsula in short order. If that happened, the United States would be faced with accepting a fait accompli or mounting a costly and hazardous amphibious landing to recover the land.

This danger was painfully apparent to MacArthur and the Joint

Chiefs of Staff. MacArthur sent an advance commander, Brigadier General John H. Church, to Suwon Airfield, a few miles south of Seoul, on June 27. Church saw at once that the South Koreans were in a state of impending dissolution. He radioed MacArthur that American troops would have to be committed. Church's report galvanized MacArthur to fly to Suwon to see for himself. When he arrived, he insisted on driving northward against the panicked flow of thousands of refugees to the Han River at Seoul, still a barrier, but wavering.

Back in Tokyo that night, MacArthur drafted a message to the Joint Chiefs. The South Korean Army was entirely incapable of defending against the North Koreans, he wrote. The fall of the republic was seriously threatened. MacArthur asked initially for commitment of a regimental combat team (about five thousand men) and later to build up to two full divisions. Truman got the message at 5 A.M. June 30 (he was already up) and approved sending the RCT at once. His decision on the two divisions was to wait till another Blair House conference of Acheson and the military leaders that morning.

At this conference Truman announced that Chiang Kai-shek had offered thirty-three thousand of his Nationalist troops to serve in Korea, and Truman was inclined to accept the offer. Acheson and the Joint Chiefs were appalled. It was evident that the implications of such a move had not dawned on the president. Acheson quickly set him straight. In the first place, accepting Nationalist troops would automatically make Chiang Kai-shek an ally, while Truman had scrupulously avoided taking that step when he quarantined the island. Also, Chinese Nationalist troops in Korea would be a flagrant sign that Chiang Kai-shek intended to march up to the Yalu River and there launch an offensive into mainland China. In other words, if the United States committed Nationalist troops to Korea, it was the equivalent of a declaration of war against Red China.

The administration suspected that China was a party to the invasion, but the Chinese had made no overt move, and it was absolutely in the interest of the United States to avoid precipitating their intervention. China had many times more troops and weapons than North Korea. The Joint Chiefs chimed in to explain to the president that the Nationalists on Taiwan were more or less military refugees and would require complete re-equipment of everything from shoes and uniforms to weapons, vehicles, food, and ammunition. Transport facilities would be required to get them to Korea. Materials and transportation could be far more effectively used to send in American troops. Truman was convinced, and agreed to turn down Chiang's offer.[14]

Now Truman made a stunning decision. He authorized MacArthur to use, not just the two divisions he asked for, but all four of the divisions forming the occupation force of Japan. These divisions were anything but battle-ready. They had been enjoying an incredibly soft life in Japan, waited upon by Japanese servants and spending little time in battle training. "Maid-sans" and "boy-sans" cost one-twentieth of a second lieutenant's pay. Excellent officers' and enlisted men's clubs featured highly professional Japanese bands and singers performing to all hours. Cocktails seldom cost more than 10 or 15 cents. There was an old occupation joke that one could simply not afford to stay sober. The four divisions were only at about 70 percent strength in personnel, each of the divisions' three infantry regiments had only two battalions instead of the normal three, and each of the divisions' five artillery battalions had only two instead of the usual three firing batteries. There were no immediately available tanks; only a few of the new HEAT (high explosive antitank) artillery rounds had been sent to the Far East, and the new 3.5-inch "super-bazooka" antitank rocket launcher was still in the States.

To the 24th Infantry Division, stationed on Kyushu, Japan's southernmost island and the closest to Korea, fell the responsibility for slowing the North Korean advance long enough for other forces to get to Korea and establish a solid defensive line. This division suffered tremendous casualties in desperate battles at key locations on the main highway and parallel railway running south from Seoul, down which the primary North Korean attack was coming.

The first collision came just north of Osan—twenty-five miles south of Seoul—on July 5, 1950. There a tiny force of 406 soldiers from the 21st Infantry Regiment, supported by 134 men in a 105mm artillery battery from the 52nd Field Artillery Battalion, challenged the entire 4th North Korean Infantry Division of 6,000 men, supported by thirty-three T-34 tanks. The force, under Lieutenant Colonel Charles B. (Brad) Smith, held off the North Koreans for much of the day, despite the fact that the tanks ran right through the position, and "Task Force Smith" was able to stop only four of them. At the end of the day, the U.S. force retreated south, having lost 180 men killed, wounded, or missing.

Elements of the 24th Division retreated in increasing disorder through Chochiwon, Pyongtaek, and Chonan. Finally, at Kongju and Taep'yong-ni on the Kum River, ninety miles south of Seoul, the 34th and 19th Infantry Regiments staged a brief defense July 14–16, 1950, before also collapsing and retreating to Taejon, about twenty miles farther south. At Taejon elements of the 24th Division put up a creditable fight on July 20, before crumpling and retreating south.

The retreats had seemed disastrous, but the fighting slowed the North Koreans just enough to allow other American forces to rush into Korea from Japan, and from other U.S. bases around the world.

By early August American and South Korean elements gained superiority of force, and stopped the North Koreans along the Naktong River, a south-flowing stream some twenty miles west of the major city of Taegu. The American commander in Korea, Lieutenant General Walton H. Walker, quickly formed the "Pusan Perimeter" covering both Taegu and the key port city of Pusan on the southern coast. New weapons, including modern tanks, had begun to arrive, and the North Koreans now crashed vainly against the United Nations defensive line.

It had been a close call. Had it not been for the defensive stands of the 24th Division, the Americans might have been driven into the sea. On July 22, when the division was finally pulled off the front line, it was down to 8,660 men. It had lost 30 percent of its strength in the seventeen days it had been in action.[15] Its losses in officers had been far heavier.

Meantime, the U.S. military forces had called back into service 250,000 men from reserve and National Guard units. The immense superiority of the United States in weapons began to show itself. The time had passed when the North Koreans could have won the war. But Kim Il Sung pressed civilians into service and committed them to battle with virtually no training. The North Koreans mounted assault after assault against the Pusan Perimeter. Although they gained some local successes, they made no breakthroughs, and their army was growing weaker by the day. Kim Il Sung did not give up, however, and continued to order one failed attack after another.[16]

The situation had degenerated into a stalemate. North Korea was not winning, but it controlled all of Korea except the small Pusan Perimeter. It was important that the United Nations go on the offensive to reconquer South Korea. Orthodox American officers began planning attacks that could exploit the vastly superior American firepower and drive the North Koreans back in a series of campaigns such as they had carried out against the Germans in World War II. But Korea was a highly mountainous country, and any straightforward offensive could easily get bogged down in repeated, expensive fights for mountaintops, as had happened to Allied forces in the Italian campaign of 1943–45.

General Douglas MacArthur, however, had thought of another, far less costly way to defeat the North Koreans. He had come up with the idea shortly after they attacked. He drew on a principle as old as warfare itself. But it was entirely unanticipated by the Joint Chiefs of Staff, and they opposed it. Since MacArthur turned out to be right and the Joint Chiefs wrong, MacArthur's status rose phenomenally. This played an immense role in the conflict that was developing between MacArthur and President Truman on American policy in the Cold War.

The principle is simplicity itself. It calls on a commander to focus the enemy's full attention on a single threat, such as an extremely strong defense or a strong attack, while he lands the real blow on the enemy's rear. The concept is mentioned in the Bible (2 Samuel 5:23–25), and it was employed frequently by Napoléon Bonaparte. He called it the *manoeuvre sur les derrières*, and he used it for the first time in the Italian campaign of 1796–97. He launched a decoy attack against Valenza on the Po River in Piedmont. This drew most of the Austrian army to block it. Meanwhile Bonaparte marched the bulk of his army fifty-five miles eastward and crossed the Po at Piacenza. He was now almost astride the Austrian supply line, forcing the Austrian army into chaotic retreat back toward Vienna.[17]

MacArthur saw that a similar opportunity existed in Korea.

Virtually the entire North Korean Army was pressing with every ounce of its strength against the Naktong River line in southern Korea. This army relied for all of its supplies on the only double-track railway in Korea, running from North Korea through Seoul southward to the battle line. MacArthur saw that if the Americans made an amphibious landing at Inchon, the port just twenty miles west of Seoul, troops could quickly capture Seoul and sever the railway. The North Korean Army, deprived of food, ammunition, and fuel, would die within days, without a shot having to be fired at it.[18]

MacArthur saw that the North Koreans had completely misread what should have become apparent when the United States entered the war. Their army was doomed the longer they persisted and the more successful they were. Somehow the North Koreans had not focused on the fact that the Korean peninsula is shaped like a sack. The farther they penetrated south, the deeper they fell into the sack and the more difficult it would be to extricate themselves if the Americans closed the sack anywhere above them. Since the Korean peninsula is surrounded by water on three sides, the United States Navy, with complete command of the sea, could land anywhere it wanted to up the coast of Korea and quickly seal off all enemy forces below it.

Seeing the jeopardy in which the North Korean generals had placed their army, MacArthur began in the first days of July 1950 to make preparations for an amphibious landing at Inchon. The Joint Chiefs of Staff were far more conventional officers than MacArthur. Like many other orthodox commanders throughout history, the Chiefs did not fully appreciate a principle of war that Alexander the Great, Hannibal, and Napoléon had used repeatedly. The renowned English strategist Basil H. Liddell Hart, summarized it in a sentence: the successful general, he wrote, chooses the line or course of least expectation and he exploits the line of least resistance.[19] The ancient Chinese military sage Sun Tzu expressed the same concept: as water seeks the easiest path to the sea, he wrote, so armies should avoid obstacles by going around them.[20] Inchon fitted this maxim perfectly. But American military practices were heavily weighted in the opposite direction—toward predictable, direct attacks supported by intense air assaults or massive artillery barrages. U.S. Army operations resembled on a military level the crude "three-yards-and-a-cloud-of-dust" kind of straight-ahead, power football being practiced by some teams, especially Ohio State University under coach Woody Hayes.

The Joint Chiefs failed to recognize the true purpose of military strategy, or the broad conduct of war. It is to diminish the possibility of resistance. MacArthur saw that he could strike at a place where he was not anticipated and thereby reduce greatly the amount of resistance the North Koreans could exert. Instead of recognizing the fantastic opportunity that MacArthur had discerned, the Chiefs looked at limiting details. They saw that Inchon suffered from extremely high tides, deep mudflats, and a very narrow approach channel.[21] These factors spelled danger to them. J. Lawton Collins, the army chief of staff, and Forrest P. Sherman, chief of naval operations, proposed instead a landing at Kunsan, a small port a hundred miles south of Inchon and only about seventy miles west of the Naktong River line. A landing there, they said, would be safer, and, moreover, the troops could connect more quickly with the Americans defending the Naktong line.

MacArthur explained patiently to Collins and Sherman that the point of the invasion was *not* to team up with the defenders of the battle line in the south, but to *sever* the supply line of the North Koreans who were attacking in the south. The invaders, in short, did not have to come anywhere near the Naktong line. The killing blow would consist of cutting the railroad at Seoul. A landing at Kunsan, MacArthur added, would permit the North Korean command to shift forces quickly from the Pusan Perimeter to form a new line across South Korea. Any American attack thereafter would have to be a direct assault on defended emplacements and would merely drive the enemy back *on* their reserves rather than severing them *from* their reserves.

Collins now raised another objection. What if the invasion force landed successfully at Inchon and then was attacked by an overwhelmingly superior enemy force? The invaders would be so far from any help by the American troops on the Naktong that they might be defeated and forced to surrender before any help could reach them.

MacArthur asked an elementary question: where was this overwhelmingly superior enemy force going to come from? American intelligence was quite certain that the North Koreans had committed practically all of their field forces to the Pusan Perimeter. Only a few isolated training and guard units existed elsewhere. These units largely consisted of raw recruits who, moreover, had extremely few weapons. Even if by some chance a portion or all of these inexperienced men were committed to action, they would be too few and too ill-trained to change the outcome.

On the other hand, MacArthur was calling for the Inchon invasion to be conducted by the 1st Marine Division, a highly skilled and equipped force whose primary mission was precisely to make landings on hostile shores. The marines, and U.S. Navy support forces, had made numerous such landings in the South Pacific in World War II. They were absolute experts on the subject.

Finally, MacArthur pointed out that the difficulty of the landing site at Inchon, with its high tides and difficult approach channel, would cause the North Koreans to disregard any possibility that the Americans would even consider landing there. This made the site all the safer. Whatever reserves the North Koreans might possess would most certainly not be posted at Inchon.

Collins and Sherman were not convinced, and they began working with the other chiefs of staff to scotch the plan. But MacArthur was certain that an invasion of Inchon would succeed, and that it would virtually eliminate the North Korean Army. An army deprived of food and fuel, and especially ammunition, cannot survive for more than a few days. More important is the loss of confidence of a cutoff army. An army that has no way to retreat stops looking at the enemy in front of it and begins glancing anxiously back over its shoulder toward the rear. An army that realizes it is trapped remains an intact force only briefly before it disintegrates into a mob of refugees frantically seeking safety.

It was during the first conference MacArthur held with Lawton Collins and Hoyt S. Vandenberg, the air force chief of staff, on July 13, 1950, that MacArthur made a revealing comment that foreshadowed the tremendous collision he was going to have with President Truman in the coming months. The UN resolution calling for force to stop North Korean aggression implied that UN members were authorized to drive the North Koreans back to the 38th parallel but not beyond. When Collins asked MacArthur how many troops he thought he would need to do this, MacArthur replied that his intention was to *destroy* the North Korean forces, not merely to repulse them.[22]

It was quite obvious that the North Korean Army could not be destroyed without invading North Korea, where the command, supply, and training centers lay. But it was clear that MacArthur meant to do far more than this. He told Collins and Vandenberg that the task after hostilities ended would be to "compose and unite Korea," and it might be necessary to occupy all of Korea.[23] To unite Korea would require the destruction of the North Korean state and would most definitely require force. Any resulting unified state would have to be protected by the United States.

This was as radical a proposal as MacArthur's June 14, 1950, memorandum calling for the United States to protect Taiwan. It called for a complete reversal of American containment policy to halt Communist aggression but not to conquer a Communist country and turn it into a democracy. MacArthur's Taiwan proposal had been put in temporary abeyance by Truman's quarantine of the island. But MacArthur's proposal to conquer North Korea—if carried out— would mean that Red China no longer would have a *cordon sanitaire* in front of its frontier on the Yalu River.

The Truman administration should have addressed this issue at once. It should have decided just how far it was going to go in Korea. A decision to conquer Korea almost certainly would make Red China an enemy, because it would gravely endanger the country's security. Unfortunately, the administration did not confront the matter in July, when it might have done so in a more calm and measured manner than it was forced to do two months later in the frenzied aftermath of the Inchon invasion. The consequences for the nation were extremely damaging.

When Collins and Vandenberg got back to Washington, the Joint Chiefs were consumed—not with MacArthur's radical plan to eliminate North Korea—but with his Inchon proposal. MacArthur was saying he wanted to launch the invasion in September, a shockingly early time in the opinion of the JCS. When the chairman, Omar Bradley, heard Collins's report, he observed that "it was the riskiest military proposal I had ever heard of." Bradley called it a "blue-sky scheme" and said "Inchon was probably the worst possible place ever selected for an amphibious landing."[24]

Bradley complained that Inchon would absorb "most of our military reserve, and a failure could be a national or even international catastrophe, not only militarily, but psychologically. For this reason and because Truman was relying on us to an extraordinary degree for military counsel, we determined to keep a close eye on the Inchon plan, and, if we felt so compelled, finally cancel it."[25]

Since so much opposition was brewing in Washington concerning the Inchon plan, MacArthur cabled the Pentagon the following message on July 23, 1950: "I am firmly convinced that an early and strong effort behind his [the enemy's] front will sever his main line of communications and enable us to deliver a decisive and crushing blow. Any material delay in such an operation may lose this opportunity. The alternative is a frontal attack which can only result in a protracted and expensive campaign to slowly drive the enemy north of the 38th parallel."[26]

This message arrived in Washington just after Taejon had fallen, and many military leaders were wondering whether the Americans could even remain in Korea, much less move over to the offensive. But MacArthur was confident in a teleconference the Chiefs hastily called, and he insisted that the invasion be done as soon as possible.

Setting the actual date depended on the tides. Naval experts stated that small landing craft would need twenty-three-foot minimum tides to operate safely over the Inchon mud flats, and a twenty-nine-foot tide before landing ships, tank (LSTs) could come in. The navy could land men and equipment only from the time an incoming tide reached twenty-three feet until the outgoing tide dropped to twenty-three feet, a period of about three hours. Troops ashore would be stranded until the next high tide, about twelve hours later.[27]

Low seas at Inchon are common from June through August. September is a month of transition. High tides prevail from October through May. This left September as the earliest when tidal conditions would be suitable for an invasion. The next opportunity wouldn't come until October, and by then bad weather would be arriving in Korea. Even in September, only four days had suitable tidal conditions: September 15 to 18. It had to be mid-September or an indefinite postponement of the invasion.[28] MacArthur picked September 15.

CHAPTER 4

MacArthur Visits Chiang Kai-shek

Toward the end of July 1950, a panic developed over a possible attack on Taiwan by the Chinese Communists. U.S. intelligence sources picked up indications of a major Chinese troop buildup opposite the island. Reports said two hundred thousand troops and four thousand craft (almost all junks and other small seagoing vessels) had been assembled. The Joint Chiefs pulled ships off the blockade of North Korea to make a demonstration in the Taiwan Strait. The JCS also recommended that urgently needed supplies be sent to Chiang at once and that a survey team be sent to the island to determine defense needs. The JCS intended MacArthur to send some expert officers to do the survey. They didn't expect MacArthur to go himself.[1]

Intelligence reports said that some of the Chinese vessels might get through and might cause defections of Nationalist troops. The Chiefs recommended that Nationalist aircraft be authorized to strike amphibious concentrations on the mainland and to mine waters off the Chinese coast opposite Taiwan. Secretary of Defense Johnson endorsed the Chiefs' recommendations, but Acheson said mining would only be acceptable if international shipping was warned, while bombing the mainland was out of the question. The United States would be manifestly responsible, and this would antagonize friendly governments, especially Britain, and might lead to war with Red China.[2]

The JCS and Johnson revealed that they were willing to abandon the position that the United States was neutral in regard to Taiwan and the Chinese civil war. This was in direct conflict with the president's Taiwan quarantine order of June 27, which prohibited offensive action by *either* side. It was also contrary to a message Truman sent to Congress on July 19 in which he said the United States had no territorial ambitions concerning Taiwan and that the neutralization was "without prejudice to political questions affecting that island."[3]

For the United States to assist the Kuomintang in preventing Reds from attacking would line the United States solidly on the KMT side and give proof that the United States was targeting Red China as an enemy. The secretary of defense was almost certainly trying to undermine the Truman administration's containment strategy. The Joint Chiefs during this period were inconsistent about containment. So it is likely that they didn't fully understand the policy and reacted to a seeming threat in the Taiwan Strait with a straightforward military recommendation for a strong response. Truman and Acheson quickly heeled the JCS in, but Johnson's position was weakening by the day.

The feared attack on Taiwan was probably an elaborate hoax on the part of the Chinese Reds to test American response. They were not about to risk an invasion with highly vulnerable junks and light vessels against the guns and aircraft of the U.S. 7th Fleet. But the scare did have a significant effect in drawing the lines of controversy between MacArthur and Truman. At the end of the event, it was clear that Truman wanted to prevent any collision with Red China, while MacArthur was virtually calling for it.

MacArthur's visit to Taiwan occurred from July 31 to August 1, 1950. Most provocatively, he brought along Vice Admiral Arthur D. (Dewey) Struble, commander of the 7th Fleet, which was guarding Taiwan against Red invasion, thus giving the strong impression that Struble was working out ways to assist Chiang Kai-shek in attacking the mainland.

The crisis grew out of a logical fallacy that was contained in Truman's treatment of Chiang Kai-shek on June 27. Officially the United States had "neutralized" the island, thus creating a Far Eastern Switzerland that was equally neutral to the United States and to Red China. Since this neutralization had been imposed by force from the United States, however, Taiwan looked to the leaders in Beijing less like a benign and unthreatening Switzerland and more like a pugnacious ally of the United States about to embark on an offensive against the mainland.

MacArthur's appearance on Taiwan with Admiral Struble in tow multiplied the suspicions of the Red Chinese many times over. Distrust was increased even more by the behavior of Chiang. As Omar Bradley wrote, "MacArthur arrived like a visiting head of state, and was entertained accordingly. Naturally, Chiang Kai-shek made propaganda hay of the visit. The net effect of the Nationalist propaganda was to give the impression that the United States was, or was going to be, far more closely allied with Chiang militarily in the struggle against Communism in the Far East; that we might even arm him for a 'return to the mainland.' This impression was distinctly at odds with the Truman-Acheson hands-off policy and the JCS view, which was merely to help Chiang deny Formosa [Taiwan] to the Communists."[4]

Chiang took immediate advantage of the bonanza. He announced that "the foundation for Sino-American military cooperation has been laid."[5] MacArthur himself did nothing to dispel an impression that the United States was identifying its interests with the Nationalists.

The fallout from the meeting infuriated Truman. Some American allies, such as Britain, who had already recognized the Beijing regime, were appalled. Several congressional members of the China lobby in Washington crowed that MacArthur might still save the China that Truman and Acheson had "lost." Truman was sure that MacArthur was encouraging the China lobby. He made two decisions. He told his ambassador-at-large W. Averell Harriman to spell out administration policies to MacArthur on a trip he was taking to the Far East in early August. And he ordered Secretary of Defense Louis Johnson to send MacArthur a pointed message that "the most vital national interest requires that no action of ours precipitate general war or give excuse to others to do so."[6]

MacArthur quickly replied that he fully understood the president's policy and his headquarters were "operating meticulously in accordance therewith."[7]

But it was clear that MacArthur had a much different view of Taiwan than had Truman. For example, while MacArthur was flying to the island, the JCS received a cable saying that in the event Taiwan was attacked, he intended to transfer three squadrons of U.S. F-80C jet fighters to the island. He reported that he had already authorized "familiarization flights for small groups of U.S. fighter aircraft to Taiwan." The landings were temporary and for refueling only, he said. These steps were in strict violation of national policy of not using American forces other than the 7th Fleet for defense of Taiwan. The JCS quickly got off a cable stressing that such action would have "strong political implications" and should not be undertaken until considered at the "highest levels" in Washington.[8] On August 14, Truman informed MacArthur that the June 27 directive was designed to limit U.S. defense of Taiwan to operations that could be carried out without committing any American forces to the island. MacArthur, therefore, was not to place fighter squadrons on the island, and no U.S. forces were to be based there without specific approval by the Joint Chiefs.[9]

When MacArthur got back to Tokyo, he denied any political significance to his visit—as if the appearance of the Far East commander and the chief of the 7th Fleet in Taiwan could be construed in any other possible way except as support of the United States for Chiang Kai-shek and the possibility of an offensive alliance with him.[10] Red leaders were already suspicious that American plans were to defeat the North Korean Army, occupy North Korea, and support an invasion of China across the Yalu River with Nationalist Chinese troops.

The visit of MacArthur with Struble made these fears appear more real. This was a threat that President Truman most definitely did not want to convey. He had already vetoed a proposal to use Chinese Nationalist troops in Korea. Thus, it is no wonder that MacArthur's visit aroused his intense anger. It was the first time that he seriously considered firing the general.[11]

Johnson naively thought that MacArthur's treading on the edge of insubordination would be quickly forgotten. He asked the Chiefs to draft a message giving MacArthur standing authority to allow the

Nationalists to attack the Chinese mainland whenever intelligence showed that a Red attack was imminent.[12]

The proposal drew Truman's wrath, and further weakened Johnson's position. In a message on August 5, under Johnson's name but by Truman's order, MacArthur was told that the June 27 neutralization order remained in effect and that Taiwan's status had not changed. The message added: "No one other than the president as commander in chief has the authority to order or authorize preventive action against concentrations on the [Chinese] mainland. . . . The most vital national interest requires that no action of ours precipitate general war or give excuse to others to do so. This message has the approval of the president and the secretary of state."[13]

MacArthur quickly denied he had any intentions of usurping the rights of the president. But his visit to Taiwan marked his first overt move outside military channels to change American policy.

Truman hoped Averell Harriman's visit with MacArthur in Tokyo on August 6–8 would clear the air and allow MacArthur to come to a full agreement with Truman in regard to policy. It didn't work out that way.

Harriman's report to the president on his talks with MacArthur included several disturbing elements. "In my first talk with MacArthur," Harriman reported, "I told him the president wanted me to tell him he must not permit Chiang to be the cause of starting a war with the Chinese Communists on the mainland, the effect of which might drag us into a world war. He answered that he would, as a soldier, obey any orders that he received from the president. . . . For reasons which are rather difficult to explain, I did not feel that we came to a full agreement on the way we believed things should be handled on Formosa and with the Generalissimo [Chiang]. He accepted the president's position and will act accordingly, but without full conviction. He has a strange idea that we should back anybody who will fight Communism, even though he could not give an argument why the Generalissimo's fighting Communists would be a contribution towards the effective dealing with the Communists of China."[14]

In his talks with Harriman, MacArthur also proposed eliminating the North Korean state and absorbing it into South Korea. Harriman reported MacArthur's words: "When Syngman Rhee's government is reestablished in Seoul, the UN-supervised election can be held within two months, and he has no doubt of an overwhelming victory for the non-Communist parties. The North Koreans will also vote for the non-Communist parties when they are sure of no Russian or Communist intervention. He said there was no need to change the Constitution, which now provides 100 seats for the North. Korea can become a strong influence in stabilizing the non-Communist movement in the East."[15]

MacArthur had already stated to J. Lawton Collins, the army chief of staff, and Hoyt S. Vandenberg, the air force chief of staff, on July 13 that he intended to destroy the North Korean Army, which could only mean destruction of the North Korean state. In both utterances MacArthur was going far beyond the mandate given by the UN. According to Acheson, the original U.S. policy was to restore the status prior to the invasion and to reestablish the peace broken by the invasion.[16]

MacArthur's talks with Harriman confirmed that he intended to conquer North Korea, thereby rolling American forces right to the frontier of China along the Yalu River and creating an all-Korean state under Syngman Rhee, allied to the United States. MacArthur's plan carried the acute danger of Soviet or Red Chinese intervention. It implied upsetting the precarious political balance in the Far East and eliminating one of the Soviet Union's client states *and* the buffer that North Korea constituted for Communist China between it and the United States. It implied abandoning the containment policy put in place by the Truman administration in 1946 to avoid precipitating war with the Communist world.

Official Washington should have focused on this startling plan and resolved it quickly. Here was the senior military commander in the Far East proposing actions that would almost certainly bring war with Red China and very possibly with the Soviet Union. Despite the radical implications of MacArthur's proposals, however, no one in Washington became sufficiently alarmed to resolve the issue. Probably the reason was that President Truman accepted MacArthur's promises of support, however incomplete, as evidence of loyalty. For example, Truman wrote: "After Harriman explained the administration's policy to MacArthur, he had said he would accept it as a good soldier. I was reassured. I told the press that the general and I saw eye to eye on Formosa policy."[17]

Upon Harriman's departure from Tokyo, MacArthur issued a statement disclaiming that he discussed any nonmilitary matters with Chiang Kai-shek. He showed no hint of regret for the uproar he had caused, and raised doubt that his aggressive aspirations had been tamed. He charged that the purpose of his trip had been "maliciously represented to the public by those who invariably in the past have propagandized a policy of defeatism and appeasement in the Pacific. I hope the American people will not be misled by sly insinuations, brash speculations and bold misstatements invariably attributed to anonymous sources, so insidiously fed them both nationally and internationally by persons 10,000 miles away from the actual events, if they are not indeed designed to promote disunity and destroy faith and confidence in American purposes and institutions and American representatives at this time of great world peril." There could be no doubt that this verbal blast was aimed at his critics in Washington.[18]

Truman made no comment about MacArthur's plan to destroy the North Korean state and absorb it into South Korea, a factor far more likely than Taiwan to set off a war with Red China. He was already working on a policy, though he did not give it the precedence it needed. On July 17 Truman had instructed the National Security Council to make recommendations on U.S. courses "after the North Korean forces have been driven back to the 38th parallel."[19] This directive led to a series of studies embodied in NSC 81, which was not circulated until September 1, an extremely long time given the fact that the Inchon operation was looming and decisions were required urgently.

Meanwhile, other persons were stirring the pot for a campaign to destroy North Korea. John M. Allison, director of northeast Asian affairs in the State Department, said, "There will be no permanent peace and stability in Korea as long as the artificial division at the 38th parallel continues." Although he wasn't sure it would be possible, Allison said he felt "we should continue right on up to the Manchurian and Siberian border, and, having done so, call for a UN-supervised election for all of Korea."[20] Syngman Rhee and the South Korean ambassador to the U.S., John M. Chang, predictably took the same tack. [21]

Herbert Feis, a historian and member of the State Department's policy-planning staff, was one of the few who took a contrary position. Feis was to receive the Pulitzer Prize in 1960 for his study of the 1945 Potsdam Conference. Now he recommended that the United States prohibit American or South Korean troops moving north of the 38th parallel. If they did, Feis wrote, the Chinese Communists and the Russians might send their troops into Korea. Allison disagreed with Feis, saying it was unrealistic to expect to return to the status quo antebellum. At the very least, he wrote, the United States should destroy the North Korean Army and hold all-Korea elections under UN auspices. John Foster Dulles, Republican consultant to Acheson (and later to become secretary of state in Dwight D. Eisenhower's administration), agreed that the 38th parallel should not be a political boundary and he thought "it would be folly to allow the North Korean army to retire in good order" behind the 38th, whence it could attack South Korea in the future.[22]

At the same time, Joseph Stalin announced a far different plan to end the Korean conflict and the problem with Taiwan in a single move. He said the UN Security Council could secure a peaceful settlement provided Red China replaced the Nationalists on the council. Jawaharlal Nehru, prime minister of India, thought Stalin's proposal offered excellent possibilities and he urged it upon the United States.[23]

Acheson hunted for allies to deflect Stalin's démarche and found a reluctant friend in Ernest Bevin, British foreign minister. Bevin agreed with Washington's position that there could be no bargain to admit Red China to the UN as the price of peace in Korea. Each issue had to be dealt with on its merits, Bevin said. However, Bevin feared that the U.S. policy of spurning Beijing, if pursued, would alienate China irrevocably from the West and turn it even more to the Soviet Union.[24] Bevin's advice was good, and the admission of Red China to the UN would almost assuredly have brought pressure by Russia and Red China to stop the North Korean attack. But Washington was incapable of such cooperation with the Communists. It chose force, not negotiation, to resolve the issue of Korea, and it insisted on the fiction that Nationalist China represented the Chinese people. Out of these twin errors, a great deal of tragedy was to spring.

The NSC study of whether the United States was going to drive over the 38th parallel into North Korea revealed enormous misconceptions about the problem the United States faced. One of the most curious aspects of the case was that at no time did any of the senior planners—with the notable exception of Herbert Feis—focus on the containment policy that the Truman administration had adopted in 1946. Containment meant just that: holding the line. It did *not* mean conquering a Communist state. Indeed, the United States was at the present moment fighting a war against North Korea for attempting to conquer a Free World state! To contemplate advancing into North Korea was a direct violation of settled policy. Instead of stopping and asking themselves what on earth they were doing, the NSC experts and the members of the Truman administration spent their energy trying to figure out ways that they *could* occupy North Korea and get away with it.

Thus, when the urgings of Douglas MacArthur to destroy North Korea came into collision with the nation's containment policy—as they were bound to do—the great bulk of the senior officials of the Truman administration opted for the illogic and danger of MacArthur's proposal, and they rejected the sense and sensibility of containment. This gross mistake was going to cost the United States dearly.

The actual studies within the State and Defense departments made other flagrant blunders. One of the most astonishing was that, from the start, they focused on how the Soviet Union might react but paid amazingly little attention to Red China. The American planners took for granted that Beijing would only act as an agent of the Kremlin and did not acknowledge that the Chinese might have separate national interests. The planners concluded on July 25 that it was unlikely the Kremlin would accept a regime in North Korea it couldn't control. They also acknowledged that public and congressional opinion in the United States would probably call for a "final" solution to the Korean problem and might want military action to continue north of the 38th parallel. The conflicting desires of the Kremlin and the United States pointed to the possibility of general war. Instead of attempting to resolve this sharp contradiction, the planners merely recommended that a decision on whether to cross the 38th be deferred until the military and political situation was clearer.[25]

From Moscow, U.S. ambassador Alan G. Kirk wrote on July 27 that he didn't believe the Soviets would risk war to preserve North Korea but felt it was premature to commit the United States to crossing the 38th parallel. Paul Nitze of the State policy-planning staff said on July 28 that the United States should wait until its troops approached the 38th before deciding whether to cross.

Defense Department drafts of July 31 and August 7 took a more aggressive line. The drafts assumed that the chief limitation to unifying Korea would be *Soviet* military countermeasures, including the possible use of Chinese Communist troops, but assumed that neither Beijing nor Moscow would overtly enter Korean hostilities and risk general war in the Far East. The drafts raised no possibility that Red China might pursue its own course of action, implying that any decision would be made by the Soviet Union, not China. The final Defense paper said the United States should take measures to establish a united Korea "oriented toward the U.S." It recommended that the UN command should occupy all Korea and that the UN should hold all-Korea elections.

The State Department draft of August 31 held that it was possible but unlikely that Chinese Communist forces would be used in Korea in the event the United States moved north of the 38th, since the Soviet Union probably regarded Korea as being in its own sphere of interest. The draft repeated that a final determination for U.S. action must be made "in light of the action or inaction of the Soviet Union and the Chinese Communists" and after consulting with U.S. allies.[26]

Thus, only two weeks before the landings at Inchon—which were going to force a decision on U.S. movement over the 38th parallel—the Defense Department was saying the Communists would probably not risk war to save North Korea, while the State Department was *still* recommending that the United States wait to see what Communist reaction would be before deciding on a course of action. These attitudes indicated an entirely opportunistic approach to the problem. The implication was that if the Kremlin decided not to intervene, the United States might go on to conquer North Korea. If the Soviets did intervene, the United States would have to reconsider its decision. There was still no indication in Washington that Communist China might pursue a course independent of the Kremlin.

The entire thrust of the State and Defense departments' proposals during this crucial period reveals an almost total lack of reality and of attention to the actual problem—that the aggressive proposal to destroy North Korea being pressed by MacArthur was totally at odds with the nation's containment policy and was almost certain to bring on war with Red China. Only a few State Department officials saw this danger, and no senior officials did anything about it.

While analysts in the State and Defense departments worked over their plans, a fierce aggressiveness seized a number of American leaders. They now began to talk openly of driving the Communists back, not merely restoring the status quo antebellum. On August 10 Warren R. Austin, U.S. ambassador to the UN Security Council, announced that American determination for a united Korea "had never wavered." On August 17 he said that the United Nations should see to the elimination of a Korea that was "half-slave" and "half-free."[27] On August 25 in a speech in Boston, Francis P. Matthews, secretary of the navy, openly advocated a preventive war "to compel cooperation for peace," adding that the United States would thus "become the first aggressor for peace."[28] Less than a week later, Major General Orvil A. Anderson, commander of the Air War College, asserted that the United States was already at war and boasted he could "break up Russia's five A-bomb nests in a week." The U.S. government promptly repudiated both Matthews's and Anderson's statements, and the Pentagon removed Anderson from his post. However, Matthews remained in his job, and no American official disowned Austin's UN statements.[29]

CHAPTER 5

MacArthur Openly Defies Truman

After Averell Harriman's visit to Tokyo and MacArthur's statement that he would accept administration policy "as a good soldier," Harry Truman assumed that all was well with the general. But he was wrong.

Truman recounted: "Before the month ended—on August 26— the White House press room brought me a copy of a statement which General MacArthur had sent to the Veterans of Foreign Wars." The statement was to be read at a VFW meeting in Chicago on August 28. But it had already been printed in the *U.S. News and World Report*, and this was the first the president had heard about it.

Truman summarized the general's message: " 'In view of misconceptions being voiced concerning the relationship of Formosa to our strategic potential in the Pacific,' MacArthur thought it desirable to put forth his own views on the subject. He argued that the oriental psychology required 'aggressive, resolute and dynamic leadership,' and 'nothing could be more fallacious than the threadbare argument by those who advocate appeasement and defeatism in the Pacific that if we defend Formosa we alienate continental Asia.' In other words, he called for a military policy of aggression, based on Formosa's position. The whole tenor of the message was critical of the very policy which he had so recently told Harriman he would support. There was no doubt in my mind that the world would read it that way and that it must have been intended that way."[1]

Truman concluded that MacArthur's statement would confuse the world as to what American policy was in regard to Taiwan—that is, the neutralization of the island that he had ordered on June 27. Truman had just reaffirmed that policy in a letter to the UN secretary-general, Trygve Lie, only the day before.

Truman's letter was in answer to a charge by the Soviet delegation of U.S. aggression in its aid to Chiang Kai-shek. The Soviets held that placing the 7th Fleet in the Taiwan Strait amounted to incorporating Taiwan into the American orbit. Truman countered with a declaration that the United States was entirely willing to have the United Nations investigate the situation. Truman's letter to the UN was designed to make it plain that the United States had no other purpose than to reduce the area of conflict in the Far East. But, as Truman wrote, "General MacArthur's message—which the world might mistake as an expression of American policy—contradicted this."[2]

Truman produced a succinct answer to the challenge that Mac-Arthur had just made: "The official position of the United States is defined by decisions and declarations of the president. There can be only one voice in stating the position of this country in the field of foreign relations. This is of fundamental constitutional significance."[3]

Truman gave serious thought to relieving MacArthur on the spot. But he decided against it to avoid the appearance of demotion—and also because the Inchon landing was only a short while away. MacArthur was wholly responsible for this operation, and an abrupt change in command would have been extremely disruptive.

The president had a meeting scheduled the same morning with Secretary of State Acheson, Secretary of Defense Johnson, Averell Harriman, and the Joint Chiefs of Staff. Truman, "lips white and compressed,"[4] read MacArthur's statement to the group, then asked each of them if he had had any advance knowledge of it. All said no, and all were deeply shocked by what they heard.[5]

Acheson said "this insubordination could not be tolerated."[6] Omar Bradley said the message seemed the height of arrogance.[7] Truman then told Johnson to send a personal message to MacArthur telling him that the president ordered him to withdraw the statement.[8] It was impossible to prevent the statement's distribution worldwide, of course, but withdrawal would make clear that it had no official standing. Withdrawal was also quite obviously a harsh and immediate disciplinary move against MacArthur.

Johnson did not like the idea of being the bearer of such tidings to the general and, according to Bradley, "spent the rest of the day trying to weasel out of it." At last, Truman called Johnson in and himself dictated the order to MacArthur.[9]

This was the message: "The President of the United States directs that you withdraw your message for national encampment of Veterans of Foreign Wars, because various features with respect to Formosa are in conflict with the policy of the United States and its position in the United Nations."[10]

MacArthur complied in withdrawing the statement, but the reprimand did not have much of an effect on him. He fired back that his message had been prepared to support the president's June 27 order neutralizing Taiwan. He asserted that the views he had expressed to the VFW were "purely my personal ones."[11] This was truly a remarkable defense. There was no possibility that the general charged with keeping Taiwan neutral could spread to the world views in direct opposition to the official position of the United States and think that they were "personal"!

MacArthur's statement did rally to his side the bellicose Republicans in the Congress whom Omar Bradley called "right-wing primitives."[12] And as David McLellan writes in his biography of Acheson, it "further reinforced MacArthur in his megalomania and in his career of insubordination."[13]

Secretary Johnson's behavior in the VFW speech controversy was the last straw for President Truman. He had learned that Johnson was conniving with Republican Senator Robert Taft for the ouster of Acheson. Truman called for Johnson's resignation and immediately asked General of the Army George C. Marshall to take the job. The wartime chief of staff, special envoy to China (1945–46), and former secretary of state (1947–49) now took on his final major responsibility for his country. The Senate quickly approved him, but in the hearings for his confirmation, Marshall had to undergo brutal attacks by members of the China lobby and some Republican extremists.[14]

The immediate result of the controversy was to give a propaganda victory to the Communists. Andrey Vyshinsky, Soviet ambassador to the United Nations, in a speech said: "None other than General MacArthur recently informed, with cynical candor, the whole world about the decision of the ruling circles in the United States at all costs to turn Taiwan into an American base in the Far East."[15]

CHAPTER 6

Inchon

While official Washington was consumed with the revolt of Douglas MacArthur over American foreign policy, the nation's military leadership was disputing how the war in Korea could best be brought to an end.

Since the first days of the war, MacArthur had been calling for an invasion of the port city of Inchon, twenty miles west of the Korean capital of Seoul. During the entire period, the Joint Chiefs of Staff had opposed the idea. They gave plausible reasons for their opposition—the narrow approach channel to Inchon, the deep mudflats just offshore, and the high tides which vastly complicated the use of LSTs and other landing craft. But the real reason they opposed the idea was that they felt it was far too bold, audacious, and risky.

MacArthur saw the invasion as a way to eliminate the North Korean Army in a stroke, without having to fire a single shot at it.

But the Joint Chiefs of Staff were a very conservative group of officers, and they thought an amphibious invasion should be made on
the safest shore, under the safest conditions, and in the safest location
possible. They had already selected an alternative site, the small port
of Kunsan, a hundred miles south of Inchon. Here tidal conditions
were ideal, the landing site was easy and accessible, and, best of all
in the eyes of J. Lawton Collins and Forrest Sherman, chiefs of the
army and navy respectively, Kunsan was only a few miles west of the
Pusan Perimeter and the U.S. 8th Army defending the Naktong
River line. A landing at Kunsan, they said, was far safer than a landing at Inchon, and the invading forces could link up quickly with
the 8th Army.

In warfare, it's rare for daring acts to gain the backing of generals. One of the principal reasons why military geniuses like Alexander, Hannibal, Napoléon, Stonewall Jackson, and Erwin Rommel
succeeded was that their opponents simply could not conceive of the
radical, dramatic, unexpected movements they undertook. The Joint
Chiefs of Staff were like the generals who were forced to face these
geniuses. They saw the obvious, traditional, orthodox solutions but
were unprepared to counter the unforeseen and the unconventional.
That's why wars are largely characterized by direct assaults on the
most heavily defended, obvious enemy positions. The repeated failed
attacks against virtually impregnable fortifications on the Western
Front in World War I were notorious examples of this mind-set. In
contrast, MacArthur was a bold commander, and he saw a much less
costly solution—an unexpected descent on the enemy's rear. Though
MacArthur's plan followed a principle of war older than history, it
seemed eccentric and precarious to the JCS.

The matter came to a head at a conference in MacArthur's headquarters in the Dai-ichi Building opposite the emperor's palace in

Tokyo on August 23. MacArthur, General Collins, and Admiral Sherman were there, along with all the top American brass in the Pacific.

At issue was whether the newly formed 10th Corps, consisting of the 1st Marine Division and the army's 7th Infantry Division, would make a landing at Inchon on September 15, 1950.

Lawton Collins gave it his best shot: "I questioned the ability of 8th Army to make a quick junction with the 10th Corps at Inchon. Failure to make this junction might result in disaster to the 10th Corps. I suggested as an alternative to Inchon, that consideration be given to a landing at Kunsan, which had few of Inchon's physical drawbacks, was close to the enemy's main supply routes through Nonsan and Taejon, and should ensure more prompt union with the 8th Army in the vicinity of Taejon. Admiral Sherman seconded my suggestion."[1]

Collins was looking at the problem from exactly the opposite direction to MacArthur. Collins was concerned about whether the 8th Army could drive up from the Naktong line "quickly enough before the enemy could concentrate an overwhelming force against the amphibious attackers. In many instances throughout military history the division of forces beyond supporting distances has led to disastrous defeats."[2]

MacArthur put down his corncob pipe and began to talk in a quiet and conversational tone. He talked for forty-five minutes. This oration has gone down as one of the most powerful and convincing arguments in American military history. The generals and admirals who heard it described its effect in awed terms. The presentation guaranteed the acceptance of MacArthur's plan and established the legend of his sagacity in military matters.

MacArthur made a number of points. The North Koreans had neglected their rear and were clinging to a thin logistical rope. This rope could be cut quickly by the capture of Seoul and the double-track railway running through it to the south. Once this rope was severed, the army would collapse within days. The North Koreans had committed nearly all of their forces against the 8th Army. They had no trained reserves to oppose a landing. Seizure of Seoul would capture the imagination of Asia. A landing at Kunsan would not sever the North Korean supply line. The North Koreans could quickly create a new front facing both the 8th Army and 10th Corps, thus requiring a direct assault against the enemy and a bitter winter campaign. An amphibious landing was the most powerful tool the United Nations possessed, and proper use of it meant to strike deep and hard into enemy-held territory.[3]

Though impressed, Collins remained worried about the ability of the North Koreans to concentrate powerful forces at Inchon and stop the invasion. But where was this "overwhelming force" going to come from? The invasion force consisted of seventy thousand men (the highly augmented 1st Marine Division and 7th Division, plus naval personnel). At sea there stood a force of 230 vessels, including cruisers and destroyers, two marine escort carriers with F4U Corsair ground support craft, three U.S. attack carriers, and a light British carrier. These carriers provided as many support aircraft as the airspace over Inchon could accommodate. Aircraft and gunfire could seal off the entire Inchon landing area from enemy reinforcements.

But there was no possibility of any substantial North Korean reinforcement. Intelligence estimates showed about 5,000 troops in Seoul, 500 at Kimpo Airfield just west of Seoul, and 1,800 to 2,500 around Inchon. Only a few units guarded the line of communication, while newly formed training groups were scattered back of the Pusan Perimeter. North Korea had no navy and only nineteen piston-driven aircraft.

Even in the Pusan Perimeter, UN forces far exceeded North Korean strength. Although U.S. intelligence credited the North Koreans with 102,000 men pressing against the perimeter, actual strength had eroded to 70,000 ill-fed men, a large number of whom were raw recruits. The 8th Army, on the other hand, had 120,000 men, with firepower six times more than the North Koreans'.

Intelligence estimated that the North Koreans might be able to divert three divisions (24,000 men) from the perimeter to go to Inchon. This was an unbelievably high figure because it would have denuded large portions of the Naktong line. More important, getting these troops to Inchon would be virtually impossible because UN command of the air ensured that trains could only run at night and had to hole up in tunnels during the day. Actually, it made little difference whether the North Koreans tried to reach Inchon or remained in place. They were doomed either way the moment the railway line was cut at Seoul. This would eliminate fuel, ammunition, and food. The North Korean Army would disintegrate wherever it was.

When Collins and Sherman got back to Washington, they and the rest of the Joint Chiefs were inclined to postpone Inchon until they were sure the 8th Army could hold the Pusan Perimeter, now under renewed attack. But Truman, Secretary Johnson, and Averell Harriman saw MacArthur's plan as daring and were certain it would succeed. So the senior military figures of the United States were extremely suspicious of the plan, while three civilians were ardent supporters.[4]

The plan, pending final JCS endorsement, called for the 1st Marine Division to make an assault landing directly into the port of Inchon, then to move rapidly to Kimpo Airfield a few miles east and seize the suburb of Yongdongpo just across the Han River from Seoul.

The 7th Division was to land after the marines and advance to secure the marines' right flank and link up with the 8th Army moving up from the south. Both marines and soldiers would capture Seoul quickly by movements from the west and the south.

As ships and men made vast final preparations in ports in Japan, the JCS was seized with last-minute fears and sent MacArthur a final warning of the disastrous consequences if the Inchon landing failed or failed to produce a quick victory. The Chiefs' message:

"While we concur in launching a counteroffensive in Korea as early as feasible, we have noted with considerable concern the recent trend of events there. In light of all factors including apparent commitment of practically all reserves available to 8th Army, we desire your estimate as to the feasibility and chance of success of projected operation if initiated on planned schedule. We are sure that you understand that all available trained army units in the United States have been allocated to you except the 82nd Airborne Division and that minimum of four months would elapse before first of partially trained National Guard divisions could reach Korea in event that junction of main 8th Army forces with 10th Corps bridgehead should not quickly be effected with forces now available to FECOM [Far East Command]."[5]

When MacArthur got the message, he said it "chilled me to the marrow of my bones," because it implied that "the whole movement be abandoned."[6] Even so, MacArthur replied calmly, stating that there was no question as to the feasibility of the operation and its chances for success.[7]

The Chiefs held a final discussion of Inchon on September 8 that included a morning conference with President Truman. "It was really too late in the game for the JCS to formally disapprove Inchon,"

Bradley said.[8] The Joint Chiefs told the president they endorsed Inchon, and the same day they flashed MacArthur the go-ahead.

D espite all the trauma leading up to the decision about Inchon, the actual operation went off like a well-organized theatrical production. No problems developed. The navy knocked out guns guarding the harbor on the island of Wolmi-do, and the marines quickly seized all of the key positions. There were few casualties. By midnight Inchon had been essentially secured, and marines moved out swiftly to capture Kimpo Airfield and occupy Yongdongpo. Meanwhile the 7th Infantry Division protected the flank against North Korean counterattacks. The response of the North Koreans was stunned surprise and inaction. They never were able to mount a single major counterstroke.[9] The few troops they held in the area disintegrated in the face of overwhelming American power.

It was September 20, five days after the invasion, before the North Korean front around the Pusan Perimeter collapsed. But when it happened, the entire North Korean Army disintegrated, just as MacArthur had anticipated. By September 23 North Korean units were in full flight northward. A few North Korean soldiers walked meekly into POW camps, while the majority melted away into the hills and mountains, avoiding combat and trying to walk back to North Korea. Some of them made it.

Meanwhile marines and soldiers launched an assault on Seoul. Its capture took nine days, September 19–28. The issue was never in doubt, but groups of North Korean soldiers built barricades in the city streets and defended them fiercely. Organized North Korean units had pulled out of the city by September 26, and the North Koreans still in the city were isolated. Though capture by UN forces was a certainty, reduction of Seoul became a series of nasty local fights that took a toll on both sides. The North Koreans stretched barricades all the way across the streets at many locations in the central part of the city, generally at intersections. Most of the barricades were about chest high and were built out of rice and fiber bags filled with earth. North Koreans mounted antitank guns and machine guns behind and to the sides of these barricades. They swept the streets with fire and made movement extremely dangerous. Other enemy soldiers hid in nearby buildings and fired from windows and doors. In front of the barricades, the enemy laid down antitank mines.

The marines and soldiers quickly developed a method for destroying these barricades. But the process involved destroying much of the neighborhood as well. U.S. troops ordered in marine and navy aircraft to rocket-bomb and strafe the positions. Then they pounded the barricades with mortar and artillery fire while engineers moved under its cover to explode the antitank mines. Then two or three medium tanks, usually M26 Pershings but also older M4A3 Shermans, pushed aside the barricades and destroyed the antitank and machine guns. Infantry following after provided the tanks with protection and dealt with snipers. It sometimes took an hour to break a barricade. When the fight was over, a shattered, burning section of Seoul remained, along with many dead bodies.[10]

The aftermath of the Inchon victory was the precipitous rise in the stature of Douglas MacArthur, along with the equally precipitous plummeting in prestige of the Joint Chiefs of Staff. MacArthur had been right all along, and the objections of the JCS seemed to have been timid and hesitant. President Truman sent the general a message glowing with compliments: "I know I speak for the entire American people when I send you my warmest congratulations on the victory which has been achieved under your leadership in Korea. Few operations in military history can match either the delaying action where you traded space for time in which to build up your forces, or the brilliant maneuver which has now resulted in the liberation of Seoul."[11] The Joint Chiefs acknowledged that "your transition from defensive to offensive operations was magnificently planned, timed and executed."[12]

The North Koreans were defeated consecutively and in detail. They were never able to concentrate for a decisive counterattack. With this evidence of careful planning by MacArthur to eliminate any possibility of a meaningful enemy response, it is astonishing that Omar Bradley called Inchon "the luckiest operation in history" and a "military miracle."[13] Scarcely any invasion could have involved less luck and more elimination of chance. At least Bradley acknowledged that he had been wrong: "In hindsight, the JCS seemed like a bunch of nervous Nellies to have doubted."[14]

But the victory at Inchon was going to have far-reaching consequences. Matthew B. Ridgway, army deputy chief of staff and later to replace MacArthur, said: "A more subtle result of the Inchon triumph was the development of an almost superstitious regard for General MacArthur's infallibility. Even his superiors, it seemed, began to doubt if they should question *any* of MacArthur's decisions."[15]

Thus, in the space of days, MacArthur's position had moved from the president considering relieving him for failing to follow national policy to almost universal acclaim in Congress and in the American press as a military genius.

CHAPTER 7

The Attempt to Conquer North Korea

Of the North Korean soldiers in South Korea when the Inchon invasion occurred, between twenty-five thousand and thirty thousand eventually got back to North Korea. With few exceptions, the escaping North Koreans lost their heavy weapons and vehicles. A few soldiers kept their rifles and light automatic weapons, but the great majority arrived back in North Korea dispirited and unarmed.

A number of survivors walked through rugged country for days to reach the two major assembly points just north of the 38th parallel—"the Iron Triangle" formed by Chorwon, Kumwha, and Pyonggang in the middle of the peninsula, and the Inje–Hwachon Reservoir region in the high Taebaek Mountains in the east. Although these men, for the moment, were essentially refugees, they would become an army in time.

A surge to occupy North Korea and absorb it into South Korea rushed over the American people immediately after the capture of Seoul. Demands arose everywhere to reunite the two Koreas. This, in the public's mind, would restore order and calm to the country and region. MacArthur had called for this twice, and some American officials had been beating the drums for it since August.

By the time of Inchon, Truman had actually made up his mind—he intended to unify North and South Korea in a single country protected by the United States. Truman did not announce this publicly, however. The resolve existed as a policy recommended by the National Security Council and approved by Truman on September 11, four days before the invasion. Truman, therefore, abandoned the containment policy the administration had been following since 1946 and set out to push back the Communist frontier to the Yalu River. It was a radical departure, exactly in line with the aggressive desires of Douglas MacArthur, and the decision paid little attention to the political realities of East Asia.

On September 1, the NSC completed its study (NSC 81) of what the United States should do once its forces got back to the 38th parallel. The NSC 81 drafters rejected the idea of restoring the status quo antebellum. They held that the United States should seek unification of Korea through free elections by the United Nations and that the South Korean government under Syngman Rhee should be recognized by the UN as the only lawful government in the country. When NSC 81 made the rounds of Washington, it received only two significant changes. Acheson got a requirement that MacArthur had to clear operations north of the 38th with Truman, and he inserted a statement that "it should be the policy" to use South Korean soldiers along the northern Korean borders with China and the Soviet Union.[1] This is the document (NSC 81/1) that President Truman approved on September 11.[2]

Truman made this decision in the face of undisguised movements of Chinese troops in large numbers into Manchuria, beginning shortly after the U.S. ambassador to the UN, Warren R. Austin, began making statements in mid-August urging North and South unification. Red Chinese alarm became unmistakable after Inchon. Intelligence officers in the Far East Command estimated that People's Liberation Army (PLA) troops in Manchuria rose to 246,000 men by August 31 and to 450,000 by September 21.[3]

It's likely that President Truman did not realize at first the full extent of what he had decided to do. Originally there was a vague idea that unification was an objective and did not necessarily imply invasion of North Korea.[4] However, Truman soon recognized that Korea was not going to be united without force. Therefore, on September 27—before the matter was submitted to the United Nations—he approved a JCS directive to MacArthur that specifically authorized military action north of the 38th. This directive stated that Mac-Arthur's objective was destruction of the North Korean armed forces.[5]

The Truman administration was thinking on the extremely narrow basis of what would be most advantageous to the United States. There was no effort to achieve a settlement of outstanding issues in East Asia in order to come to a sustainable peace. What is worse, the administration assumed that only Russia might intervene, and that this was unlikely. It did not seriously consider the possibility that Red China might respond on its own.

Omar Bradley summed up the administration's position. He said that Red China was a satellite of the Kremlin and that "the Russians were not ready to risk global war over Korea." Red China would not move on its own, he said, because if it ever intended to move it would be to seize Taiwan, not "help solve Russia's problem in North Korea."[6] In other words, the administration simply disregarded the issue that was consuming Red China—the fear that the United States would seize North Korea and use it to launch attacks against North China.

In his memoirs, Bradley admitted to two flaws in his logic. "The first was our belief that Red China was a Soviet satellite under tight Moscow control. Not enough consideration was given the view that Red China could, or might want to, act independently of Moscow or that a dramatic Red Chinese military rescue of North Korea could in effect turn North Korea into a Chinese Communist satellite, greatly enhancing Red China's power and prestige in the Far East. The second flaw was the all too widespread belief that Red China acting alone could not make a decisive difference; in fact, might even suffer a humiliating defeat, and further, that the most favorable time militarily for intervention (when we were hanging on in the Pusan Perimeter) had passed."[7]

This revealed a complete misreading of China and China's interests. Red China had already concluded that America was hostile, on the strength of three brazen acts—the quarantine of Taiwan, Douglas MacArthur's highly trumpeted visit to Chiang Kai-shek, and MacArthur's widely disseminated speech to the VFW that implied occupation of Taiwan and using it as an offensive base against the Chinese mainland. These acts aroused the highest suspicion that the United States was going to team up with Chiang and launch an invasion of North China across the Yalu River frontier.

"I would very much like to write," Bradley said in his memoirs, "that the military establishment had seen the flaws in this logic and held a different view. Such was not the case. Our military intelligence estimates had contributed substantially to the CIA's conclusions. We wrongly continued to focus too much emphasis on enemy intentions and not enough on his capabilities."[8]

The conclusion must be that it did not occur to the top leaders of the United States that the most provocative act they could commit against Red China was to threaten to eliminate the North Korean state.

No one in the administration talked to a China scholar, who could have told the planners that Korea was crucial to China's security. From the Han Dynasty in the time of Christ onward, Chinese emperors had tried to keep Korea as a buffer in front of the North China Plain, China's heartland. About 100 B.C., the Han Emperor Wu-ti extended Chinese control down to a line that almost traces the modern 38th parallel.[9] For two thousand years Korea had kept its independence by serving as a shield for China. King Yi Sung-gai, the founder of the Korean Yi Dynasty, for example, accepted the status of "civilized tributary state" from China in 1392. He said: "Our little kingdom may well serve as fence and wall and still do grace to the wide and limitless favor of the Emperor."[10] In 1910 Japan annexed Korea and used it to invade Manchuria and North China. In 1945 this peril ended with Japan's defeat. China most definitely did not want the United States to replace Japan as the occupier of Korea and the threat from the sea.

All things considered, it was absurd to think that Red China would quietly acquiesce to the movement of the world's most powerful military force right up to its most vulnerable frontier, particularly since the owner of this force had already signaled its hostility in many ways.

The NSC 81/1 decision had been made in part because of the pressure exerted by Douglas MacArthur to conquer North Korea. It had been abetted by the bellicose demands of Republicans in Congress and other figures in the public eye. After Inchon, American public opinion reinforced this attitude by swinging toward its traditional one-dimensional desire for total victory. On September 18, the *New York Times* demanded that the North Korean aggressors be destroyed.

On September 25, *Time* magazine predicted the United States would urge the United Nations to authorize crossing the 38th parallel. After Inchon, *U.S. News and World Report* also urged crossing. One of the few voices in opposition was Hanson W. Baldwin, military writer for the *New York Times*. On September 27, he said if UN troops crossed the parallel, "we will surely be accused of aggression and the Chinese Communists might well be provoked to action."[11]

The administration's delay in coming to a decision about conquering North Korea contributed to its failure to examine the situation adequately. But witless oblivion also played a role. Any sensible, informed citizen could have seen that Beijing would not accept a forcible unification of North and South Korea. Any such government would be dominated by the United States and almost certainly hostile to Communist China.

It would have been much more sensible for the administration to face the problem head-on and decide where American national interests lay. Conquering a Communist state might be dazzling, but it would add very little to American strategic strength. Yet any realistic appraisal—not the wishful thinking and pseudo-analysis carried out by Omar Bradley—should have shown the real likelihood of Red China's intervention. If sincere, objective evaluation had been done by the people in charge, NSC 81/1 could easily have been set aside, and a rational program to bring peace to East Asia could have been worked out.

The unequivocal warnings coming from Beijing, coupled with massive troop movements right up to the Korean frontier that were not hidden from intelligence agents, prove that Washington had ample notification of China's anxiety and probable response.[12] The Truman administration had the responsibility for evaluating war threats and determining the proper course to follow. This job did not lie with MacArthur or with the Joint Chiefs of Staff. Washington did not need to depend on them entirely for information and guidance. Reliable information came in constantly from diplomatic and intelligence sources. The Truman administration and especially the State Department chose to ignore these warnings and to discount ominous intelligence reports. The administration was responsible for weighing the dangers to the United States and deciding whether it would invade North Korea or seek an accommodation with Beijing. But it failed miserably.

Although Russia lurked in the wings, nearly everyone in authority had concluded correctly that Joseph Stalin was not interested in committing his forces to such a doubtful and marginal enterprise. Stalin had given Kim Il Sung weapons in the hopes he could achieve an easy victory. Once the United States entered the war, there was no chance of that. So Stalin wisely backed out entirely. Red China, however, could not be expected to accept a loss of its buffer state in front of the Yalu. But Beijing was no more interested in a warlike North Korea than the United States. It might well have acquiesced to a quick UN strike into North Korea to abolish the rebuilding North Korean Army and Kim Il Sung's government—but not to eliminate the North Korean state. Then the United States and Red China might have stood patron for a less aggressive North Korea.

But this was not to be, to the great tragedy of the world. Douglas MacArthur's extremely hostile attitude toward Red China found willing acolytes in the halls of Congress and in much of the press. The wild, unfounded charges of Senator Joseph McCarthy added to the unreasoned fear pervading the country. So the Truman administration marched off, disregarding its own containment policy, to conquer a Communist state.

The United States wanted UN approval for what it intended to do. The Soviet Union had returned to the Security Council on August 1, so there was no chance of getting a resolution through that chamber. The United States turned instead to the General Assembly. The case was building in the UN for eliminating North Korea, but members shied away from expressing this wish in such blunt terms. Accordingly, Secretary of State Acheson worked out a deal with the British representative to introduce a resolution on September 30, 1950, sponsored by seven other countries, but not the United States. Acheson probably drafted the resolution, since it bears telltale marks of his habit of obscuring the real intent of his actions wherever possible. Since no one was willing to say frankly what he wanted to happen, the measure was misleading and ambivalent. It recommended that "all appropriate steps be taken to ensure conditions of stability throughout Korea" and that "all sections and representative bodies of the population of Korea, South and North, be invited to cooperate with the organs of the United Nations in the restoration of peace in the holding of elections, and the establishment of a unified government."[13]

Clearly this all-Korea election was not going to take place without force, but UN members deliberately avoided using the term. MacArthur had no doubts. In Senate committee hearings in May 1951, he said: "My mission was to clear out all North Korea, to unify it, and to liberalize it."[14] As James F. Schnabel and Robert J. Watson write in their history of the Joint Chiefs of Staff, "General MacArthur could readily conclude that the Assembly meant for him to impose unity on Korea by the sword."[15]

While the debate was going on in the UN General Assembly, Red China firmly and emphatically made its position known. On October 1, 1950, Premier Zhou Enlai gave an official speech in Beijing that crossing the parallel was a possible cause for war. The Chinese people, Zhou asserted, "absolutely will not tolerate foreign aggression, nor will they supinely tolerate seeing their neighbors being savagely invaded by the imperialists."[16]

Red China's strongest warning came in the early hours of October 3, 1950. Zhou Enlai summoned K. M. Panikkar, the Indian ambassador, to his residence. Zhou informed him that the People's Republic would intervene in Korea if American troops crossed the 38th parallel, but not if South Korean troops did so alone. Panikkar immediately notified his government and also the diplomatic representatives of Britain and Burma.[17]

Zhou's warning reached Washington through British channels early on October 3. Panikkar's message got nothing like the attention it deserved. Official Washington didn't like Panikkar because it thought he favored the Communists too much. Truman said Zhou's warning might be a propaganda ploy to keep the UN Assembly from approving the North Korean intervention resolution. Acheson thought Zhou's message was part of a Soviet-Chinese effort to get all UN forces withdrawn. Only one rational voice cried out in the intellectual wilderness. U. Alexis Johnson, Far Eastern expert for the State Department, said the U.S. should not assume that Zhou's threat was all bluff. He recommended that South Korean forces be used exclusively in North Korea, with UN air and naval support.[18]

The Truman administration essentially ignored Zhou Enlai's warning. This failure to pay attention to a clear threat was one of the greatest political disasters in modern times. The warning was a direct refutation of the rationalizations the administration had been manufacturing to justify its resolve to destroy North Korea. For that reason alone, the administration should have stopped in its tracks and reevaluated its entire strategic plan.

Zhou had actually left the United States a huge loophole through which it could have jumped to solve the problem of North Korea.

He said Red China would not intervene if only South Korean troops entered North Korea. This showed that Red China was less interested in saving North Korea's government than it was in preventing an American army on the banks of the Yalu River. The South Koreans were capable of destroying the North Korean army remnants, especially if they were given more artillery, tanks, and air support.

Alexis Johnson was the only American official who recommended this solution. If he had been listened to, the Korean War could probably have ended in a couple months' time. In that case North Korea would have been disarmed, but the North Korean state would still have stood as a buffer in front of the Yalu.

That was not what MacArthur and the Truman administration wanted. They wanted to destroy North Korea.

On October 7, 1950, the Korean resolution passed the UN Assembly by a vote of forty-seven to five, with seven abstentions. On October 9, MacArthur launched his forces into North Korea.

The plans MacArthur came up with to destroy the remaining North Korean forces were quite bad. He took his only rested force, 10th Corps around Seoul, and sent it on a long, circuitous, and time-consuming voyage to make an amphibious landing at Wonsan on Korea's east coast. He assigned the 8th Army, exhausted and out of supplies after driving up from the Naktong line, the task of advancing directly north from Seoul on the North Korean capital of Pyongyang and to the Yalu River beyond. The 10th Corps thus occupied the two ports, Inchon and Pusan, needed to bring in greatly needed supplies, while the 8th Army had to reorganize and resupply before it could launch its drive northward.

The result was predictable. The 8th Army was unable to overrun the two North Korean assembly sites in the Iron Triangle and Hwachon-Inje before the enemy soldiers were able to get away, and South Korean soldiers walking on foot captured Wonsan before the marines and soldiers of 10th Corps had even gotten into their ships.

MacArthur sent the newly arrived 3rd Infantry Division to occupy Wonsan, and diverted the 1st Marine Division and parts of the army 7th Infantry Division to land at Hungnam on Korea's northeastern coast and drive through Hamhung northward through the Changjin or Chosin Reservoir to the Yalu. The rest of the 7th Division he landed at Iwon, northeast of Hungnam, with instructions to drive up the coast to the Soviet frontier, along with South Korean forces.[19] Meanwhile the 8th Army continued on its drive toward the Yalu, encountering small and lessening amounts of resistance the farther north it pressed.[20]

The offensive into North Korea had just gotten under way when President Truman decided he needed a meeting with General MacArthur. Since the success of Inchon, MacArthur's status had soared to stratospheric heights in the United States. Everywhere people were acclaiming him as an infallible military genius. All his judgments and comments were being viewed as expressions of great wisdom and insight. The public and most civilian members of the administration were not aware of the blunders he had made in launching the invasion of North Korea. Truman felt that in a face-to-face meeting he would have better success in conveying his administration's foreign policy.

And there was one important question he wanted to ask MacArthur directly. Although he had accepted his advisers' opinions that the United States could achieve a quick victory and roll back Communism's borders in Korea, he still wanted to get MacArthur's personal appraisal as to whether Red China would, in fact, intervene.[21]

For the meeting, Truman selected Wake Island, a tiny U.S.-owned atoll twenty-three hundred miles west of Hawaii and two thousand miles southeast of Tokyo. The meeting took place on Sunday, October 15, 1950.

Many persons in the State Department opposed Truman going so far to meet MacArthur, because it implied raising the general almost to the same level as the president. Dean Acheson refused to go. "While General MacArthur had many of the attributes of a foreign sovereign," he wrote, "it did not seem wise to recognize him as one."[22] The Joint Chiefs of Staff also didn't want to go, so Omar Bradley agreed to represent them all. Others in the group included Dean Rusk, assistant secretary of state; W. Averell Harriman, special assistant to the president; and Admiral Arthur W. Radford, Pacific Fleet commander.

Here is Truman's account of their first meeting: "General MacArthur was at the ramp of the plane as I came down. His shirt was unbuttoned, and he was wearing a cap that had evidently seen a good deal of use. We greeted each other cordially, and after the photographers had finished their usual picture orgy we got into an old two-door sedan and drove to the office of the airline manager on the island. We talked for more than an hour alone. We discussed the Japanese and the Korean situations. The general assured me that the victory was won in Korea. He also informed me that the Chinese Communists would not attack and that Japan was ready for a peace treaty."[23]

Before they drove back to another small building where the other members of the party had gathered, MacArthur repeated to Truman that the Korean conflict was won and there was little possibility of the Chinese Communists coming in.

At the gathering with the assembled officials, MacArthur stated his firm belief that all resistance would end by Thanksgiving. This, he said, would enable him to withdraw the 8th Army to Japan by Christmas, leaving two divisions in Korea until elections had been held.

Truman now gave MacArthur a chance to repeat what he had told the president in their private meeting. He asked: what chances were there of Chinese or Soviet interference? MacArthur answered that there was no danger of Russian action. As for the Chinese, MacArthur said there was very little chance they would come in. At most, he said, they might be able to get fifty or sixty thousand men into Korea, but since they had no air force, "if the Chinese tried to get down to Pyongyang, there would be the greatest slaughter."[24]

General MacArthur very shortly was going to be proved very wrong in his predictions. But no one at the Wake Island conference, including the president, contradicted anything he said. He had become bigger than life because of his success at Inchon, and everyone received his views with great respect.

On October 22, 1950, in the west, elements of the 8th Army reached the Chongchon River, about sixty miles south of the Yalu. Meanwhile, in the east, 10th Corps (the 1st Marine Division, with elements of the army's 7th Infantry Division) was heading toward the Chosin or Changjin Reservoir up a narrow, difficult mountain road from the port of Hungnam.

There was spotty resistance by isolated small groups of North Koreans against 8th Army units, but almost none on the road to the Chosin Reservoir. The war seemed to be nearly over. On October 24, MacArthur canceled the provision in NSC 81/1 that called for only South Korean troops to operate close to the Yalu, and ordered all UN forces to press to the northern limits of Korea.

MacArthur's order opened the gates for the 8th Army. UN forces crossed the Chongchon at several places and struck out at full speed. The attack resembled a series of rapier thrusts by individual units, advancing along any roads that promised speedy penetration. There was virtually no contact between the various thrusts. Each column advanced on its own without any concern for the other columns.

There had been no evidence of Chinese troops. But their absence was deceptive. The mountainous region between the Chongchon and the Yalu held a vast secret.

On October 6, 1950, the Chinese Communist Party's ruling politburo decided to send "volunteers" to Korea under one of its most seasoned officers, Marshal Peng Dehuai.[25]

No one actually volunteered, and all forces were regulars in the People's Liberation Army (PLA), dressed in their standard padded cotton winter uniforms. Mao Zedong had made a most astute calculation. He reasoned that calling Chinese troops "volunteers" would deter the Truman administration from claiming that China had entered the war. If so, the United States would have no excuse to attack China directly. Mao hoped that the United States also sought to confine the war to Korea, and would accept the fiction. He was proved right. Truman aspired to conquer North Korea, but he did not want to start a war with China.[26]

The movement by the Chinese commenced on the night of October 18. A vast force slipped into North Korea, unit by unit. The troops were entirely unseen by American air reconnaissance. They marched by night and hid by day. In the west the troops moved into blocking positions on the southern face of the high mountain mass fifty miles south of the Yalu and a few miles north of the Chongchon. In the east they moved to positions below the Chosin Reservoir.

As the 8th Army advanced across the Chongchon, three Chinese

Left: Madame Chiang and Chiang Kai-shek. Chiang ruled the right-wing Nationalist party that sought to keep control of China in the hands of a small privileged minority of landlords, industrialists, and merchants, while saddling the peasants and the workers with the vast majority of taxes. In 1927 Chiang killed all the Communists in China that he could find. Thousands of people lost their lives. *National Archives photo*

Right: Zhou Enlai (left) and Mao Zedong. Mao seized full control of the Chinese Communist Party in 1935 by taking up the cause of the Chinese peasants and the small urban proletariat. In doing so, he eliminated all influence by Joseph Stalin and the Kremlin. Zhou barely escaped Chiang Kai-shek's massacre of Communists in 1927, and served as Mao's main deputy. *National Archives photo*

(Seated, from left) Winston Churchill, Franklin D. Roosevelt, and Joseph Stalin at the Yalta Conference February 4–11, 1945. At this conference Stalin agreed to enter the Pacific war against Japan three months after the end of World War II in Europe. In exchange Roosevelt granted him huge land acquisitions and privileges in the Far East, but Stalin agreed to recognize Chiang Kai-shek's Nationalist government and to ignore the Chinese Communists. *National Archives photo*

Left: A sign made by a U.S. Army unit denoting the 38th parallel boundary. The line was drawn by the Allies in August 1945 separating North Korea, occupied by the Soviet Union, from South Korea, occupied by the United States. Picture taken by the author near Uijongbu, north of Seoul in November 1951. *Author's personal collection*

Right: Soviet expert George F. Kennan, attaché in the American embassy in Moscow, wrote the "long telegram" on February 22, 1946, which outlined the containment policy the United States followed during the Cold War. The policy avoided attempts to regain lands seized by the Communists, but aimed to keep them from making any more advances. *National Archives photo*

Reviewing stand at Army Day parade in Washington on April 6, 1949. (From left) General Omar N. Bradley, chairman of the Joint Chiefs of Staff; Louis A. Johnson, secretary of defense; President Harry S. Truman, and an unidentified official. Secretary Johnson became closely associated with Republicans who wanted to protect Chiang Kai-shek on Taiwan, to which the Nationalists retreated after being ousted from the mainland by the Chinese Communists in October 1949. Truman, however, wanted to abandon Chiang. Johnson's efforts to undermine President Truman led to his ouster in September 1950 and his replacement by General George C. Marshall. *National Archives photo*

The Joint Chiefs of Staff, the senior military officials of the United States during the Korean War. (From left) Generals Omar N. Bradley, chairman; Hoyt Vandenberg, air force; J. Lawton Collins, army; and Admiral Forrest P. Sherman, navy. *National Archives photo*

The leading officials in the Truman administration during the MacArthur-Truman controversy. Here President Truman shakes hands with W. Averell Harriman, special assistant to the president, in a Rose Garden ceremony in 1951. Flanking them are Dean Acheson, secretary of state (left), and George C. Marshall, secretary of defense (right). *National Archives photo*

Marines move around North Korean T-34 tank knocked out in Pusan Perimeter battle in late summer 1950. A dead North Korean soldier lies on the tank in the foreground. *U.S. Marine Corps photo*

Bagpipers of the Argyll and Sutherland Highlanders on August 8, 1950, pipe ashore at Pusan a battalion of their Scottish regiment and a battalion of the English Middlesex Regiment, the first United Nations ground troops to join the Americans and South Koreans. *U.S. Army photo*

Marines seek cover behind an M26 Pershing tank west of Masan during a Pusan Perimeter engagement in the summer of 1950. A dead North Korean soldier lies on the ledge at left. *U.S. Marine Corps photo*

Brigadier General F. W. Farrell, Korean Military Advisory Group commander, confers with Lieutenant General Walton H. Walker (seated in jeep), 8th Army commander, during the height of the Pusan Perimeter battle. *U.S. Army photo*

During the North Korean offensive in the summer of 1950, an American F-80 jet strafes an enemy T-34 tank and jeep in the road and vehicles and troops in the village.
U.S. Air Force photo

A U.S. Navy Corsair shepherds part of the armada assembled for the Inchon invasion on September 15, 1950, the world's last great amphibious landing.   *U.S. Navy photo*

General Douglas MacArthur watches bombardment of Inchon from the bridge of the USS *Mount McKinley*. He is flanked by (from left) Vice Admiral A. D. Struble, Major General E. K. Wright, and Major General Edward M. Almond, 10th Corps commander. *U.S. Navy photo*

Four LSTs unload on the beach at Inchon as marines gather equipment to move rapidly inland on September 15, 1950. Landing ships were stuck in the deep mud flats between one high tide and the next. *U.S. Navy photo*

General Douglas MacArthur (in leather jacket) and an entourage of press and brass examine bodies of North Korean soldiers at advanced marine positions east of Inchon on September 17, 1950. The marine in camouflage helmet holds a Russian-made submachine gun known to Americans as a burp gun. *U.S. Army photo*

Marines carry a wounded comrade while other marines hold positions on the outskirts of Seoul in September 1950.   *U.S. Marine Corps photo*

A marine infantryman keeps cover as he looks over the Han River valley near Seoul four days after the landing at Inchon.   *U.S. Navy photo*

U.S. 7th Division infantry wait as an army M4A3 Sherman tank clears a gap in a barricade during the street-by-street North Korean defense of Seoul in September 1950. *U.S. Army photo*

Breakout from the Pusan Perimeter. Koreans move back to their homes at Waegwan as U.S. infantrymen advance after the fleeing North Koreans. The soldier in the foreground is carrying a Browning Automatic Rifle. *U.S. Army photo*

Frozen bodies of American marines, British commandos, and South Korean soldiers are gathered for group burial at Koto-ri on the retreat of the 1st Marine Division and elements of the 7th Infantry Division from Chosin Reservoir after a massive Chinese attack in late November 1950. *U.S. Marine Corps photo*

This C-47 is being unloaded at the tiny Hagaru-ri airstrip at Chosin Reservoir, while wounded and frostbitten marines and soldiers wait to get on board. From this airstrip 4,312 wounded and frostbitten men were evacuated by air in the five days before the retreat to the sea began. *U.S. Marine Corps photo*

The marine and army retreat from the Chosin Reservoir in December 1950 occurred in temperatures that were often down to zero degree Fahrenheit.   *U.S. Marine Corps photo*

Korean refugees pack the road south of Seoul on January 5, 1951, trying to get away from advancing Chinese troops.   *U.S. Army photo*

Winter battle 1951: A machine-gun crew rests above a Korean village after assaulting a Chinese position.   *U.S. Army photo*

Men of the 25th Infantry Division observe an artillery concentration beginning to land on a Chinese position in central Korea in March 1951.   *U.S. Army photo*

General Douglas MacArthur (in front seat of jeep) with Lieutenant General Matthew Ridgway and Major General Doyle Hickey (in the rear seat), on a visit of MacArthur to the front in Korea on April 3, 1951. *National Archives photo*

General Douglas MacArthur speaking before the United States Congress on April 19, 1951, eight days after President Truman relieved him of his command in the Far East. Vice President Alben W. Barkley (left) and House Speaker Sam Rayburn are in the background. *National Archives photo*

A battery of self-propelled 155mm Long Tom rifles fires north of Seoul in May 1951, as United Nations troops move up behind withdrawing Chinese forces.   *U.S. Army photo*

Left: Major General William M. Hoge (right), commander of 9th Corps, studies a map at Chunchon airstrip, May 1951, with General Matthew B. Ridgway, Far East commander, and Lieutenant General James A. Van Fleet, 8th Army commander.   *U.S. Army photo*

Right: To protect against American artillery fire and air attacks, the Chinese and North Koreans created deep underground tunnels, rooms, and bunkers nearly impervious to all but direct hits by heavy-caliber weapons. These Chinese soldiers are armed with "potato masher" hand grenades. *Eastphoto*

Historical Detachment commanders Captain Pierce W. Briscoe (left) and Lieutenant Bevin Alexander beside the moat surrounding the emperor's palace in Tokyo in early May 1951. In the background is the Dai-ichi Building, Far East Command headquarters. Douglas MacArthur had departed Tokyo for the United States only a couple weeks before this picture was taken. Seven U.S. Army Historical Detachments, each commanded by a combat historian, operated along the front in Korea producing authentic on-the-spot accounts of battle actions. *Author's personal collection*

Above: Refugees on a street in Pusan, South Korea, in early June 1951. Millions of South Koreans were displaced from their homes and fled southward into areas not occupied by the North Koreans and Chinese. A vast number of these people had no shelter whatsoever. *Author's personal collection*

Right: Historical Detachment commanders John Mewha (left) and Bevin Alexander at 10th Corps headquarters in the Taebaek Mountains of eastern Korea in early June 1951. *Author's personal collection.*

armies (each with thirty thousand men) faced them in hidden positions. Two additional armies lay concealed in the mountains in reserve. On the 10th Corps front, one Chinese army was deployed south of the reservoir, but only one of its three divisions was in a position to challenge the marines and soldiers advancing up the narrow road from the coast.

The primary reason the Chinese had not been detected was that they had very little artillery and vehicles and generally walked to their destinations. They made a very small visual imprint on the environment, and their moving only at night made their concealment easier. They carried only light weapons, and they transported them, their ammunition, and their food, sometimes on the backs of animals, but mainly on the ubiquitous wooden A-frame carriers that Chinese and Korean farmers strapped to their backs.

Although their primitive logistical system was extremely limiting, the Chinese soldiers were liberated from roads and they could fight anywhere they could walk. UN forces, on the other hand, were tied to the roads because their supplies arrived by truck on those roads.

The Chinese struck without warning on October 25. The pattern was almost always the same: an advancing South Korean, American, or British force encountered a roadblock on the route it was advancing. This stopped all forward progress. While the unit tried to break this block, another Chinese force swept around to the rear and set up another roadblock. Unless the UN unit could crack the rear block, it was trapped. Some units disintegrated, others abandoned their weapons and vehicles and fled across country to safety in the rear.

No Westerners had ever encountered a military force like the People's Liberation Army, or PLA. In keeping with the new kind of army Mao Zedong and Zhu De had created in the Ruijin soviet in southeastern China between 1928 and 1934, the Chinese actively discouraged a military caste system. They recruited leaders from the ranks and encouraged common soldiers to solve everyday problems on their own. The leadership gave extensive pre-combat briefings to ordinary soldiers about the tactical situation and the battle plans of the unit, something seldom done in Western armies. This information contributed greatly to the soldiers' sense of responsibility and ability to work as part of a larger operation.[27]

The Chinese organized their forces around small combat units. Rifle squads, for example, were based on a "three-times-three" pattern in which three men formed a team, with each man assigned to watch (and watch out for) the other two. Three teams plus a leader made up the squad. This team system greatly simplified command in small units and helped to solve the problem of getting the individual soldier actually to fight. In the PLA, there was an official ban on beatings and abuse of men. The army attempted to prevent gross disparities of food by rank, it reduced excessive forms of military courtesy, and it encouraged comradeship between soldiers and leaders.

The weapons the Chinese used were extremely modest and uncomplicated compared to American and even South Korean weapons. UN forces depended on heavy artillery and on trucks and vehicles, including tanks and tracked and armored carriers. The Chinese used very little artillery, and almost no trucks. In place of artillery, they relied on American-made 60mm and 81mm mortars (captured from the Nationalists) and occasionally on heavy 120mm Russian mortars. All mortars could be broken down and carried by individual soldiers. Their main assault weapons were rifles, machine guns, hand grenades, and satchel charges of explosives (to use against tanks). These weapons required no trucks to transport them; they went with the soldiers. This gave the Chinese immense flexibility and high mobility in battle situations, and the Chinese soldiers could ignore the roads.

In tactics, the Chinese employed extremely simple but effective methods that they had developed in their guerrilla warfare against the Chinese Nationalists. Doctrine was based on cutting the defending force into small fractions and attacking these fractions with local superiority in numbers. The Chinese favored the ambush. Since they could not counter United Nations airpower, they usually shifted their main attacks to nighttime. Their general method of attacking an advancing enemy force was to stop it in front by means of a roadblock and get another force on the rear of enemy positions to cut off escape routes and supplies.

They used similar methods against an enemy force in a defensive position. They broke up their attack into many small segments to approach individual enemy defensive positions or outposts. They then sent in both frontal and flank attacks in the darkness to bring the enemy to grips. Chinese soldiers closed in on a small enemy element until they either destroyed it or forced the defenders to withdraw. The Chinese then crept forward against the open flanks of the next small unit and repeated the process.

Advancing Chinese units generally followed the easiest and most accessible terrain in making their approaches—valleys or draws or streambeds. As soon as they met resistance, they peeled off selected small units to engage the opposition. But if they met no opposition, an entire column often moved in the darkness right past defensive emplacements deep into the rear of UN positions. There were many examples of this. In some cases entire Chinese regiments marched in column formation right into the UN rear.

Chinese doctrine did not call for fighting slugging matches with Americans, because they would lose badly to overwhelming U.S.

firepower. Although there were many reports that the Chinese used "hordes of troops" in "human-wave tactics" to storm UN positions, the real Chinese advantage was not mass attack but deception, surprise, and stealthy infiltration by small units at night. The Chinese did use headlong attacks by very small units (platoons or companies of fifty to two hundred men) to make decisive penetrations, but the aim almost always was to hold defending troops in place while other Chinese units slipped around their flanks or set up roadblocks in the rear. The official U.S. Marine Corps history of the war cited the sarcastic comment of one marine: "How many hordes are there in a Chinese platoon?"[28]

The best defense of UN forces against the Chinese tactics was somehow to maintain their positions until daybreak. Then, with visibility restored, the Chinese attacks ceased, and American superiority in weapons and dominance in the air usually could safeguard front-line emplacements by hitting known Chinese positions with artillery and air strikes. However, Chinese night attacks were so effective that counsel to hold on till daylight often went unheeded, and many UN forces retreated in haste or were simply overrun and destroyed.[29]

In a series of devastating engagements, Chinese troops tore apart a three-division South Korean corps, hit one South Korean division so hard it virtually ceased to exist, caused two South Korean regiments to disappear as effective fighting units, and shattered one American regiment (the 8th Cavalry), causing one of its battalions to be abandoned for lost. The unexpected onslaughts were so crushing that General Walker, commander of the 8th Army, ordered all forces to retreat back across the Chongchon except for two small bridgeheads.

On the 10th Corps front, Chinese forces occupied a hill twenty miles south of the reservoir. The hill dominated the only road north. The 7th Marine Regiment launched repeated attacks against the hill, but the Chinese stopped them all.

The reaction of both the 8th Army and the Far East Command to the attacks was disbelief and denial. Even as irrefutable evidence of severe setbacks came in, the high commands were reluctant to accept the forces as organized Chinese units. The periodic intelligence report (PIR) of the 8th Army on October 26, 1950, viewed the events merely as "some further reinforcement of North Korean units with personnel taken from the Chinese Communist forces."[30] Major General Charles A. Willoughby, intelligence officer (G-2) for the Far East Command, dismissed the news with the observation that "the auspicious time for intervention has long since passed."[31] The UN command (coextensive with the Far East Command) reported the capture of Chinese prisoners but concluded that "there is no positive evidence that Chinese Communist units, as such, have entered Korea."[32] Reality, however, finally forced commanders to recognize that substantial Chinese forces had intervened. The Far East Command didn't acknowledge the fact, but MacArthur had been dead wrong.

Then, on November 6, an astonishing and unprecedented event took place. The Chinese Army in the full flush of its success abruptly broke contact and marched entirely away from the fight. Australian soldiers with the 27th British Brigade on the far west saw the Chinese soldiers plainly march away. By the end of the day all had vanished back into the high mountains.

The only credible explanation for this remarkable event was that the Chinese leadership had attacked the UN forces as a warning, and that they backed off to give the UN command a chance to reconsider what it was doing and withdraw. Whatever intention Beijing had in mind, the reaction in Washington and Tokyo was to ignore the evidence in front of their faces and to pretend that nothing had changed. The ensuing lull, which lasted for nearly three weeks, gave the Truman administration ample time to readjust its policy to an altered situation. But it did nothing, despite the fact that large questions were being asked in Washington concerning MacArthur's competence.

MacArthur had told President Truman on October 15 at Wake Island that the Chinese were unlikely to intervene, and that if they did, they would be beaten badly. Ten days later they shattered large military formations with seeming ease. MacArthur's predictions were entirely incorrect. His reputation for omniscience plunged in Washington.

And MacArthur was getting irrational. A bulletin he issued on November 6 charged the Communists with having "committed one of the most offensive acts of international lawlessness of historic record by moving without any notice of belligerency elements of alien Communist forces across the Yalu River into North Korea." This bulletin also charged the Chinese Reds with massing a great concentration of troops "within the sanctuary of Manchuria."[33] Of course, the Chinese *had* warned that they would strike if the United States invaded North Korea.

MacArthur insisted that the march to the Yalu be continued. In a message to the Joint Chiefs on November 7, he urged that the United Nations should condemn Red China for defiance of its resolutions and should threaten military sanctions—presumably attacks on Chinese territory—if Chinese forces were not withdrawn.[34] Senior officials in Washington were not interested in taking such drastic action, but they were also not willing to call MacArthur down.

The critical administration failure occurred on November 9, 1950, at a meeting of the National Security Council, presided over by Acheson in the absence of Truman. The Joint Chiefs had sent a report to Secretary of Defense Marshall that said the UN command had three choices: to press on to the Yalu, to hold a line short of the Yalu, or to withdraw. They did not recommend any action but implied that they preferred holding positions below the Yalu "pending clarification of the military and political problems raised by Chinese intervention."[35] If this had been done, it is unlikely that the Chinese would have attacked, and the United States would have had time to come to a reasonable solution. But the Chiefs did not recommend a specific action.

In the NSC meeting, there was a lot of discussion about various potential courses of action, including holding a line south of the Yalu. But in the end the NSC decided not to order MacArthur to change his plans. MacArthur, the council ruled, was to act at his discretion. He was constrained only by a prohibition against attacking Manchuria.[36]

The NSC made no effort to change its decision over the next few days, even though a stream of warnings of likely Chinese resistance flowed into the State Department from U.S. allies. The most significant came from the Dutch government on November 17. It said that the Chinese were motivated by fear of aggression against Manchuria, and if the UN halted fifty miles south of the Yalu, there would be no further intervention.[37] The Communist Party of China also issued a most-revealing statement on November 4 that compared the United States to Japan's strategy of using Korea as a base to attack China. This statement presented a direct challenge to the United States, yet it, too, went unheeded.[38]

Secretary of State Acheson attempted a belated, and entirely unconvincing, defense of government inaction in his memoirs. "The government missed its last chance to halt the march to disaster in

Korea," he wrote. "All the president's advisers in this matter, civilian and military, knew that something was badly wrong, though what it was, how to find out, and what to do about it they muffed."[39]

It was much more than a muff. It was a total failure on the part of the government to take responsibility and to devise a solution. The Chinese had given the United States a breathing spell. But, as James F. Schnabel and Robert J. Watson write in their official history of the Joint Chiefs of Staff, "Through indecision, vacillation, and faulty judgment that opportunity was lost."[40]

MacArthur informed the JSC on November 18 that the offensive would get under way on November 24.[41]

In a message to the Joint Chiefs just as the offensive was about to start, MacArthur said that completing the UN mission of occupying all Korea provided "the best—indeed only—hope that Soviet and Chinese aggressive designs may be checked before these countries are committed to a course from which for political reasons they cannot withdraw."[42] So MacArthur held that the *only* way to keep the Chinese from entering the war was to advance to the Yalu. But they had *already* entered the war because Americans had already marched toward the Yalu, and the Chinese had already struck UN forces. No better evidence of MacArthur's disconnect with reality could be offered.

In his memoirs Secretary Acheson has another apologetic and equally unconvincing passage about the course of events in Washington between the first appearance of Chinese troops and MacArthur's final announcement of his "end-the-war" offensive. Acheson summarizes the excuses that leaders in Washington were making, and he also illuminates their continuing failure of leadership. Here is what he wrote:

"All the dangers from dispersal of our own forces and intervention by the Chinese were manifest. We were all deeply apprehensive.

We were frank with one another, but not quite frank enough. I was unwilling to urge on the president a military course that his military advisers would not propose. They would not propose it because it ran counter to American military tradition of the proper powers of the theater commander. . . . If General Marshall and the Chiefs had proposed withdrawal to the Pyongyang-Wonsan line [the narrow waist of Korea] and a continuous defensive position under united command across it—and if the president had backed them, as he undoubtedly would have—disaster would probably have been averted. But it would have meant a fight with MacArthur, charges by him that they had denied him victory—and his relief under arguable circumstances. So they were hesitant, wavered, and the chance was lost. While everyone acted correctly, no one, I suspect, was ever quite satisfied with himself afterward."[43]

As UN forces were gathering supplies for the drive to the Yalu, the Chinese concentrated 180,000 men west of the Nangnim-sanmaek Mountains, a high, trackless extension of the Taebaek Mountains running from Wonsan northward to the Yalu, and 120,000 men east of the mountains. Against this force, the UN command had assembled 247,000 men, most of them American.[44]

The UN offensive opened on the morning of November 24. The Chinese met it at once. On the west they stopped with strong attacks all of the UN elements advancing northward across the Chongchon River. This held the UN forces in a fierce battle embrace, from which they could not easily extricate themselves. Meanwhile, a major Chinese force executed a decisive indirect blow against a South Korean division holding Tokchon, on the extreme east near the high mountains. Tokchon was well south of the Chongchon River and well east of the main UN concentration along the river. This was a massive—and completely unanticipated—strategic flanking move designed to dislodge the entire UN position on the river. It achieved total success. The Chinese shattered the South Korean division, quickly penetrated deep into the rear of the 8th Army, and unhinged the whole line.[45]

Meanwhile, in the 10th Corps sector east of the mountain divide, Chinese forces surrounded individual marine and army units around the Chosin Reservoir and cut their lines of supply and retreat.

On the 8th Army front along the Chongchon, all the UN forces were able to disengage and escape back across the river, except the U.S. 2nd Infantry Division and the Turkish Brigade. The 2nd Division was along the upper Chongchon around Kujang-dong where no roads led away from the river. Its only escape route was to move downstream for twenty-five miles to Kunu-ri. Meanwhile, the attached Turkish Brigade had been sent out on the road to Tokchon in a fruitless effort to stop the Chinese advance. The brigade was briefly surrounded but broke free and was retreating toward Kunu-ri. From this village there were two exit routes—a tiny road winding through mountains then along the Taedong River to Sunchon, eighteen miles south, and a road continuing down the Chongchon Valley to Anju, where other roads led south.

By November 29, the 2nd Division had withdrawn under heavy attack to the vicinity of Kunu-ri, while the Turkish Brigade continued to back down the road from Tokchon. Both the 2nd Division and the Turks had suffered heavy losses. The division consolidated at Kunu-ri with the intention of withdrawing down the road to Sunchon, while the division commander, Major General Laurence B. Keiser, ordered the Turkish Brigade to close up and retreat with them.

But during the morning division headquarters got shocking news: a Chinese roadblock had been set up about ten miles south of Kunu-ri on the road to Sunchon. General Keiser sent both his 2nd Reconnaissance Company and a company of the 38th Regiment to break the block, but they failed. Keiser asked 9th Corps to send a force up from Sunchon to crack open the block, but no troops were in position to move immediately.

The situation was now getting desperate. Keiser ordered the 9th Regiment to attack south on the Sunchon Road at 7:30 A.M. the next day, November 30. The 9th Regiment's commanding officer, Colonel Charles C. Sloane Jr., assembled his pitifully reduced regiment, now down to four hundred men, less than an eighth of its normal strength, and launched the attack.

By now, all 8th Army forces except the 2nd Division and the Turks had successfully withdrawn from the Chongchon. The army's reserve force, the 1st Cavalry Division, had moved up to hold Sunchon open for the 2nd Division and the Turks to come through. The big question was whether the Kunu-ri-to-Sunchon road could be used. If not, the only exit route was to continue fourteen miles on down the Chongchon Valley to Anju, where the 5th Regimental Combat Team was holding open roads south.

Both routes had their perils. The Kunu-ri-to-Sunchon road was much shorter, and American officers believed only a few Chinese troops had been able to infiltrate through to form a roadblock. The road to Anju ran along the south bank of the Chongchon, and Chinese troops could be expected to encircle any retreating column and cut it to pieces with roadblocks. The decision was made more difficult because the 9th Regiment was making slow progress against fanatical Chinese resistance. But a decision had to be made. Keiser decided on the Sunchon road. He designated the 23rd Regiment and the Engineer Battalion to form the rear guard, then to follow the rest of the division.

Chinese forces were closing in. Intense sniper fire from all directions began to fall into the division command post. The 2nd Division *War Diary* described the situation: "By 1300 [1 P.M.], the remaining known alternatives were limited to either fighting south to break the roadblock or to button up in the vicinity of the division command post for a futile last-ditch stand. The decision was made to fight out to the south and at 1330 the column moved out."

By this time the Turkish Brigade had reached the division area, and its soldiers and some South Koreans joined the column.

Leading elements of the column had moved about three-fourths of a mile when heavy Chinese fire rained down from both sides of the road. It was evident that the roadblock had not been broken. The men soon discovered that it was not an ordinary roadblock at all, that Chinese troops were arrayed on both sides of the road for seven miles. It was an avenue of death and mayhem. Whenever fire would commence from hidden Chinese soldiers, the men in and on the vehicles would hit the ditches. The men of the 17th Field Artillery Battalion, an eight-inch howitzer outfit attached to the division, reported that a twin-40mm antiaircraft artillery half-track started spraying the roadsides with fire. But the biggest reason the column was able to move was that U.S. fighter aircraft (mainly F-51 Mustangs) continually ranged up and down the road, savaging anything on the sides that looked suspicious. When a fighter was on a run, the Chinese mortars and guns fell silent. But as soon as the nose of the aircraft turned up after a strafing run, the Chinese gunners opened fire once more. Progress thus came in short spurts, followed by halts. Burning or disabled vehicles had to be bypassed or pushed aside. Remaining vehicles soon became loaded with wounded. The dead were of necessity left strewn along the sides of the road.

Some of the men of the 17th Artillery remembered that a jeep carrying a military police lieutenant attempted to pass their vehicles. A sniper hit the driver and killed him instantly. The lieutenant was badly shocked and was placed by members of the battalion atop a jeep trailer.

The Engineer Battalion continued to hold two critical hills just southwest of the old division command post at Kunu-ri until well after dark. Not a man escaped from the northernmost of the hills, but the remainder of the engineers got away to follow the rear of the column. As the tail of the column moved on south, Chinese troops closed in, using bayonets, small arms, grenades, and mortars.

When the 23rd Regiment, also forming the rear guard, got radioed word to withdraw, the commander, Colonel Paul L. Freeman Jr., decided it was hopeless to try to follow the division down the Sunchon road. He told his tanks and artillery to fire off all their reserves of ammunition while the remainder of the regiment got a motorized column together to move out fast. The tankers and gunners quickly fired off three thousand rounds in twenty minutes. The Chinese, thinking an attack was about to be launched, began digging in. When the regiment moved out, the Chinese made no effort to come after them. Colonel Freeman led his regiment in the darkness down the Chongchon Valley to Anju, where the 5th RCT was holding open the road. Both the 23rd and the 5th RCT turned south and escaped.

Near the head of the column the 17th Artillery was driving about 8:15 P.M. with no lights except blackout lamps. The battalion reached a stream where the bridge had been blown. A bypass had a good approach from the north but a steep approach over rice paddies to the south. Three vehicles had become stuck there and restricted passage. The first 17th Artillery tractor was uncoupled to pull out the trucks. As this was taking place, two 1st Cavalry tanks drove up from Sunchon, to the south, with their lights blazing, illuminating the 17th Artillery tractor. At once 60mm Chinese mortar rounds began to land and machine guns opened fire.

A Chinese sniper was standing in the road only thirty feet from Captain Roland D. Judd, executive officer of Battery A, and was aiming his rifle at him. At that moment a gunner shot him down. The tanks quickly shut off their lights and fired into the general direction of the Chinese. The 17th Artillery tractor pulled out the stuck trucks, and the retreat was able to continue. This broken bridge marked the end of the Chinese roadblock. There was no more firing on into Sunchon.

The division filed into Sunchon with wounded on top of trailers, on howitzers, and on fenders. An estimated four hundred dead UN troops had been counted along the sides of the road. The division and the Turks had survived, but at heavy cost. The division lost five thousand men and was combat-ineffective. The Turks also lost a large portion of their five-thousand-man force.

The 8th Army moved back in full flight. By the middle of December it was holding an unsteady line below the 38th parallel and along the frozen Imjin River, only a few miles north of Seoul. It had been the longest retreat in American history, 120 miles. The initiative had passed over entirely to the Chinese.

Meanwhile, around the Chosin Reservoir, the 1st Marine Division and elements of the 7th Infantry Division at last cracked through the Chinese forces surrounding them and staged a "breakout to the coast." The marines and soldiers broke every Chinese roadblock along the narrow road leading south to Hungnam and the sea. It was a perilous, difficult, and exhausting operation, but the vast majority of the men got through. The last elements arrived at Hungnam on December 11.

While the retreat of the marines and soldiers to the coast was going on, all other UN forces in northeast Korea withdrew by ship. A huge fleet evacuated the marines and soldiers from Hungnam. On the day before Christmas 1950, the last troops fired off their last rounds, climbed into waiting landing craft, and pulled away to protecting warships. At 2:36 P.M. December 24, the U.S. fleet turned southward. The great attempt to conquer North Korea had ended in failure.[46]

Only two days later, on December 26, MacArthur issued a communiqué that absolved him from all responsibility. UN forces, he claimed, were "suddenly and without the customary notice of belligerency" confronted by Communist China. Yet he said that the UN command had "survived without marked diminution of its strength and resources or loss of its fluidity of movement and maneuver." MacArthur declared that he was unable to assess enemy strength largely because "field intelligence was handicapped by the severest limitations. Aerial reconnaissance beyond the border [into Manchuria], which was the normal source of field intelligence, was forbidden. Avenues of advance from border sanctuary to battle area, only a night's march, provided maximum natural concealment. No intelligence service in the world could have surmounted such handicaps to determine to any substantial degree enemy strength, movements, and intentions."[47]

Thus MacArthur denied that UN forces had suffered a defeat— which was an absolute falsehood. Besides, he argued, whatever had happened was not his fault in the least.

CHAPTER 8

Return to Containment

The intervention of Red China had been a devastating blow to General MacArthur. It was an equal blow to President Truman. He had been assured by MacArthur, the Joint Chiefs of Staff, and most of his advisers that neither Russia nor Red China would likely intervene if the United States conquered North Korea and reunited it with South Korea. This was a most attractive goal that would suit the wishes of the American people, quiet opposition of Republicans in Congress, and, best of all, cost very little, since the North Korean Army was to all intents and purposes defunct.

It had seemed to Truman, therefore, that he could safely ignore the containment policy that he had been following ever since George Kennan had sent his long telegram outlining its elements on February 22, 1946. In coming to the decision, Truman had disregarded the complaints of Red China; indeed, he had disregarded everything except the most selfish interests of the United States. However, he was still uncertain enough of the decision to travel halfway around the world to have a personal conference with MacArthur to reassure himself that Red China would not intervene, or could be easily beaten if it did.

But MacArthur had been wrong. The JCS had been wrong. All his advisers had been wrong, with the single exception of Alexis Johnson in the State Department. And he had been ignored.

Now the United States had suffered a catastrophe. And it was self-imposed. Not only had the idea of conquering North Korea vanished like a puff of smoke, but the American military had sustained large casualties. The 2nd Infantry Division had lost one-third of its strength and had been rendered combat-ineffective. The 1st Marine Division and parts of the 7th Infantry Division were fighting for their lives, and would soon embark on a perilous retreat down a narrow mountain road in terrible winter conditions.

The Truman administration had also suffered a major blow in the November 7, 1950, elections. Voters reduced the Democratic seats in the Senate to 49 against 47 Republican seats, for a GOP gain of 5, and elected 235 Democrats, 199 Republicans, and 1 Independent in the House, for a Republican gain of 28. Foreign policy had been the chief issue in the campaign, and the GOP leadership now felt the public was rallying around their hard line in the Far East.[1]

President Truman was thus in a bleak mood when he held a press conference on November 30, 1950. Trying to put as good a face on the situation as possible, Truman issued a statement that the UN forces had "no intention of abandoning their mission in Korea." Reporters began intensive questioning of the president, leading him to say that the United States would take any steps necessary to meet the military situation, including use of "every weapon that we have."

Did that mean, a reporter asked, that use of the atomic bomb was being considered? The president answered that "there has always been active consideration of its use." He went on further to imply that the decision to drop the A-bomb would be left to General MacArthur.[2]

Truman had been led along the path by a reporter, but he had actually spoken the unspeakable. He had said that if the United States suffered a military reverse, it might use the atomic bomb to redress the situation. The defeat in North Korea had cost the United States dearly, but it was not threatening the very existence of the nation. To consider using the A-bomb in such circumstances was so incredibly irresponsible that it defied belief. In the burgeoning moral revulsion to nuclear weapons that was sweeping the world, and the terrifying fear of a fateful confrontation now that the Soviet Union had exploded an atomic bomb, such a statement could have only the most chilling effects everywhere.

The damage was magnified exponentially by Truman's implication that the decision to use the A-bomb would not rest with him, but with General MacArthur. The general already had developed a reputation throughout the world as a trigger-happy warrior with little regard for restraint or concern for consequences. Furthermore, he was seen as determined to achieve the destruction of Red China's capacity to make war. To leave this decision in his hands was frightening beyond measure.

Reaction was swift across the world. Acheson assembled a "damage-control party" and released a statement on behalf of the White House that assured the world that only the president could authorize the use of nuclear weapons, that the mere possession of any weapon necessarily entailed "consideration" of its use, and that the situation regarding the weapons had in no way changed as a result of the press conference. It was a solid effort, but it paled compared to the worldwide tumult Truman's utterance had spawned.[3]

The blunder caused a sensation in the British House of Commons. A hundred Labour MPs signed a letter to Prime Minister Clement Attlee protesting the possibility of the use of the atomic bomb. The U.S. embassy described the deliberation that followed as "the most serious, anxious, and responsible debate on foreign affairs conducted by the House of Commons since the Labour Party came to power in 1945." Not only the Labour MPs, but also Conservative members, including Winston Churchill and Anthony Eden, joined in the furor. The Commons wanted to be assured that events in Korea would not propel the world into a major war. After a hurried telegraphic exchange with the White House, Attlee announced to the Commons that he was flying to Washington for a conference with the president.[4]

Truman's statement had also horrified the French. Réné Pleven, the prime minister, made a quick trip to London on December 2, and he and Attlee achieved a "general identify of view." Attlee thus carried the authoritative positions of Britain and France when he arrived in Washington.[5]

Truman was not the only official to make stupid statements at this time. Washington quite plainly was getting hysterical. For example, at a meeting of the administration's major political and military advisers on December 1, Dean Acheson suggested that the United States might offer to withdraw from Korea if Red China withdrew its military forces from Manchuria![6] A proposal for mutual withdrawal from Korea had some promise, but to expect China to pull its troops out of an integral part of its own country—and that part considered by its leaders as the most vulnerable—was ridiculous.

President Truman's meetings with Prime Minister Attlee and his closest advisers on December 4–8 were most effective. They righted the ship of state and turned it in a more rational and reasonable direction.

The British and the French and, for that matter, most of the Western world had more complaints with the United States than the fear that it would launch the atomic bomb. One of the biggest was universal anger over repeated public protests MacArthur was making to numerous reporters about the "privileged sanctuaries" of China that he was forbidden to bomb or attack, and the failure of European countries to support an aggressive stance in the Far East.

For example, on two occasions on December 1, MacArthur publicly criticized limitations against hot pursuit of enemy forces across the Yalu River and against attacks on Manchurian bases. He accused Washington of giving enemy aircraft safe refuge in Manchuria and called this "an enormous handicap" for him, one "without precedent in military history." He made these complaints in an interview with editors of *U.S. News and World Report* and a message he sent to Hugh Baillie, president of United Press. MacArthur came dangerously close to impugning the motives of European allies. He spoke of their "selfish" and "short-sighted" viewpoints, and implied that they were responsible for orders withholding of support for his forces.[7]

On December 3, the *New York Post* observed that MacArthur had also found time to reply to a cable from Ray Henle, a lesser known radio commentator, and to answer an inquiry from Arthur Krock, *New York Times* Washington correspondent. The main premise of these messages was that all his troubles had stemmed from being ordered to limit the war to Korea. It was not, he said, faulty intelligence or faulty evaluation that forced the retreat from the Yalu, but "extraordinary inhibitions" from Washington that kept him from pursuing the Chinese across the Manchurian borders and from bombing supply bases there.[8]

In all of these statements MacArthur denied any responsibility for any of the defeats and blamed everything on restrictions he was getting from Washington not to extend the war beyond the Korean peninsula. He accepted no guilt for insisting that the offensive be launched on November 24, to drive to the Yalu—the very order that set off the Chinese counteroffensive. For example, in a message to Arthur Krock on November 30, 1950, MacArthur said: "It is historically inaccurate to attribute any degree of responsibility for the onslaught of Chinese Communist armies to the strategic course of the campaign itself. The decision of the Chinese Communist leaders to wage war against the United Nations could only have been a basic one, long premeditated and carried into execution as direct result of the defeat of their satellite North Korean armies."[9]

Along with its allies, the Truman administration was getting distressed with these diatribes, and Truman issued a directive on December 5 addressed to all U.S. officials, but plainly meant for MacArthur, that they must clear all public statements relating to foreign or military policy with the State and Defense departments.[10] In the event, MacArthur disobeyed this directive.

The British proposed that Taiwan should be ceded to Red China as a price of peace. This was not acceptable to the Americans, and it was dropped. But the British continued to favor admission of Red China to the UN.[11]

In the matter of nuclear weapons, the two sides came to a better understanding than might have been expected. The British wanted the Americans never to use the bomb without consulting the United Kingdom, something the administration would not agree to. The two nations finally settled on a statement in a joint communiqué that mentioned President Truman's hope "that world conditions would never call for the use of the atomic bomb," and his desire to keep the British prime minister at all times "informed of developments which might bring about a change in the situation."[12] Bland as this statement appeared on paper, it marked a decisive move by the U.S. government never again to get caught making unthinking statements about nuclear weapons. Conferring with the British provided a sturdy backstop and guard against some irresponsible official spreading some outlandish threat to the public.

The most important benefit of the British-American talks was a solid agreement to end the Korean War on the basis of the old border on the 38th parallel. In other words, the United States officially abandoned its desire to conquer North Korea and absorb it into a reunited Korea.[13] This abruptly ended the American resolve to roll back the frontiers of Communism, and immediately reinstated George Kennan's containment strategy as the formal policy of the nation.[14]

The decision of the American-British conference led at once to an effort in the United Nations by Sir Benegal N. Rau, the Indian delegate, to get thirteen Asian and Arab states to ask the Chinese and North Koreans not to cross the 38th parallel. Beijing and Pyongyang did not respond directly, but private talks went on for several days. The Indians explored the idea of a cease-fire with China. The New York Times reported on December 8 that "responsible officials" in Washington gave assurances that UN forces would not renew their invasion of North Korea if Communist forces stopped at the parallel.[15]

The thirteen-nation cease-fire proposal passed the UN Political and Security Committee (the First Committee) on December 13 and the full UN General Assembly on December 14, in both cases with U.S. support. Now the Beijing government, in the flush of victory and after winning its primary aim, its buffer in front of the Yalu, made a major and costly mistake. On December 21, the Red Chinese rejected the UN cease-fire proposal on the grounds that all UN actions taken without Communist China's participation were illegal.

On December 23, Premier Zhou Enlai broadcast the text of a telegram he sent to the thirteen-nation group in which he said the 38th parallel boundary had been obliterated forever by the UN invasion of North Korea. He asserted that Red China would not consider a cease-fire unless there was an agreement on the withdrawal of foreign troops from the peninsula, settlement of Korean affairs by the Korean people themselves, withdrawal of "American aggression forces" from Taiwan, and the seating of Red China in the United Nations.[16]

If Red China had accepted the cease-fire, its stock would have soared so high it would have been virtually impossible for the United States to bar Red China's admission to the UN. And world opinion would have made it politically unwise for the United States to continue to support Chiang Kai-shek on Taiwan. Thus the Red Chinese, by demanding too much, got nothing. And the war nobody wanted went on.

Red China's rejection of a cease-fire played no part in a proposal MacArthur presented to the Joint Chiefs on December 30, 1950. This statement was the clearest he had yet made as to his goals and aspirations. It was a total rejection of containment and a cease-fire. It was a call to war.[17]

In the proposal, MacArthur claimed that the "entire military resource of the Chinese nation" had been committed against the UN command. But MacArthur noted that Chinese forces were concentrated in Korea and Manchuria, leaving other parts of the country vulnerable. Existing policies prevented exploitation of these opportunities. He proposed that restrictions on striking mainland China be lifted in case the administration decided "to recognize the state of war which has been forced upon us by the Chinese authorities."

His recommendations would have brought on full-scale war with China and possibly the Soviet Union. He told the JCS that the United States should blockade China's coast, destroy the country's industrial war-making capacity through air and naval bombardment, reinforce the UN command in Korea with Chinese Nationalist units, and allow the Nationalists to undertake diversionary action against the mainland.

By these means, MacArthur held, the United States "could severely cripple and largely neutralize China's capability to wage aggressive war and thus save Asia from the engulfment otherwise facing it."

MacArthur recognized that such a course of action—which he called "defending ourselves by way of military retaliation"—had been rejected earlier as likely to provoke a major war. But, he argued, China was now fully committed, and "nothing we can do would further aggravate the situation."

Dreadful as these proposals were, they would not have driven China to its knees. A naval blockade would have had little effect. Red China had captured from the defeated Nationalists large quantities of the weapons it used—rifles, machine guns, mortars, hand grenades, and satchel charges—along with big stocks of ammunition. It manufactured additional ammunition in widely scattered domestic factories. Most other needed materials and weapons came overland from the Soviet Union, not by sea. A bombing campaign using ordinary explosives against Chinese cities would have resulted in abysmal casualties among civilians. But saturation bombing had not kept Germany from waging war, and a similar air assault on Chinese cities would have had no more success. It would, however, have outraged world opinion and alienated America's allies. Unless China launched an assault on the United States outside of Korea, the Truman administration was not going to approve aggressive measures directly against China.

MacArthur's proposal far exceeded the now-abandoned plan to conquer North Korea. Truman never wanted to extend the war beyond the peninsula. And once it failed, he was quick to return to Kennan's containment that would avoid all aggressive war. The lines between MacArthur and Truman were now clearly drawn.

MacArthur's attitude toward war was so stark, single-minded, and unyielding that it strongly resembled the ruthless policy of conquest followed by the Roman Republic from its earliest days. As the nineteenth-century military historian Theodore Ayrault Dodge writes in his account of the Second Punic War against Carthage (219–202 B.C.), "Rome and all her officials were constantly on the outlook for opportunities for conquest; she always stuck her fingers into every pie, and never ceased to breed quarrels in order herself to benefit by eventual interference. . . . Once at war, she carried on war with all her might; once victorious, her opponent was ground into the dust."[18]

CHAPTER 9

The Search for a Way Out

General MacArthur's stature had declined drastically after the Chinese intervened in Korea. It declined even further among members of the Truman administration after his December 30, 1950, call for extending the war to mainland China. The administration had looked at the same facts as MacArthur and had decided not on extended war, but on a search for a cease-fire.

MacArthur also had become the object of scathing public criticism. Clement Attlee and Jawaharlal Nehru, the British and Indian leaders, and Lester Pearson, the Canadian minister of external affairs, implied that MacArthur had become the tool of forces in the United States bent on the destruction of Red China. Henry Luce's *Time* magazine said he was responsible for one of the greatest military catastrophes of all time. *Look* magazine said MacArthur had "grossly miscalculated the intentions, strength, and capabilities of the forces against him." The *New York Herald Tribune* blamed MacArthur for a disaster in which he had "compounded blunder by confusion of facts and intelligence."[1]

Now MacArthur was arrayed directly against the Truman administration. But it was not a simple case of ordering a soldier to obey orders. The defeat in Korea had shocked the American people greatly. The traditional American response to a military setback was to rearm and drive on to total victory. MacArthur's December 30 proposal reflected this attitude exactly.

There were many who shared this resolve. Admiral Forrest P. Sherman, chief of naval operations, for example, was opposed to asking for a cease-fire. At a meeting of State and Defense leaders on December 3, 1950, Sherman said the United States had lost a battle but not a war. He believed the United States should warn the Chinese to stop their attack or face war. Any other course, he said, would lead other nations to "push us around." Secretary of State Acheson responded that, if the United States followed Sherman's recommendation, it would be "fighting the second team." The real enemy, Acheson said, was the Soviet Union, which would be delighted to see the United States embroiled in a full-scale war with Communist China. Sherman's view did not prevail, but his attitude reflected a large element of the American public who wanted to pursue war to the finish.[2]

Although the administration had decided against MacArthur's proposal, it had not figured any way to end the war. The Chinese Communists had been successful in driving the UN forces back almost to Seoul. Now, having rejected a cease-fire urged by the United Nations, they decided to exploit their gains by undertaking a powerful new offensive.

In Washington, there was real doubt whether the United States could even maintain its position in Korea. Most of this doubt was caused by the intensely pessimistic reports coming from MacArthur. Shortly after the Chinese attacked, MacArthur told the JCS that the present UN force was "not sufficient to meet this undeclared war by the Chinese. The resulting situation presents an entirely new picture which broadens the potentialities to world-embracing considerations beyond the sphere of decision by the theater commander."[3] A few days later MacArthur sent another flash to the Joint Chiefs stating that further withdrawals of UN forces were required because the Chinese had as their objective "the complete destruction of United Nations forces and the securing of all Korea."[4] He gave no evidence to show how he'd come to this conclusion.

MacArthur's gloomy assessments caused the American military leaders and the Truman administration to conclude that UN forces were in danger of annihilation. In light of these somber claims, the Joint Chiefs sent a directive to MacArthur on December 29, approved by Truman, that told MacArthur to defend successive positions, but if the line was forced back to the Kum River near Taejon, and if the Chinese massed large forces, "it then would be necessary, under these conditions, to direct you to commence the withdrawal to Japan."[5]

MacArthur had made all of his dire prophecies from his office in the Dai-ichi Building in downtown Tokyo. But on the ground in Korea, nothing like his doleful attitude prevailed. The soldiers and marines had been solidly defeated and badly bloodied, but none thought they were facing disaster. Commanders were beginning to realize that the Chinese were severely hamstrung by their primitive supply system and would have an impossible time driving the United Nations out of Korea. The Chinese could move easily around UN forces and could inflict fearsome casualties. And they had deflated puffed up attitudes of Western superiority. But commanders there saw strong evidence that the Chinese dependence on human transport meant that they could not sustain an offensive long enough to drive the UN forces into the sea.

Besides, an entirely new outlook was emerging in Korea. On December 23, the 8th Army commander, Lieutenant General Walton H. Walker, was killed when his jeep was struck by a truck north of Seoul. The Joint Chiefs immediately named a charismatic new commander, Lieutenant General Matthew B. Ridgway, until then army deputy chief of staff. Ridgway had created a spectacular reputation as commander of the 82nd Airborne Division and an airborne corps in World War II and had won high praise for his work within the Joint Chiefs of Staff organization.

Ridgway's spirit of offensive warfare arrived in Korea at a crucial time. He quickly re-created a sense of pride and confidence in the 8th Army. He stopped all talk of defeat and retreat. He talked entirely of attack and victory. His most memorable affectation was a grenade he strapped to his combat jacket. Nobody thought the field commander in Korea would have occasion to assault a Chinese bunker head-on, but the grenade got the message across: it was the business of the army to fight and the 8th Army was now being run by an officer who knew how to do it.

All ideas that the army was beaten quickly vanished after Ridgway took over, and a sense of military professionalism and purpose returned.

The Chinese Communists, now with the help of some reorganized North Korean troops, unleashed a New Year's Eve offensive against the 8th Army. The Chinese had been building up their troops and supplies behind the line where the 8th Army had finally stopped its retreat—along the Imjin River in the west and extending more or less along the 38th parallel eastward to the Sea of Japan.

The recently evacuated troops of 10th Corps, now incorporated into the 8th Army, were reorganizing in southern Korea.

The Chinese Communist Politburo had rejected a cease-fire. But despite the dire predictions of MacArthur, it was never clear that Mao Zedong had any intention of occupying all of Korea. This is not what Beijing was saying publicly, but the Chinese never massed enough troops to do more than push back UN forces. In the first six months of 1951, the Communists had seven hundred thousand troops in Korea, the vast bulk of them Chinese. But in no offensive did they use more than half of them.[6] Because of their crude logistical system, a full-scale invasion to drive the UN out of Korea would have required a series of offensives, followed by repeated reorganizations and resupplies. This would have necessitated enormous costs, which the Chinese were not in a position to bear.

Mao saw the political realities in the Far East better than Harry Truman. The president wanted to seize all of Korea and roll back the Communist frontier to the Yalu. This turned out to be too great a challenge for the United States. Mao saw that an attempt by China to roll back the Free World frontier to the strait separating Korea from Japan was also too great a challenge. And unlike Truman he did not attempt it. Most likely what Mao was really trying to do was to parlay a battlefield victory into withdrawal by the United States of its protection of Taiwan and its blocking of a Red Chinese seat in the UN. It turned out to be the wrong strategy.

Nevertheless, the Chinese offensive that rolled out on New Year's Eve was massive, and it was completely convincing to the severely weakened 8th Army, which had received very few reinforcements since its defeat in North Korea. Those that had been added were concentrated under 10th Corps in the high mountains in the east, close to the Sea of Japan. These were 2nd Infantry Division, which had been brought back to strength by heavy replacements; the 187th Airborne Regimental Combat Team, which had recently arrived from the States; and parts of the 7th Infantry Division not caught up in the retreat from the Chosin Reservoir.

The Chinese, less anxious about the opposition they might receive, advanced much faster than they had done in the November attack. They hit mainly 1st Corps to the north of Seoul and 9th Corps around Chunchon in the center of the peninsula. Seven Chinese armies of three divisions each (210,000 men) and two North Korean corps penetrated deeply around Seoul and toward the rail and road center of Wonju in the central sector, forty-five miles south of Chunchon.

South Korean forces north of Seoul panicked and their units dissolved, despite frantic efforts by General Ridgway to stop the collapse. The Americans, the British 29th Brigade, and the Turkish Brigade retreated in good order. By January 3, 1951, Ridgway realized it would be impossible to hold Seoul, and he ordered its evacuation. He also ordered 9th Corps in the center to pull back level with the retreating 1st Corps.

The retreat was causing a mass exodus of Korean civilians from Seoul and points north of the Han River. Ridgway realized that a rush of refugees could clog the two pontoon bridges that spanned the river (the permanent bridges had been broken in the fighting in 1950). This might trap combat forces north of the river. To prevent this, Ridgway kept open for civilians a footbridge across the river, but he closed the pontoon bridges to all but military traffic. He placed Brigadier General Charles D. Palmer, assistant division commander of the 1st Cavalry Division, in charge of both pontoon bridges, with full authority to use Ridgway's name to keep military traffic moving.

While military police under Palmer's command guarded the northern approaches and kept the tide of Korean refugees at bay, long, slow lines of infantrymen, trucks, tanks, artillery, and carriers moved over the bridges to the south bank. At last, Palmer allowed the heaviest of the equipment to roll across the bridges: eight-inch howitzers and Centurion tanks of the British 29th Brigade. The Centurions exceeded the rated tonnage of the bridges, and the pontoons sagged ominously into the ice-choked river. But the pontoons held, and the last of the 8th Army forces crossed safely. Directly behind them came a flood of refugees.[7]

Many hundreds of thousands of Korean civilians fled. Seoul became almost a ghost town. Many died in the bitter cold. Many tried to reach Pusan in the extreme south, but this city was already jammed with homeless people. The exodus could not be stopped. The people clogged highways and endangered military operations, but they were terrified of being under North Korean and Chinese control. At last, the 8th Army set up traffic points to channel the people into the southwestern provinces, away from the military lines of communication and all potential fighting.

UN forces all across Korea retreated southward to the vicinity of the 37th parallel. Although there was chaotic fighting in the east against North Koreans who had infiltrated through the high Taebaek Mountains, the Communists were unable to sustain the offensive. It stalled just below the 37th.

The familiar Chinese weaknesses reappeared. They had few vehicles and couldn't use them anyway because Americans had complete command of the sky and could destroy any vehicles on the roads in daylight. Accordingly, the Chinese had to advance on foot and carry their supplies the same way. Few Chinese pushed south of Seoul. As the 8th Army withdrew farther south, contacts with the Chinese fell off sharply. As early as January 7, an American task force pushed north from Pyongtaek toward Osan without finding a single enemy soldier.

The results of the New Year's offensive were not as dismal as the doomsayers, especially MacArthur, had predicted. In Washington a new spirit of confidence emerged. This was reinforced by the realization that the Chinese Communists, despite their aggressive moves, were restricting all their activities to Korea. James F. Schnabel writes in his official history of policy in the first year of the war: "Thus far, the Chinese government had not declared war against the United States and had, in fact, disclaimed responsibility for the actions of Chinese armies in Korea. While this was purely a technicality it was an important one. Confining the fighting in Asia to a limited arena in Korea and preserving the unity of a bloc of nations allied with the United States against Communist aggression were basic principles of established policy."[8]

Accordingly, on January 9, the administration and the Joint Chiefs formally turned down MacArthur's December 30 call for carrying the war to mainland China. The Chiefs were extremely patient in illuminating their reasons to MacArthur. Any blockade of the Chinese coast, they explained, would require approval of the British, who traded with China through their colony of Hong Kong. A blockade would also require acceptance by the United Nations. It was absolutely certain that Britain and the UN would veto any aggressive move toward China. The JCS also told MacArthur that naval and air attacks would be authorized only if China attacked U.S. forces outside of Korea. Finally, they rejected MacArthur's request to have Nationalist Chinese troops shipped to Korea and used against the Chinese Reds. The JCS ordered MacArthur to defend successive positions in Korea as previously decided, while attempting to inflict maximum damage on Communist forces.[9]

MacArthur's hopes for extending the war to China were foiled. He responded with a damning criticism of the situation he was facing. It was "self-evident," he wrote, that the UN command was not strong enough to hold Korea and also protect Japan. He said a beach-head could be maintained in Korea for some time, but with inevitable losses. "Whether such losses were regarded as 'severe' or not," he wrote, "would to a certain extent depend upon the connotation one gives the term."

The UN command, MacArthur said, had accomplished its original mission of destroying the North Korean Army. It had never been intended to "engage the armies of the Chinese nation." He then followed up with a devastating evaluation of the morale of the troops in Korea. He made the charge without substantiation. Here is what he said:

"The troops are tired from a long and difficult campaign, embittered by the shameful propaganda which has falsely condemned their courage and fighting qualities in misunderstood retrograde maneuver, and their morale will become a serious threat to their battle efficiency unless the political basis upon which they are asked to trade life for time is clearly delineated, fully understood, and so impelling that the hazards of battle are cheerfully accepted."

MacArthur tried to force the administration to decide at once whether to remain in Korea. He said the decision was "of highest national and international importance. . . . My query therefore amounts to this: is it the present objective of United States political policy to maintain a military position in Korea—indefinitely, for a limited time, or to minimize losses by evacuation as soon as it can be accomplished?"

MacArthur concluded: "As I have before pointed out, under the extraordinary limitations and conditions imposed upon the command in Korea, its position is untenable, but it can hold for any length of time up to its complete destruction if overriding political considerations so dictate."

In effect, MacArthur was claiming that the morale of the troops was in perilous jeopardy, and he could not sustain a position in Korea.[10]

MacArthur's message produced profound dismay in Washington. President Truman called a meeting of the National Security Council on January 12. Secretary Acheson interpreted MacArthur's statement as a "posterity paper" designed to shift the blame from him if things went wrong. It was also, Acheson wrote, designed to put "the maximum pressure on Washington to reverse itself and adopt his proposals for widening the war against China." This was positive proof, Acheson wrote, that MacArthur was "incurably recalcitrant and basically disloyal to the purposes of his commander in chief."[11]

The Joint Chiefs acted at once. With the approval of Secretary of Defense George Marshall, they decided to send J. Lawton Collins, army chief of staff, to Korea to determine firsthand whether MacArthur's charges were correct. Hoyt S. Vandenberg, the air force chief of staff, volunteered to go along. Before departing, however, they attended the National Security Council meeting Truman had called. Truman approved a JCS draft, sent at once to MacArthur, telling him to follow national policy. It said that if his charges were true, it was still extremely important to American prestige "that Korea not be evacuated unless actually forced by military considerations, and that maximum practicable punishment be inflicted on Communist aggressors."[12]

Because of MacArthur's pessimistic reports, the JCS produced a tentative plan on January 12 that called for a vast increase in actions against China in case UN forces were about to be driven off the peninsula. Among other things, it called for the U.S. to deny Taiwan to the Communists, delay a general war with the Soviet Union until more U.S. forces could be mobilized, prevent the spread of Communism on the mainland of Asia, and support establishment of a government in China friendly to the United States.[13]

But the true situation in Korea was nothing whatsoever like what MacArthur, sitting in Tokyo, was claiming. He was insisting that UN forces could not hold out in Korea. But they were doing just that.

While the 8th Army was stemming the Communist offensive, and the Joint Chiefs were girding to fight as long as possible in Korea, a wholly new threat descended on the Truman administration. The thirteen-nation UN cease-fire commission had not accepted as final Beijing's earlier rejection of a cease-fire. It drew up a new peace plan, designed to meet some of Red China's demands. The group presented the plan to the UN First Committee on January 11, 1951, only hours after U.S. officials first learned of it. It proposed a six-step program for peace: an immediate cease-fire, exploration of measures to promote peace, withdrawal of armed forces from Korea, arrangements for Koreans to express their views on government, interim arrangements for a unified Korea, and setting up an "appropriate body" to settle Far Eastern problems, including the status of Taiwan and China's representation in the United Nations. The "appropriate body" was to consist of representatives from the United States, Britain, the Soviet Union, and Communist China.[14]

The "appropriate body" was clearly stacked against the United States. Britain wanted a cease-fire, wanted the United States to recognize Red China as the legitimate holder of China's seat in the UN, and wanted Taiwan reunited with the mainland. Its vote could not be counted on, and the two Communist states would vote against the United States. Even if the United States could stop any formal action by the appropriate body, it would suffer a shattering defeat in world opinion.

The proposal was contrary to American policy, but it offered a remarkably sensible and logical answer to the dilemma facing the Far East. Korea could be reunited with a government that would almost certainly be moderate, rejecting Communism and the right-wing authoritarianism of Syngman Rhee. The seating of Red China in the UN would be achieved by world consensus, and foreign troops would get out of the peninsula and cease using it as a pawn in the Cold War.

The proposal offered a wonderful bonanza to Red China. This was an open invitation to world acceptance; it would have answered all Red China's main aims in Korea, it would have propelled China into the UN with the blessings of most of the world, and it would ultimately have solved the problem of Taiwan—for the United States could not have indefinitely held a Chinese province against the opinion of the world.

Secretary of State Acheson, however, saw the proposal as "murderous," because of bellicose Republicans and the China lobby who wanted no change of status for Taiwan and were pugnaciously pushing for a stronger military stance against China.[15]

Acheson had noted the intransigent attitude Red China had assumed in the UN cease-fire proposal in December. Then, as well, Red China could have gotten practically everything it wanted if it had made only the slightest of concessions. From this Acheson had concluded that the Red Chinese leaders were ideologues who were greatly lacking in political savvy of the kind practiced in democratic parliaments around the world. The Reds approached every issue on the basis of some abstract principle and were unable to work in the give-and-take compromise atmosphere of legislative bodies.

Acheson saw this as a fatal weakness. He reasoned that the Red Chinese would reject this new offer as well. He recommended to the president that the United States accept the proposal. This would gain a major propaganda victory in world opinion; and when China rebuffed the plan, other countries would join with the United States in labeling Red China as an aggressor. Truman endorsed the idea.

The UN First Committee quickly approved the plan after Warren Austin, the American ambassador, praised it and said the United States would vote for it. The First Committee asked the UN secretary-general to transmit it to Beijing. The Red Chinese reply came on January 17: a cease-fire without political negotiations was wholly unacceptable. Red China's counterproposals were basically what they had been in December: admission to the United Nations and removal of American forces from Taiwan.

Acheson had won. The Red Chinese had demonstrated they were amateurs in international affairs. Acheson had gained the upper hand. He was able to pronounce: "We must now face squarely and soberly the fact that the Chinese Communists have no intention of ceasing their defiance of the United Nations."[16]

It was the opening the United States needed. On January 20, Ambassador Austin submitted a resolution to the First Committee that called Red China an aggressor. The First Committee approved the measure on January 30, and the UN General Assembly endorsed it on February 1. The resolution called for members to consider "additional measures" to meet Chinese aggression. It had been a neat finesse by Acheson. But some UN members were not pleased. They said Red China had been thrust into pariah status, while the United States had suffered no political consequences at home.[17]

Generals Collins and Vandenberg arrived in Tokyo on January 15. After a quick conference with MacArthur they flew to Korea. Both officers strongly doubted MacArthur's claim that the morale of the 8th Army was shot and the troops were in danger of being driven out of Korea. Vandenberg visited air force bases, where he found morale excellent. Collins met up with General Ridgway, and together they toured headquarters of a number of U.S., UN, and South Korean units. Collins found morale in the 8th Army good and improving daily under Ridgway's vigorous, offensive-minded leadership. The South Koreans had a traditional fear of Chinese soldiers, and they were shakier. But leaders assured Collins that they would remain solid, so long as they were sure the United States would not abandon the country. Ridgway also told Collins that he didn't think the Chinese were capable of driving the UN out of Korea. Even if they pushed farther with larger forces, he said, he was confident the UN could hold a defensive line indefinitely. So, in Ridgway's eyes, MacArthur's fears were wholly unfounded.[18]

Collins and Vandenberg got back to Washington on January 18. The next day they recounted to the JCS and to the president and his cabinet the reassuring comments and appraisals they had received in Korea. The mood of the American leadership abruptly changed from gloom to high confidence. Collins wrote afterward: "For the first time since the previous November, responsible authorities in Washington were no longer pessimistic about our being driven out of Korea."[19]

While Collins and Vandenberg were in the Far East, the National Security Council commenced a study of the January 12 JCS plan for expanding the war in case UN forces were driven from the peninsula. The NSC toned down a number of the proposals and turned others into "plans" to be implemented only if the worst came to pass. After getting the positive reports from Collins and Vandenberg, the NSC, deciding that the grim prospects were not going to happen, sent the entire plan back to the JCS for study and revision.[20] There it languished and died.

Confidence blossomed that the United States would not have to make the awful choice of striking directly at China. General Ridgway was providing time for the administration to seek ways to persuade the Chinese to end the war on the basis of status quo antebellum. There was no danger that the UN forces would be driven into the sea. Thus armistice negotiations now became a distinct prospect.[21]

James F. Schnabel and Robert J. Watson, in their history of the Joint Chiefs, write that Collins's appraisal contradicting MacArthur was a watershed in the Korean War. During the weeks after the Chinese counteroffensive of November 25, 1950, they write, "there had been an invisible but important alteration in the command relationships involved in the Korean conflict. The organizational charts remained unaltered, except for the insertion of a new name in the box representing the commanding general 8th Army. But the imposing figure in Tokyo no longer towered quite so impressively. In every previous decision of crucial import—commitment of U.S. troops in Korea, selection of the Inchon landing site, separation of 10th Corps from 8th Army, advance of UN forces to the Yalu—the recommendations of General MacArthur had proved decisive. Now, however, his prestige, which had gained an extraordinary luster after Inchon, was badly tarnished. His credibility declined further when General Collins contradicted his assertions about the sinking morale of 8th Army. There was indeed some reason to believe that General MacArthur's own morale had been affected. Certainly his frequently changing appraisals of the military prospects in Korea seemed difficult to account for on any other basis. And his superiors, their patience tried by numerous arguments necessitating the sending of emissaries to Tokyo, no longer reposed full confidence in him."[22]

Secretary of State Acheson summarized the situation quite succinctly. "The effort to stabilize the Korean War," he wrote, "involved nearly simultaneous efforts on three fronts: the front in Korea, the front in the United Nations, and the front in Tokyo. The most intractable was the last."[23]

On the ground in Korea, conditions had become fairly quiet. The Chinese had run out of supplies and were withdrawing to build up their strength again. They were also bringing up replacements for the casualties they had suffered in the offensive. The characteristic of this phase of Chinese operations was to use only light screening troops between the 8th Army forward positions and the withdrawal positions they had established far in the rear. Contact between the two armies virtually ceased.

General Ridgway was unhappy with the intelligence reports he was getting. "All our vigorous patrolling, all our constant air reconnaissance had failed to locate any trace" of the Chinese forces. The commander of the 5th Air Force, Major General Earle E. (Pat) Partridge, offered to take Ridgway up in an old AT-6 advanced trainer that he himself flew, so that Ridgway could see the situation for himself. The two generals proceeded north twenty miles deep in front of the 8th Army's positions. They flew often at treetop height. "Hardly a moving creature did we spot," Ridgway wrote, "not a campfire smoke, no wheel tracks, not even trampled snow to indicate the presence of a large number of troops."[24]

The only way to determine what was out there was to advance. On January 25, Ridgway launched "Operation Thunderbolt." Each corps was to use an American division and a South Korean regiment to push north to seek out the enemy. Ridgway abandoned MacArthur's system of isolated columns that advanced without any connection to neighboring units, which he had used in his drive for the

Yalu in October 1950. Ridgway reverted to the traditional American method. Tanks, antiaircraft automatic weapons, and artillery covered a certain number of hills with fire. Under the cover of this fire the infantry advanced and swept the ground clear of enemy troops before moving on to the next objective. Any enemy force flushed out was set upon by air force or marine fighters. Ridgway also insisted that advancing units had to keep a solid front, with units maintaining contact left and right with other units as they moved forward. The purpose was to prevent the Chinese from flanking road-bound columns or moving behind them to set up roadblocks. MacArthur's habit of allowing columns to advance down roads without flank protection was a major reason why Chinese troops had been able to slip behind UN forces and set up devastating barriers.

The carefully staged advance encountered little resistance in 1st Corps on the west and 9th Corps in the center. On February 10, 1st Corps troops seized Inchon and Kimpo Airfield and reached the south bank of the Han River, where they could look across at Seoul. In 10th Corps in the east, however, UN troops got into a chaotic series of battles with North Korean and Chinese troops in the vicinity of Hoengsong, some fifteen miles north of Wonju. Determined Chinese attacks were finally broken on February 15 by the brilliant defensive stand of 2nd Division's 23rd Infantry Regiment with the attached French Battalion in the "twin-tunnels" area near Chipyong-ni, about twenty miles northwest of Wonju.

On February 18, Major General Bryant M. Moore, commander of 9th Corps, informed Ridgway that some of his troops had found enemy positions in front of them vacant. Patrols quickly confirmed that enemy forces along the entire central front were beginning a general retreat. Since the Chinese relied on withdrawal to regain their strength before advancing again, Ridgway hit upon a method of countering this device—a general, but cautious, pursuit on the heels of the retreating enemy, to give him neither time nor an opportunity to restock his supplies. Ridgway planned this operation, code-named Killer, on February 18, two days before a visit by MacArthur to his front.

MacArthur arrived in Korea on February 20, the eve of the attack. He and Ridgway went up to the front. Ridgway describes what happened: "Standing before some ten or more correspondents met at the 10th Corps tactical command post, with me leaning against a table in the rear, MacArthur said calmly, 'I have just ordered a resumption of the offensive.' There was no undue emphasis on the personal pronoun, but the implication was clear: he had just flown in from Tokyo, had surveyed the situation, discussed it with his subordinates, and had then ordered the 8th Army to attack."[25] Thus MacArthur managed to take credit before the press corps for an offensive wholly thought up and already ordered by General Ridgway. MacArthur knew that the headlines in the States would say that it was MacArthur who was responsible for any success.

The UN advance encountered few enemy troops, but it was slowed by a thaw accompanied by heavy rains that turned roads and the landscape into mud and caused streams to reach flood stages. The UN advance halted.

CHAPTER 10

MacArthur Stops a Cease-Fire

By the beginning of March 1951, a remarkable set of circumstances had come to pass in Korea. The 8th Army was moving northward, step by step, while the Communists, largely Chinese, were withdrawing behind a cloud of delaying troops. On the map it looked like a giant defeat of the Communists and a burgeoning victory for the UN forces. But commanders on the ground knew this was not the true picture.

It was becoming clear that the Communists were recoiling in preparation for a massive new offensive in the spring. The focal point of the counterstroke was the Iron Triangle—the mountain-girded region a few miles north of the 38th parallel bounded by Chorwon, Kumwha, and Pyonggang. The Iron Triangle was well served by a railway and roads coming in from the north, which permitted the Communists to build up a large base of supplies. But the Iron Triangle was extremely difficult to approach from the south, east, and west. Most of the country was high and extremely rough. The only open approach was the so-called Uijongbu Corridor, a cleft in the mountains running from Wonsan on the Sea of Japan almost due south to Seoul. This had been the historic invasion route into Korea for a thousand years. But Chorwon blocked any movement back up this corridor from Uijongbu and Seoul. In other directions, the roads were universally bad. The few roads leading from Chunchon, about forty miles southeast of Chorwon, were steep, crooked, and dangerous. There was just one (also difficult) road leading from Hwachon and Inje to the east.

Consequently, the Communists believed they could hold the Iron Triangle and use it not only to mount an offensive south, but also to form the anchor of a solid defensive line running east to west all the way across the peninsula.

By pulling their forces into these rough, almost trackless mountains, the Communist commanders placed UN forces at a maximum disadvantage. Supply was limited to a few approach roads, and all of these were expected to be in poor condition with the spring rains.

However, the movement back to the Iron Triangle gave General Ridgway the opportunity to occupy most of the remainder of Communist-dominated South Korea. Ridgway quickly took advantage of the chance. He aimed his main thrust at Chunchon. This small city was the major road junction in central Korea. Its capture would cut off most easy routes of enemy retreat, and it would also flank enemy troops holding Seoul as well as the mostly North Korean troops holding the eastern mountains.

The UN attack, which Ridgway code-named Ripper, began on March 7, 1951, with an assault of the 25th Infantry Division across the Han River near its junction with the Pukhan River, about twenty miles east of Seoul. The Chinese contested the penetration for three days, but then withdrew in some disorder. UN advances elsewhere were rapid and strong. Troops moved on both sides of Chunchon. This advance placed the Chinese forces holding Seoul in peril, for Ridgway could turn west and cut off their retreat to the Iron Triangle. The Chinese did not wait for this to happen; they abandoned the capital on March 13 and 14. Seoul had now changed hands four times in nine months of war.

As American, British Commonwealth, and South Korean troops approached the southern reaches of the Iron Triangle, they began to encounter antitank mines in the roads, innumerable machine gun nests, bunkers made of heavy timber and covered with thick layers of soil, and trenches with overhead cover. These heavy field fortifications foreshadowed grinding positional warfare along the 38th parallel.

By the middle of March, UN forces had reoccupied virtually all of prewar South Korea. Troops were on or slightly above the 38th parallel everywhere except in the extreme west near the Yellow Sea. President Truman, Acheson, and the Joint Chiefs saw this as a great opportunity to offer a cease-fire without prejudice to the U.S. position on Taiwan or the admission of the Red Chinese into the UN. If the guns could fall silent, they reasoned, talks about political settlement could go on to everyone's heart's content, but soldiers would no longer be dying, and it would be extremely unlikely that war would start again.[1]

As James F. Schnabel writes, "The Chinese Communists were, in effect, to be invited to cease fire and to negotiate a settlement of the outstanding issues. They were also to be warned that if they refused to negotiate, the United Nations would be forced to continue the fighting."[2]

On March 20, the Joint Chiefs informed MacArthur of what was afoot with the following message: "State planning Presidential announcement shortly that, with clearing of bulk of South Korea of aggressors, United Nations now prepared to discuss conditions of settlement in Korea. Strong UN feeling persists that further diplomatic effort towards settlement should be made before any advance with major forces north of the 38th parallel. Time will be required to determine diplomatic reactions and permit new negotiations that may develop. Recognizing that parallel has no military significance, State has asked JCS what authority you should have to permit sufficient freedom of action for next few weeks to provide security for UN forces and maintain contact with enemy. Your recommendations desired."[3]

MacArthur replied with a complaint about any restrictions on his operations, along with a gratuitous comment that he was unable to conquer North Korea, which, of course, was not what was being asked of him.

Thus MacArthur had been officially informed that the United States government was seeking a cease-fire and was searching assiduously for the views and recommendations of its allies. Once an agreement was reached, the president was planning to broadcast a message to the Chinese Communists offering peace and some degree of reconciliation. There seemed to be a real chance to end the war.

The draft of Truman's planned speech to the Chinese Reds included these comments: "The Unified Command is prepared to enter into arrangements which would conclude the fighting and ensure against its resumption. Such arrangements would open the way for a broader settlement for Korea, including the withdrawal of foreign forces from Korea. . . . A prompt settlement of the Korean problem would greatly reduce international tension in the Far East and would open the way for the consideration of other problems in that area by the processes of peaceful settlement envisaged in the Charter of the United Nations."[4]

Four days later, on March 24 Far East time, MacArthur, without any notice whatsoever to the JCS or the president, issued his own public statement in the form of an ultimatum aimed at the Chinese authorities that threatened extension of the war unless Red China sued for peace. The statement was in direct defiance of the national policy of the United States and was clearly designed to wreck the president's peace initiative. MacArthur was attempting to establish a new policy by the United States that offered no hint of compromise. Here is what MacArthur said:

"Operations continue according to schedule and plan. We have substantially cleared South Korea of organized Communist forces. It is becoming increasingly evident that the heavy destruction along the enemy's lines of supply, caused by our round-the-clock massive air and naval bombardment, has left his troops in the forward battle area deficient in requirements to sustain his operations. This weakness is being brilliantly exploited by our ground forces. The enemy's human wave tactics have definitely failed him as our own forces have become seasoned to this form of warfare; his tactics of infiltration are but contributing to his piecemeal losses, and he is showing less stamina than our own troops under the rigors of climate, terrain and battle.

"Of even greater significance than our tactical successes has been the clear revelation that this new enemy, Red China, of such exaggerated and vaunted military power, lacks the industrial capacity to provide adequately many critical items necessary to the conduct of modern war. He lacks the manufacturing base and those raw materials needed to produce, maintain and operate even moderate air and naval power, and he cannot provide the essentials for successful ground operations, such as tanks, heavy artillery and other refinements science has introduced into the conduct of military campaigns. Formerly his great numerical potential might well have filled this gap but with the development of existing methods of mass destruction, numbers alone do not offset the vulnerability inherent in such deficiencies. Control of the seas and the air, which in turn means control over supplies, communications, and transportation, are no less essential and decisive now than in the past. When this control exists as in our case, and is coupled with an inferiority of ground fire power as in the enemy's case, the resulting disparity is such that it cannot be overcome by bravery, however fanatical, or the most gross indifference to human loss.

"These military weaknesses have been clearly and definitely revealed since Red China entered upon its undeclared war in Korea. Even under the inhibitions which now restrict the activity of the United Nations forces and the corresponding military advantages which accrue to Red China, it has been shown its complete inability to accomplish by force of arms the conquest of Korea. The enemy, therefore, must by now be painfully aware that a decision of the United Nations to depart from its tolerant effort to contain the war to the area of Korea, through an expansion of our military operations to its coastal areas and interior bases, would doom Red China to the risk of imminent military collapse. These basic facts being established, there should be no insuperable difficulty in arriving at decisions on the Korean problem if the issues are resolved on their own merits, without being burdened by extraneous matters not directly related to Korea, such as Formosa or China's seat in the United Nations.

"The Korean nation and people, which have been so cruelly ravaged, must not be sacrificed. This is a paramount concern. Apart from the military area of the problem where issues are resolved in the course of combat, the fundamental questions continue to be political in nature and must find their answer in the diplomatic sphere. Within the area of my authority as the military commander, however, it would be needless to say that I stand ready at any time to confer in the field with the commander-in-chief of the enemy forces in the earnest effort to find any military means whereby realization of the political objectives of the United Nations in Korea, to which no nation may justly take exceptions, might be accomplished without further bloodshed."[5]

Historian John W. Spanier notes that MacArthur's claim that the allies were actually the victors, and that all that Beijing had to do was to recognize this fact, made certain that Red China would not lay down its arms. "Great nations," Spanier writes, "do not generally broadcast their defeat or appearance of defeat. To call upon Communist China to confess its defeat, therefore, was to ensure its rejection and the continuation of the war. This, it would seem, was the real purpose of MacArthur's statement of March 24, and in that respect it was successful."[6]

MacArthur's unilateral ultimatum absolutely stunned official Washington. Omar Bradley wrote in his memoirs: "I do not know what went on in MacArthur's mind at this time. His memoirs and books of his associates shed little light. He had been made a fool of by the Chinese Communist armies; now, as all the world had seen, Ridgway's brilliant leadership had bailed him out. In January he may have convinced himself that Washington might adopt his views on widening the war. Our cable indicating that Truman was going to ask for a settlement doubtless shattered that hope. There would be no all-out war with China directed from Tokyo. Perhaps that realization snapped his brilliant but brittle mind."[7]

MacArthur's biographer, William Manchester, has perhaps a deeper understanding of what was driving the general. "He simply could not bear to end his career in checkmate," Manchester writes. "It would, in his view, be a betrayal of his mission, an acknowledgment that MacArthur was imperfect."[8]

The State Department immediately announced that the political matters enunciated by MacArthur were beyond his responsibility as a field commander. The issues, it said, were being dealt with in the United Nations and "by intergovernmental consultations." On March 29 Red Chinese radio termed MacArthur's ultimatum a "bluff" and an "insult to the Chinese people."[9]

Truman reacted to MacArthur's proclamation as follows: "This was a most extraordinary statement for a military commander of the United Nations to issue on his own responsibility. It was an act totally disregarding all directives to abstain from any declarations on foreign policy. It was an open defiance of my orders as president and as commander in chief. This was a challenge to the authority of the president under the Constitution. It also flouted the policy of the United Nations."[10]

It was thus impossible for Truman to make the offer to the Chinese that he had planned. Acheson tersely summarized the matter: if he had done so, everyone would have compared his statement to MacArthur's and asked, who is speaking for the United States?[11]

It appears to be unbelievable, but only four days previously, MacArthur had taken an additional position in direct conflict with American policy, in a letter to Joseph W. Martin Jr., Republican leader in the House of Representatives.

On February 12, 1951, Martin had delivered a speech in Brooklyn in which he charged that Truman was preventing "800,000 [sic] trained men" on Taiwan from opening "a second front" against the Chinese Reds. Martin said there was good reason to believe that MacArthur and "people in the Pentagon" favored this course. "If we are not in Korea to win," Martin went on, "then the Truman administration should be indicted for the murder of thousands of American boys." Martin had included a copy of this speech in a March 8 letter to MacArthur, and had invited his comments.[12]

On March 20, MacArthur replied, endorsing Martin's proposal to use Nationalist Chinese troops, thanking him for the speech, and saying he had read it "with much interest, and find that with the passage of years you have certainly lost none of your old-time punch."

MacArthur then added a most provocative criticism of American policy: "It seems strangely difficult for some to realize that here in Asia is where the Communist conspirators have elected to make their play for global conquest, and that we have joined the issue thus raised on the battlefield; that here we fight Europe's war with arms while the diplomats there still fight with words; that if we lose this war to Communism in Asia, the fall of Europe is inevitable; win it and Europe most probably would avoid war and yet preserve freedom. As you pointed out, we must win. There is no substitute for victory." [13]

MacArthur should not have been surprised that Martin read the general's letter on the floor of the House on April 5. Thus, Martin announced publicly that MacArthur was opposed to the administration's policy. But Martin did not explain the administration's reasons for not wanting to use Nationalist Chinese troops. It was a direct bid to put the Truman administration in as bad a light as possible, and the political ploy had been aided and abetted by MacArthur.

The Associated Press issued a quick bulletin: "House Republican Leader Martin of Massachusetts told the House today General MacArthur favors use of Chinese Nationalist troops in Korean fighting."[14] The general's letter made headlines around the world. The *Times* of London called it the most dangerous of an "apparently unending series of indiscretions." The *Observer* reported that the British government had strongly objected and described it "as foreshadowing an extension of the war to the mainland of Asia." Other nations lodged similar, though less public, protests with the State Department. But Republican Senator Robert A. Taft of Ohio said "it is ridiculous not to let Chiang Kai-shek's troops loose," and Republican Senator Homer Ferguson of Michigan proposed that a congressional committee fly to Tokyo and ask MacArthur how the war should be conducted.[15]

The next day, Friday, April 6, Truman called a meeting in his office.[16] Attending were Ambassador Harriman, Secretary of State Acheson, Secretary of Defense Marshall, and General Bradley. "I put the matter squarely before them," Truman wrote. "We discussed the question for an hour. Everyone thought that the government faced a serious situation." Harriman said MacArthur should have been fired earlier. Marshall urged caution. But Bradley saw a clear case of insubordination and said the general should be relieved. Acheson also said MacArthur should be relieved, but he thought it essential for all of the Joint Chiefs of Staff to agree. "If you relieve MacArthur," Acheson said, "you will have the biggest fight of your administration." He also advised the president to discuss the matter with congressional leaders of both parties before making a decision.

The group met again at 9 A.M. Monday, April 9. Truman said he'd talked with congressional leaders over the weekend. Bradley reported that the JCS was unanimous in recommending that MacArthur be fired. All the advisers present endorsed this view. Truman only then announced that he had made up his mind to relieve MacArthur when he made his statement on March 24.

Truman wrote later: "If there is one basic element in our Constitution, it is civilian control of the military. Policies are to be made by the elected political officials, not the generals or the admirals. Yet time and again General MacArthur had shown that he was unwilling to accept the policies of the administration. By his repeated public statements he was not only confusing our allies as to the true course of our policies, but, in fact, was also setting his policy against the president's."[17]

Somehow MacArthur, for all of his brilliance, had missed the fundamentals of the American political system, which is founded on democratically elected representatives. Any substantial deviation from this system threatens the American political balance. It made no difference whether MacArthur was right or wrong. By taking it on himself to make policy unilaterally, and in defiance of the policy adopted by the government, he was operating outside the American political system.

Although MacArthur received much support from Republicans, his actions had effectively isolated him, and therefore rendered him powerless. Quite obviously MacArthur did not see this. The only way military men can take over a democratic society is by force, or by a great groundswell of support from the people. Force was not in the cards. Not only was defiance by the military totally contrary to American values and tradition, but the hierarchy of the U.S. military was directly opposed to MacArthur's views. A groundswell also had not occurred, and MacArthur's Republican friends were by no means ready to step forward and lead a popular revolt.

Who was to replace MacArthur? Bradley, Collins, and Marshall thought it should be Ridgway. Truman agreed, and instructed Collins to prepare draft messages to MacArthur, Ridgway, and Lieutenant General James A. Van Fleet, who already had been designated as Ridgway's successor if the need arose.

The administration planned to have Frank Pace, the secretary of the army, who was in Korea at the moment, deliver the dismissal to MacArthur personally. But the plan misfired because of a breakdown in communications. Then the White House learned that the *Chicago Tribune* somehow had got wind of the firing and was preparing to print it in the next morning's edition. Truman decided at once to send the orders to MacArthur directly, using army communications.

He also directed that a press conference be held quickly. Thus, at the strange hour of 1 A.M. on Wednesday, April 11, reporters were handed the announcement.

The president's order went on the army wires an hour before the press conference. Signed by Omar Bradley, it read: "I have been directed to relay to you the following message to you from President Truman: I deeply regret that it becomes my duty as president and commander in chief of the United States military forces to replace you as supreme commander, allied powers; commander in chief, United Nations command; commander in chief, Far East; and commanding general, U.S. Army, Far East. You will turn over your commands effective at once to Lieutenant General Matthew B. Ridgway. You are authorized to have issued such orders as are necessary to complete desired travel to such place as you may select. My reasons for your replacement will be made public concurrently with the delivery to you of the foregoing order, and are contained in the next-following message. Signed Harry S. Truman."

The "next-following message" was: "With deep regret I have concluded that General of the Army Douglas MacArthur is unable to give his wholehearted support to the policies of the United States government and the United Nations in matters pertaining to his official duties. In view of the specific responsibilities imposed upon me by the Constitution of the United States and the added responsibility which has been entrusted to me by the United Nations, I have decided that I must make a change of command in the Far East. I have, therefore, relieved General MacArthur of his command and have designated Lieutenant General Matthew B. Ridgway as his successor.

"Full and vigorous debate on matters of national policy is a vital element in the constitutional system of our free democracy. It is fundamental, however, that military commanders must be governed by the policies and directives issued to them in the manner provided for by our laws and Constitution. In time of crisis, this consideration is particularly compelling.

"General MacArthur's place in history as one of our greatest commanders is fully established. The nation owes him a debt of gratitude for the distinguished and exceptional service which he has rendered his country in posts of great responsibility. For that reason I repeat my regret at the necessity for the action I feel compelled to take in his case. Signed Harry S. Truman."[18]

Commercial communications still beat army communications. News services got the story to Tokyo first. Before the official message reached MacArthur, results of the Washington news conference had been broadcast over Tokyo radio. An aide to the general, hearing the broadcast, telephoned Mrs. MacArthur, and it was she who informed MacArthur of his relief.[19]

General Ridgway also got first news of his appointment from a correspondent. He borrowed Secretary Pace's Constellation, which was much faster than his old B-17 bomber. MacArthur received him at once in the Dai-ichi Building. Ridgway wrote later: "He was entirely himself—composed, quiet, temperate, friendly, and helpful to the man who was to succeed him. . . . I thought it was a fine tribute to the resilience of this great man that he could accept so calmly, with no outward sign of shock, what must have been a devastating blow to a professional soldier standing at the peak of his career."[20]

CHAPTER 11

Return of the Hero

The reasons for the removal of General MacArthur were not at all apparent to the American people. When President Truman addressed the nation on radio and television on April 11, he made no reference to his effort to seek a cease-fire. He emphasized that "we must try to limit the war to Korea" and gave only the briefest explanation why he had fired MacArthur: "A number of events have made it evident that General MacArthur did not agree with that policy. I have therefore considered it essential to relieve General MacArthur so that there would be no doubt or confusion as to the real purpose and aim of our policy."[1]

Accordingly, the news shocked the American public. And it was Truman who caught the blame. Thousands of people wired their protests to representatives in Congress and to the White House. In San Gabriel, California, the president was burned in effigy. The City

Council of Los Angeles bemoaned "the political assassination" of General MacArthur. The Illinois Senate condemned "the irresponsible and capricious action of the president." The Michigan, California, and Florida legislatures approved similar resolutions.[2]

At 10:00 A.M. on April 11, Joseph Martin, minority leader in the House, emerged from a meeting with leading Republicans and announced they had agreed that Congress should investigate the administration's foreign and military policy "in light of the latest tragic development" and that MacArthur should be invited to give his complete views to Congress.[3]

On Monday, April 16, Emperor Hirohito personally visited MacArthur at the American embassy. Afterward, thousands of Japanese witnessed MacArthur's last trip through the city, with his wife, Jean, and their thirteen-year-old son, Arthur. At the airport, MacArthur received a nineteen-gun salute, eighteen jet fighters circled overhead, and four B-29 Superfortress bombers flew over the field in formation. At 7:20 A.M. MacArthur's Lockheed Constellation named *Bataan* took off with the general and his party for Hawaii, the first leg of the journey home. The Constellation was the premier airliner in the world, with four piston-driven engines, pressurized cabin, range of over thirty-five hundred miles, and top speed of 330 miles per hour. In Hawaii, many thousands of people lined a parade route and cheered as the general passed by. MacArthur and party arrived in San Francisco at 8:29 P.M. on April 17. There another enormous crowd awaited him.[4]

Meanwhile, Congressman Martin was negotiating to have MacArthur invited to speak to a joint session of Congress. The Democrats did not resist the plan and joined with the Republicans in sponsoring the invitation. They did, however, insist that the general be invited to address a joint "meeting" of Congress, not a formal session. It was a small technical point, and only the parliamentarians noticed.

The arrangements for the hearings caused more difficulty. The Republicans wanted the sessions open to the public and the press, but the Democrats restricted them to joint hearings of the Military Affairs and Foreign Relations committees of the Senate. And they were to be closed to the public. But transcripts—censored to remove any secret information—were to be made available in the Senate office building press room within an hour after the testimony had been given.[5]

MacArthur and family arrived in Washington just after midnight on April 19. An enormous crowd gave the general an almost hysterical reception. The welcoming party included Secretary of Defense Marshall, the Joint Chiefs of Staff, and Major General Harry Vaughan, the president's personal representative.

The nation's attention was focused on Congress on April 19, when MacArthur spoke shortly after noon. The speech was broadcast on radio and television (there were 12 million TV sets in the country at the time[6]), and a huge portion of the country's population listened to or watched the event. As historian John W. Spanier writes, MacArthur projected a forceful image: "MacArthur's strength of character, deeply felt convictions, and unshakable self-confidence were apparent from his opening sentence."[7]

MacArthur knew that he had the full attention of the nation, and he used it to make his case. The public did not quite realize that it was a case directly contrary to the position of the United States government. This would have to come out later in the Senate hearings. In the House chamber, therefore, he was able to state his position without any refutation or counterargument.[8]

In a general discussion of events in the Far East, MacArthur repeated his call that Taiwan not be allowed to fall under Communist control. "Such an eventuality," he said, "would at once threaten the freedom of the Philippines and the loss of Japan, and might well force our western frontier back to the coasts of California, Oregon, and Washington." He said that Red China had "become aggressively imperialistic with a lust for expansion and increased power." He said this aggressiveness was being "displayed not only in Korea, but also in Indochina and Tibet and pointing potentially toward the south." This, he claimed, "reflects predominantly the same lust for the expansion of power which has animated every would-be conqueror since the beginning of time."

Although MacArthur stated these claims as fact, they were false. Taiwan had nothing like the strategic importance that he asserted. China, with no navy, had no possibility whatsoever of forcing the United States back to the West Coast. Also, China had controlled Tibet for centuries, it was making no aggressive moves in Indochina or points south, and its intervention in Korea was entirely defensive—to guard against potential American aggression.

MacArthur now turned to the intervention of Red China in Korea. "Apart from the military need, as I saw it, to neutralize the sanctuary protection given the enemy north of the Yalu, I felt that military necessity in the conduct of the war made necessary, first, the intensification of our economic blockade against China; second, the imposition of a naval reconnaissance of China's coastal areas and of Manchuria; third, removal of restrictions on air reconnaissance of China's coastal areas and of Manchuria; fourth, removal of restrictions on the forces of the Republic of China [Nationalists] on Formosa with logistical support to contribute to their effective operations against the Chinese mainland."

MacArthur asserted that he had been severely criticized by "lay circles, principally abroad," for these recommendations. But, he said, they were "all professionally designed to support our forces committed to Korea and bring hostilities to an end with the least possible delay and at a saving of countless American and allied lives." He said that his "views have been fully shared in the past by practically every military leader concerned with the Korean campaign, including our own Joint Chiefs of Staff." This, of course, was not true.

MacArthur went on: "I called for reinforcements, but was informed that reinforcements were not available. I made clear that, if not permitted to destroy the enemy built-up bases north of the Yalu, if not permitted to utilize the friendly Chinese force of some 600,000 men on Formosa, if not permitted to blockade the China coast to prevent the Chinese Reds from getting succor from without, and if there were to be no hope of major reinforcements, the position of the command from the military standpoint forbade victory."

In these circumstances, MacArthur continued, "we could hope at best for only an indecisive campaign with its terrible and constant attrition upon our forces if the enemy utilized his full military potential."

MacArthur insisted that he was not a warmonger. "But once war is forced upon us," he said, "there is no other alternative than to apply every available means to bring it to a swift end. War's very object is victory, not prolonged indecision. In war there is no substitute for victory.[9]

"There are some who, for varying reasons, would appease Red China. They are blind to history's clear lesson, for history teaches, with unmistakable emphasis, that appeasement but begets new and bloodier war. It points to no single instance where this end has justified that means—where appeasement has led to more than a sham peace. Like blackmail, it lays the basis for new and successively greater demands, until, as in blackmail, violence becomes the only other alternative. Why, my soldiers asked of me, surrender military advantages to an enemy in the field? I could not answer. Some may say to avoid spread of the conflict into an all-out war with China; others, to avoid Soviet intervention. Neither explanation seems valid. For China is already engaging with the maximum power it can commit and the Soviet will not necessarily mesh its actions with our moves."

MacArthur concluded his address as follows: "The world has turned over many times since I took the oath on the plain of West Point, and the hopes and dreams have long since vanished, but I still remember the refrain of one of the most popular barracks ballads of that day which proclaimed most proudly that old soldiers never die, they just fade away. And like the old soldier of that ballad, I now close my military career and just fade away, an old soldier who tried to do his duty as God gave him the light to see that duty. Good bye."

It was an unforgettable performance. It immediately brought a brief resurgence of the song among the American people. It was less popular in Korea, where young soldiers *were* dying.

The next day, New York City gave the general the biggest ticker-tape parade in its history. Hundreds of thousands of people lined the parade route to cheer him.

CHAPTER 12

No Vindication in Congress

The Senate committee hearings, which began May 3 and ended on June 27, 1951, were essentially a collision between Douglas MacArthur's concept of total war leading to complete victory and the Truman administration's concept of a war limited to specific goals and designed to prevent a widespread conflict that could escalate to atomic war.

The hearings were thus an argument about the nature of war. MacArthur represented a feeling strong in some people that war is a cataclysmic event aimed at the destruction of an enemy. This perception sees war as a crusade to destroy evil. The Truman administration defined war in Clausewitzian terms as an extension of national policy—that is, war carried out only to achieve specific, limited ends of state.

In the world of nuclear confrontation that was looming in 1951, the Truman administration's idea of limited war was far more realistic and far safer than MacArthur's view of total war.

But MacArthur had much American opinion on his side—represented vociferously by aggressive Republicans in Congress who had not come to grips with the reality of nuclear bombs and how they had changed the nature of warfare.

The conflict over American policy emerged on the very first day of the hearings. Senator Leverett Saltonstall, Republican of Massachusetts, asked MacArthur his opinion of a public statement Dean Rusk, assistant secretary of state, had made on April 15.

Rusk said: "What we are trying to do is to maintain peace and security without a general war. We are saying to the aggressor, 'You will not be able to get away with your crime. You must stop it.' At the same time we are trying to prevent a general conflagration which would consume the very things we are trying to defend."

MacArthur condemned Rusk's position as "the concept of appeasement, the concept that, when you use force, you can limit that force." With such a policy, MacArthur went on, "you would not have the potentialities of destroying the enemy's military power, and bringing the conflict to a decisive close in the minimum of time, and with a minimum of loss. It seems to me the worst possible concept, militarily, that we would simply stay there, resisting aggression, so-called, although I do not know what you mean by 'resisting aggression.' The very term of 'resisting aggression,' it seems to me that you destroy the potentialities of the aggressor to continually hit you. If that is the concept of a continued and indefinite campaign in Korea, with no definite purpose of stopping it until the enemy gets tired or you yield to his terms, I think that introduces into the military sphere a political control such as I have never known in my life or have ever studied."[1]

This, of course, was a ridiculous claim. Nearly all wars have political motives, and innumerable wars throughout history have had limited goals. The American Revolution, the War of 1812, the Mexican War, and the Spanish-American War all had extremely limited aims, and all were directly driven by political considerations.

MacArthur quickly revealed his aggressive attitude toward Red China. When the presiding officer, Senator Richard B. Russell, Democrat of Georgia, asked what MacArthur would have done about Chinese Red troops massing in Manchuria in August and September 1950, MacArthur answered: "I would have warned China that, if she intervened [in Korea], we would have regarded it as war and we would have bombed her and taken every possible step to prevent it."[2]

MacArthur also disclaimed any responsibility for the tremendous defeat UN forces had suffered when the Chinese Communists did intervene. He asserted that prior to the launching of his offensive on November 24, 1950, he had made plans to retreat if he found the enemy in force.

"The concept that our forces withdrew in disorder or were badly defeated is one of the most violent prevarications of truth that ever was made. These troops withdrew in magnificent order and shape. It was a planned withdrawal from the beginning. The forces in the northeast, the 10th Corps, were withdrawn in the same way. The losses we had in that withdrawal were less than the losses we had in our victorious attack at Inchon."[3]

This was an almost totally false statement. It indicates either a divorce from reality or a conscious effort on MacArthur's part to suppress the facts about his role in the catastrophe. There is no evidence whatsoever that MacArthur anticipated a major Chinese counteroffensive and thus planned for a possible UN retreat. And U.S. battle losses were three times greater than Inchon—more than eleven thousand, compared to thirty-two hundred in the entire Inchon operation.

MacArthur had grossly underestimated the number of Chinese troops facing him—saying there were between forty thousand and seventy-one thousand, when in fact three hundred thousand Chinese were hidden in the mountains above the Chongchon River and opposite 10th Corps in the Chosin Reservoir region.[4] On November 18, 1950, MacArthur informed the Joint Chiefs that U.S. air attacks had largely "isolated" the battle area from enemy reinforcements and had greatly diminished the flow of enemy supplies.[5]

Just prior to the start of the offensive on November 24, 1950, he flew over the region between the Chongchon and Yalu rivers. Seeing no evidence of large enemy forces anywhere on the snow-covered landscape, MacArthur decided to allow the offensive to take its course.[6] He boasted to press correspondents accompanying him on the airplane that the attack was going to be easy, telling them that he hoped to have the troops "home by Christmas."[7] This, in fact, was the ironic name that UN troops in Korea used in referring to the offensive.

Although he later claimed in his memoirs that he had directed 8th Army commander Walton H. Walker to prepare for voluntary withdrawal if it turned out that Chinese troops were entering Korea in "determined force,"[8] there is no evidence that such plans were prepared. As James F. Schnabel and Robert J. Watson write in their official history of the Joint Chiefs, "Had they been in existence, the subsequent forced withdrawal of UN forces might have been more orderly."[9]

MacArthur's own communiqué, issued on November 28, 1950, three days after the Chinese counterattacked, revealed that he had not anticipated the Chinese offensive. "We face an entirely new war," he stated. "This has shattered high hopes we entertained that the intervention of the Chinese was only of a token nature on a volunteer and individual basis as publicly announced, and that therefore the war in Korea could be brought to a rapid close."[10] In a message the same day to the Joint Chiefs, MacArthur said that "our present strength of force is not sufficient to meet this undeclared war by the Chinese."[11]

UN forces most definitely were thrown back in great disorder. In the west, 8th Army troops withdrew in extreme haste 120 miles to the south—the longest retreat in American history. In the east, 10th Corps endured immense peril and enormous difficulty in a retreat in subzero weather from the Chosin Reservoir down a narrow mountain road that was contested almost every step of the way by Chinese troops.

The casualty figures do not include thousands of frostbite cases, which were often more debilitating than battle wounds. Between December 1 and December 4, 1950, just prior to the breakout from the Chosin Reservoir to the coast, C-47 transports evacuated 4,312 wounded or frostbitten marines and soldiers from a small landing strip at Hagaru-ri, just south of the reservoir.[12]

MacArthur told the senators that he believed the war in Korea should be brought to an end in the quickest possible way through a military victory. "If you practice appeasement in the use of force, you are doomed to disaster," he said.[13]

The general repeated the recommendations he had made in his speech to the Congress: imposing a naval blockade on China, tightening the economic embargo, allowing Nationalist troops to strike the mainland, and bombing airfields, depots, and assembly points in Manchuria and on the mainland. MacArthur said his proposals were "fully shared" by the Joint Chiefs of Staff—which they denied when they testified.[14]

MacArthur implied that the Joint Chiefs had been forced to abandon their backing of him because their proposals must have been vetoed by President Truman or Secretary of Defense George Marshall.[15]

MacArthur used as evidence of JCS support a memorandum of January 12, 1951, that outlined tentative actions that might be taken in the event the United States was about to be pushed off the Korean peninsula and got embroiled in an all-out war with China. Among others, these actions would include denying Taiwan to the Communists, assisting South Korea as long as practicable, backing a government in China friendly to the United States, imposing a naval blockade of Red China, removing restrictions for air reconnaissance of the China coast and Manchuria, removing restrictions on Chinese Nationalist forces, giving them logistical underpinning to attack the mainland, and furnishing covert aid for Nationalist guerrilla forces operating in China.

But Bradley, in his testimony, said that it was clear to him and to the other members of the JCS that the memo was contingent and not a directive, and that they had conveyed its provisional nature to MacArthur.[16]

Secretary of Defense George C. Marshall, in his testimony, denied that he had overruled the Joint Chiefs of Staff. Moreover, he emphasized that the January 12 memo was written when the United States was "faced with the very real possibility of having to evacuate our forces from Korea," and the JCS recommendations were to be considered "if and when this possibility came closer to reality." The situation in Korea improved almost immediately thereafter, and it turned out to be unnecessary to put any of the provisional remedies into effect.[17]

Accordingly, MacArthur's insistence on the January 12 memorandum as signifying endorsement by the JCS was revealed to be false by Marshall and the Joint Chiefs. Republicans on the committees, foiled in their effort to find a means to attack the Truman administration, backed off. MacArthur's reputation declined further.

General Marshall confirmed that the administration was closely following two concerns dear to the China lobby in the Congress. It was denying Taiwan to Communist China and it was opposing seating Red China in the United Nations. Moreover, these two matters were not to be included in any armistice or cease-fire terms.[18] General Marshall pointed out that the Joint Chiefs, the secretary of defense, and the president were responsible for American security around the world. MacArthur's mission, he noted, was limited to the Far East and a particular adversary.[19]

Hoyt Vandenberg, the air force chief of staff, called MacArthur's bombing strategy "pecking at the periphery." To commit the U.S. Air Force to China, he said, "would fix it so that, should we have to operate in any other area with full power we would not be able to do so." Vandenberg went on: "The fact is that the United States is operating a shoestring air force in view of its global responsibilities. . . . The aircraft industry is unable until almost 1953 to do much of a job toward supplying the airplanes that we would lose in war against any major opposition. In my opinion, the United States Air Force is the single potential that has kept the balance of power in our favor. It is the one thing that has, up to date, kept the Russians from deciding to go to war. . . . While we can lay the industrial potential of Russia waste, or we can lay the Manchurian countryside waste, as well as the principal cities of China, we cannot do both, again because we have a shoestring air force. We are trying to run a 20-million-dollar business with about $20,000."[20]

Vandenberg was speaking about the fundamental strategy that

the West had devised to prevent Soviet aggression, which all Western military leaders (except MacArthur) were certain would be aimed at Western Europe. Western defense relied almost totally on air power. The United States got itself in this dependence methodically and deliberately after World War II. Until Russia exploded its own A-bomb in August 1949, the United States had a monopoly on nuclear weapons. As David B. McLellan writes in his astute analysis of Secretary of State Dean Acheson, Truman annually added up all the expected expenditures of the civilian government, and anything left over went to the military. "Given the choice of spending money on ground forces or on air power, the American people and the Congress had given a preference to air power," McLellan writes.[21]

American and NATO ground forces in Western Europe were wholly incapable of stemming a massive Soviet offensive backed by thousands of tanks. The sole purpose of Western army elements was to set off an alarm if Soviet troops crashed over the frontiers. This would immediately send bombers of the American Strategic Air Command straight at Moscow and other Soviet targets. And these bombers would almost certainly be armed with atomic bombs. Western strategy relied wholly on the atomic deterrent to keep Soviet armies from marching.

In this context, Korea and China were irrelevant to the defense of the West. In a total war with Russia, Korea would not be defensible, and American forces would almost certainly be withdrawn to defend the American containment line in the Far East—Japan, the Ryukyus, and the Philippines. The fate of Korea would be decided by the results of Western battles fought in other theaters. Vandenberg's testimony, therefore, was a stern reminder to the senators that the United States faced its most critical challenges in Western Europe, not in Korea and not in China. His words had the effect of showing just how limited, parochial, and inaccurate MacArthur's thinking was.

American military planners, as historian John W. Spanier writes, thought of the Korean War "only as a strategic diversion cleverly planned by the Kremlin as a means to weaken American power and divert it from Europe."[22] Western officials still had not figured out that the war probably had no deeper cause than the belief of Kim Il Sung that he could seize South Korea because the United States was not going to defend it—and Joseph Stalin had gone along with the idea.

Nevertheless, the Korean War was important to show the Soviet leaders that aggression, even far beyond the main arena, would not pay. It was also vital to hold the Western alliance together—for if any vulnerable country felt that the United States would not come to its aid if attacked, it would no longer have faith in the alliance.

When Omar Bradley got on the stand, he focused directly on the issues in the Far East. He felt almost everything MacArthur was advocating was wrong. Taking on Red China, Bradley said, would not necessarily end the war in Korea and almost surely would not bring China to its knees. One had only to look at Japan, Bradley pointed out. Between 1937 and 1941 (when Japan attacked the United States, Britain, and the Dutch East Indies), Japan had almost full control of a large part of China and yet was never able to finish the war successfully. Immense China (almost the size of the United States with Alaska) absorbed the Japanese armies. Japanese troops could move at will, but they could hold only the ground on which they stood. All the rest of China was free. Bradley implied that a similar condition would face American forces if they tried to conquer China. Bradley concluded: "We believe that every effort should be made to settle the present conflict, without extending it outside Korea."[23]

Marshall enlarged on Bradley's point: "General MacArthur would have us, on our own initiative, carry the conflict beyond Korea against the mainland of Communist China, both from the sea and from the air. He would have us accept the risk of involvement not only in an extension of the war to Red China, but in an all-out war with the Soviet Union. He would have us do this even at the expense of losing our allies and wrecking the coalition of free peoples throughout the world. He would have us do this even though the effect of such action might expose Western Europe to attack from the millions of Soviet troops poised in Middle and Eastern Europe."

Marshall continued: "What is new, and what has brought about the necessity for General MacArthur's removal, is the wholly unprecedented situation of a local theater commander publicly expressing his displeasure at and his disagreement with the foreign and military policy of the United States."

Marshall concluded: "It became apparent that General MacArthur had grown so far out of sympathy with the established policies of the United States that there was great doubt as to whether he could any longer be permitted to exercise the authority in making decisions that normal command functions would assign to a theater commander. In this situation, there was no other recourse but to relieve him."[24]

The JCS felt that an attack on China would pose enormous risk of general war and American commitment to a potentially endless stalemate on the China mainland—a war of attrition against an enemy with unlimited manpower operating guerrilla-fashion in vast areas that could never be conquered. Not only had Japan not been able to defeat China, but Chiang Kai-shek also had been unable to eradicate the Chinese Communists, in twenty-two years of conflict.

General Bradley testified that the Joint Chiefs were in complete agreement with the administration policy toward the war in Korea. The fundamental military consideration, he said, was "whether to increase the risk of global war by taking additional measures that are open to the United States and its allies." There were two major centers of power in the world today, he said—Soviet Russia and its satellites and the United States and its allies.

"From a global viewpoint," Bradley went on, "our military mission is to support a policy of preventing Communism from gaining the manpower, the resources, the raw materials, and the industrial capacity essential to world domination. If Soviet Russia ever controls the entire Eurasian land mass, then the Soviet-satellite imperialism may have the broad base upon which to build the military power to rule the world.

"Three times in the past five years, the Kremlin-inspired imperialism has been thwarted by direct action.

"In Berlin, Greece, and Korea, the free nations have opposed Communist aggression with a different type of action. But each time the power of the United States has been called upon and we have become involved. Each incident has cost us money, resources, and some lives.

"But in each instance we have prevented the domination of one more area, and the absorption of another source of manpower, raw materials, and resources.

"Korea, in spite of the importance of the engagement, must be looked upon with proper perspective. It is just one engagement, just one phase of this battle that we are having with the other power center which opposes us and all we stand for. For five years this 'guerrilla diplomacy' has been going on. In each of the actions in which we have participated to oppose this gangster conduct, we have risked world war III. But each time we have used methods short of total war. As costly as Berlin and Greece and Korea may be, they are less expensive than the vast destruction which would be inflicted upon all sides if a total war were to be precipitated.

"I am under no illusion that our present strategy of using means short of total war to achieve our ends and oppose Communism is a guarantee that a world war will not be thrust upon us. But a policy of patience and determination without provoking a world war, while we improve our military power, is one which we believe we must follow.

"As long as we keep the present conflict within its present scope, we are holding to a minimum the forces we must commit and tie down.

"The strategic alternative, enlargement of the war in Korea to include Red China, would probably delight the Kremlin more than anything else we could do."[25]

Bradley finally summed up the whole matter with a single short statement: "The course of action often described as a 'limited' war with Red China would increase the risk we are running on engaging too much of our power in an area that is not the critical strategic prize. . . . Frankly, in the opinion of the Joint Chiefs of Staff, this strategy would involve us in the wrong war, at the wrong place, at the wrong time, and with the wrong enemy."[26]

He directly disputed MacArthur's claim that any refusal to attack mainland China was "appeasement." Bradley testified: "From a military viewpoint, appeasement occurs when you give up something, which is rightfully free, to an aggressor without putting up a struggle, or making him pay a price. Forsaking Korea—withdrawing from the fight unless we are forced out—would be appeasement to aggression. Refusing to enlarge the quarrel to the point where our global capabilities are diminished, is certainly not appeasement but is a militarily sound course of action under the present circumstances."[27]

Bradley went on to testify that all members of the Joint Chiefs favored relieving MacArthur—because he had made plain he was not in sympathy with the administration's decision to limit the war to Korea, because he failed to follow the president's directive to clear statements of policy in advance, and because the JCS members "have felt and feel now that the military must be controlled by civilian authority in this country. They have always adhered to this principle and they felt that General MacArthur's actions were continuing to jeopardize the civilian control over the military authorities."[28]

General Bradley was a homespun soldier not usually given to oratory. But he emerged in the Senate committee hearings as the most eloquent and convincing speaker of them all. In one sentence, he had managed to state the entire case for preventing a military figure, no matter how impressive, to decide the policies the nation must follow.

The sheer weight of argument finally wore down nearly everyone. The two committees heard more than two million words of testimony from fourteen witnesses, including MacArthur, the secretary of state, the secretary of defense, and all the Joint Chiefs of Staff. The results did not support the ideas of MacArthur.

Rather, MacArthur's reputation suffered when it became clear that the Joint Chiefs did not agree with his ideas on war—although MacArthur had assured the committees that they did. This revelation was a great disappointment to the extreme Republicans. They had hoped to find a major conflict between the military establishment and the Truman administration to use as an election issue. When they found that the JCS solidly supported the president's concept of a limited war, their involvement in the proceedings diminished rapidly.

By the time the last witnesses had appeared on June 27, 1951, ten weeks had passed since MacArthur had been fired. By the end of the hearings most of the public had lost interest and had turned away. The two committees decided not to produce a formal report. However, eight of the twenty-six senators issued their own report that praised MacArthur and criticized the administration.[29]

The minority report made no impact whatsoever. The eight senators could extol MacArthur to the heavens, but MacArthur's ideas had not been upheld. Americans had seen clearly that the Truman administration was seeking to limit U.S. commitment to Korea. The great majority of Americans supported this view. Dean Acheson had the last word. The hearings, he said, "exhausted both committees, bored the press and the public, published a considerable amount of classified material, and successfully defused the explosive 'MacArthur issue.'"[30]

The hearings were a decisive turning point in American feelings about the war, and they also were decisive in determining the kind of policy the nation should follow into the foreseeable future. After his congressional testimony, MacArthur embarked on a nationwide speaking tour. Though he drew immense crowds and much adulation, he aroused no national movement to overturn American foreign policy. Truman's containment strategy had won.

By June 27, UN troops in Korea had turned back another Chinese offensive and had moved up to or over the 38th parallel except on the extreme west. The Chinese Communists abandoned completely their offensive efforts and turned entirely to defensive warfare. A situation eerily like the stalemate on the Western Front in World

War I descended on Korea. All across the peninsula, from the Yellow Sea to the Sea of Japan, a deep series of heavily reinforced bunkers lay hidden on the mountainsides. Protected by massive timbers and covered with thick layers of earth, they were almost impossible to see and were almost impossible to destroy by ordinary artillery fire and air strikes. Even if they were located, only direct hits by the few American flat-trajectory 155mm Long Tom rifles could break them. These bunkers were protected by automatic weapons trained on the narrow ridgelines that were the only means of approach. The bunkers were further protected by hidden 81mm and 120mm mortars that could bring down preregistered rounds on the avenues of approach.

Positional, static war now ruled Korea. The days of swift campaigns had ended. Every battle became a gruesome contest, marked by exceedingly high casualties, to capture a single mountaintop. For example, the battles to seize just two ridges, Bloody and Heartbreak, in eastern Korea from August to October 1951 cost sixty-four hundred UN casualties, mostly American, and possibly forty thousand Communist casualties. Peace talks began on July 10, 1951, at Kaesong, but were moved later to Panmunjom. It would take two more excruciating years of bloodletting and negotiation to end the war. It finally happened on July 27, 1953, almost on the 38th parallel, where the war had started. Except for MacArthur's treachery, it might have ended two years earlier at the same place.

The Triumph of Civilian Control

The United States had been involved in a gigantic battle in which a very famous and talented general was trying to snatch control from the president and from the people. In ability MacArthur was head and shoulders above the run of power-mad generals who have afflicted nations around the world for centuries. But he shared with each of these autocrats the feeling that he knew what was right for his country and that the other leaders and the people should follow what he told them they should do.

The fate of every nation that succumbs to the lure of a charismatic and able military leader is dictatorship. If MacArthur had gotten his way, all of the established means of decision-making in the United States would have been distorted. Once a military leader is granted the authority to make a unilateral decision, other decisions, equally unilateral, are almost certain to follow.

Military leaders expect to be obeyed. When somebody under their command starts to disobey orders, the instinct of all military commanders is to force them to get back in line. MacArthur was an extreme example of this tendency. Clare Boothe Luce observed that he "demanded obedience" and "plainly relished idolatry."[1] It is only a step from forcing an individual to abide by the rules to forcing an entire nation to abide by the rules. The path of all military leaders is straight to coercion and dictatorship. The Founding Fathers knew this, and they wisely made a civilian, an elected president, chief of the armed forces.

MacArthur made his fundamental position quite plain before the Senate committee hearings on May 3, 1951. When a country commits itself to force, he said, "the minute you reach the killing stage," the military assumes control. "A theater commander, in any campaign, is not merely limited to a handling of his troops; he commands that whole area politically, economically, and militarily. You have to trust at this stage of the game, when politics fail, and the military takes over, you must trust the military."[2]

The *New York Times* quickly caught the significance of what MacArthur was claiming. In an editorial two days later it said: "General MacArthur advances the thesis that once war has broken out the balance of control must be put in the hands of the military . . . while the administration holds that in peace or war, the civil administration remains supreme."

MacArthur recognized that his statement had expressed his feelings too bluntly, and he answered that he meant "that there should be no non-professional military interference in the handling of troops in a campaign."[3]

The questions went on to other topics, and the issue was never joined by the Senate committees. But the episode was a revealing exposition of MacArthur's true feelings. One of the basic arguments of military leaders is that they are "professionals" who know how to deal with problems, while civilian leaders are "nonprofessionals" who don't understand complicated matters of war and state. In his speech to Congress on April 19, 1951, for example, MacArthur lambasted "lay circles" that had criticized his actions. He insisted that he himself had "professionally designed" these actions.[4]

Of course, it is sheer nonsense to claim that military leaders are in possession of arcane knowledge inaccessible to civilians. But some people are taken in by the claims of military leaders, and see them as uniquely gifted.

For example, at the end of MacArthur's address to Congress, Representative Dewey Short, a Missouri Republican, announced: "We saw a great hunk of God in the flesh, and we heard the voice of God." A woman in New Jersey agreed. She announced that the general had "the attributes of God; he is kind and merciful and firm and just. That is my idea of God." Former Republican President Herbert Hoover exclaimed that MacArthur was "the reincarnation of Saint Paul into a great General of the Army who came out of the East." Just prior to MacArthur's ouster, Republican Senator Homer Ferguson of Michigan proposed that a congressional committee fly to Tokyo and ask MacArthur how the war should be conducted. After the general was fired, Americans phoned their newspapers, insisting that they "defy the bankrupt haberdasher [Truman]" and the "traitorous" State Department, which wanted to "sell us down the river to Great Britain, Europe, and the Communists." When MacArthur got to his suite in the Waldorf Astoria Hotel in New York City on April 19, 1951, 150,000 letters and 20,000 telegrams awaited him from the American public.[5]

The Republicans in Congress were hoping that the Senate committee hearings would demonstrate a sharp cleavage in opinion between the military establishment and the Truman administration. MacArthur had intimated that he had the backing of the Joint Chiefs of Staff and that their views had been overruled by Truman and Secretary of Defense Marshall.

But when the Republicans found that none of the Joint Chiefs backed MacArthur's desire to attack China, they quickly dropped their support of him. And as the administration meticulously brought before the Senate committees witness after witness who refuted virtually everything that MacArthur had claimed, Republican enthusiasm for a headlong challenge of the Truman administration on the matter of China vanished, and MacArthur—their putative champion—was left standing alone and isolated.

This indicates that the Republicans' main interest in MacArthur had been to single out an issue with which they could attack the Democrats in the 1952 presidential election. When they didn't find one in the general, they moved on to search for other subjects.

MacArthur thus had been used by the Republicans. He didn't see this, and he was sincere in his recommendations. But the all-out war that he wanted to inaugurate would have had terrible and lasting consequences, not only for the United States, but also for most of the world. MacArthur's aim was to attack half a billion Chinese, whose ally, the Soviet Union, possessed the atomic bomb and might intervene or might attack Western Europe while U.S. forces were tied down in the interior of China. All the people involved on both sides would have suffered vast destruction of life, property, and economic well-being.

So those two eventful years of 1950 and 1951 were immensely significant to people everywhere. President Truman saw plainly that MacArthur was trying to subvert the American political system.

Truman wrote that his effort "was an open defiance of my orders as president and as commander in chief. This was a challenge to the authority of the president under the Constitution."[6] Truman wrote later: "If there is one basic element in our Constitution, it is civilian control of the military. Policies are to be made by the elected political officials, not the generals or the admirals."[7]

This sharp division of constitutional authority is the bedrock of the American political system. Truman saw it. So did Dean Acheson, George Marshall, and the Joint Chiefs of Staff. Indeed, Omar Bradley's culminating statement in the Senate committee hearings may be taken as a summary or coda of the entire MacArthur-Truman controversy. The Joint Chiefs, he said, "have felt and feel now that the military must be controlled by civilian authority in this country."[8]

This was the whole issue in a nutshell. MacArthur had tried to take control from the elected civilian leaders. But because of soldiers like Bradley, who was unpretentious but wholly dedicated to his country, the nation made the right decision. It rejected MacArthur's claims and avoided a terrible catastrophe.

NOTES

In these notes, some references give only the last name of the author or editor or the last name and a short title. These works are cited in full in the Selected Bibliography. References not listed in the bibliography are cited in full the first time they appear in the notes of each chapter, and then are cited by author and short title afterward. Numbers in the notes refer to the pages.

INTRODUCTION: WHO WILL RULE:
A GENERAL OR A PRESIDENT?

1. Collins, 81.
2. *Military Situation in the Far East*, 3553–58. As early as 1931 MacArthur told a congressional committee that "the objective of any warring nation is victory, immediate and complete." See Manchester, 629.
3. Fear of Communism dramatically affected American affairs. Alger Hiss, a former State Department official, was accused of being a Communist spy. In January 1950, Hiss was convicted of perjury for denying that he had passed classified documents in the 1930s to a former Communist, Whittaker Chambers. In February 1950, Wisconsin Republican Senator Joseph McCarthy waved an infamous sheet of paper in Wheeling, West Virginia, which, he claimed, contained the names of 205 Communists working in the State Department. His charges set off virulent anti-Communist witch hunts in Washington that continued to 1954. This was despite the fact that, as United Press reporter George Reedy wrote, "Joe couldn't find a Communist in Red Square—he didn't know Karl Marx from Groucho." In July 1950 a Senate committee reported that McCarthy's allegations were "a fraud and a hoax." But, as D. Clayton James writes: "During the six months before the Korean War, McCarthyism spread like wildfire, forcing the Truman administration, particularly [Dean] Acheson and his department, to

defend its foreign and securities policies repeatedly." The administration's position on China was a favorite target of McCarthy and his supporters. In July 1954 the Senate voted 67–22 to censure McCarthy. With that, McCarthy lost his power. An alcoholic, McCarthy died in 1957. See Halberstam, 52, 55; James, 406; Gaddis, 387–88.

4. Spanier, 3.

5. A facsimile of this telegram is shown opposite page 498 in Gaddis.

6. Communism as an economic theory has a fatal flaw. Since Communist doctrine requires the state to possess all land, buildings, machinery, and other assets, each factory, collective farm, and other enterprise is directed by the state's bureaucracy. This is known as a command economy and is actually state capitalism. In effect, the state becomes one giant corporation that owns everything and directs all economic activities. The state bureaucracy dictates what each factory and farm will produce, and it allocates resources to each operation based, not on market demand, but on bureaucratic rules and targets. Workers are paid for hours worked at state-directed projects. There is no connection between worker output and the actual needs and desires of the public. In a command economy, the purposes of the state are preeminent. The demands of the public have much lower priority. Since workers are employees of the state, they cannot take advantage of opportunities for personal profit. They have little incentive to work harder at their state jobs, because they are unlikely to gain personally from such exertions. This is the exact opposite of a market economy, in which individuals are free to search out needs of the people and to profit personally by producing goods and services to meet these needs. A command economy can concentrate resources on major goals of the state, like armaments and large construction projects. But, since the people have no say in the state's allocation of resources and thus no say in what is being made, production of consumer goods inescapably lags far behind public demand. In contrast, a market-based economy, as is practiced in the capitalistic West, focuses most of its efforts on satisfying the demands of consumers. A command economy will inevitably produce more capital goods than can be used and fewer consumer goods than are needed by the people. Over time, a command economy will collapse.

7. The essential elements of the containment strategy were printed in the July 1947 issue of *Foreign Affairs* magazine under the title, "Sources of Soviet Conduct." Kennan wrote the article but, being a part of the State Department, could not sign it. Accordingly, it was attributed to "X." For a discussion of how the article came to be published, see Gaddis, 258–62.

8. Ibid., 235.

9. Carl von Clausewitz, *On War,* edited with an introduction by Anatol Rapoport (Hammondsworth, UK: Penguin Books, 1968), 119, 402. Clausewitz also said: "The subordination of the political point of view to the military would be contrary

to common sense, for policy has declared the war; it is the intelligent faculty, war only the instrument, and not the reverse. The subordination of the military point of view to the political is, therefore, the only thing which is possible." See ibid., 405. The implications of this concept are that civilians must control the military. It is not for the soldier to make final decisions. As John W. Spanier writes: "In the United States, it is the president and his chosen advisers who, both formally and effectively, determine the overall grand strategy which the country pursues. The military man executes the orders." See Spanier, 13.

10. The first two sentences of Sun Tzu's book, *The Art of War,* are: "Warfare is the greatest affair of state, the basis of life and death, the way to survival or extinction. It must be thoroughly pondered." Wars should be avoided if at all possible. If wars cannot be avoided, Sun Tzu urges nations to conduct swift campaigns with as little damage as possible. In all history, he emphasizes, "there is no instance of a country having benefited from prolonged war." See Bevin Alexander, *Sun Tzu at Gettysburg* (New York: W.W. Norton, 2011), xvi.

11. Gaddis, 245.

12. Ibid., 216, 217, 226.

13. Ibid., 225, 256; Alexander, *How America Got It Right,* 145. The fear was that if Communists succeeded in winning the civil war in Greece, the infection would spread to France and Italy on the west and to Iran on the east. See Gaddis, 255. Here was the first manifestation of the "falling domino" theory that was to bedevil U.S. thinking in the years ahead.

14. FRUS, *White Paper,* xvi-xvii. In June 1949, Mao Zedong announced that the Communist Chinese regime would "lean" to the side of the Soviet Union. Mao did this because the U.S. was still aiding the Nationalists, thereby signifying to Mao that it opposed the Communists. In fact, the Truman administration's motivation in publicly supporting the Nationalists was to deflect animosity of the China lobby in the U.S., which wanted to protect Chiang Kai-shek, while at the same time the administration was trying to extract the U.S. from China. This was far too subtle a point for Mao Zedong, and, getting no support from the U.S., he sought it from the Soviet Union. At the same time, Mao's move was too subtle a point for Dean Acheson, the secretary of state. He regarded Mao's "leaning" as real, and felt secure in claiming that Red China was a Soviet satellite. See *Cambridge,* vol. 14, 65; Gaddis, 355-56.

15. Alexander, *How Great Generals Win,* 202.

16. Dulles, 41.

17. Schnabel and Watson, 34, 37; Barnett, 171; Dulles, 66. The United States had adopted this line well over a year previously, but it attracted little attention until the Republicans began pushing for aid to Chiang Kai-shek after he withdrew to Taiwan in October 1949. On November 3, 1947, George C. Marshall, secretary of state, advised President Truman that massive assistance—more than was

contemplated for all of Western Europe—would be required to save the Nationalist Chinese. Marshall said China was not the place to confront the Soviet Union, and the United States should not keep Chiang Kai-shek's regime in power. He recommended that aid should be extended to Chiang only at a level that would appease Chiang's supporters in the United States (the China lobby). Truman quietly accepted Marshall's recommendations. See Gaddis, 298; Schnabel and Watson, 29–35; Barnett, 167; Dulles, 27–28. Although nothing was said publicly, this was the decision that marked U.S. abandonment of Nationalist China.

18. Although the Truman administration failed to seek Republican endorsement of its China policy, a leading Republican, Senator Arthur H. Vandenberg of Michigan, said: "It is easy to sympathize with Chiang. But it is quite a different thing to plan resultful aid short of armed American intervention with American combat troops (which I have never favored and probably never shall)." See Spanier, 50. This indicates that there was by no means unanimous Republican support for all-out aid to Chiang.

19. This decision came during a conference December 4–8, 1950, between the Truman administration and a British delegation, headed by Prime Minister Clement Attlee. In it the officials placed themselves firmly on the record as being willing to end the war on the basis of the old border between North and South Korea— the 38th parallel. The hope of unifying Korea by force had been finally laid to rest. See Schnabel and Watson, 362–78.

20. Alexander, *Korea*, 299; Schnabel and Watson, 280; Appleman, 673, 675–78.

21. Peng Dehuai, *Memoirs of a Chinese Marshal* (Beijing: Foreign Languages Press, 1984), vol. 2, 473. Peng Dehuai consistently referred to the troops he commanded in Korea as "Chinese People's Volunteers." See ibid., 474–75, 478.

22. As James Westfall Thompson and Edgar Nathaniel Johnson write in their epic study, *An Introduction to Medieval Europe 300–1500* (New York: W. W. Norton, 1937), 6, Julius Caesar and his successor, Augustus, who destroyed the Roman republic a few decades before the birth of Christ, "meant to return to the very old principle of military dictatorship, which had been worked out by the despots of the east. . . . Augustus preserved the magistracies of the Roman republic, reserving the most important for himself. In particular, his control of the army and of finances assured him a monopoly of authority and made him the actual master of the state."

23. Walter Phelps Hall, Robert Greenhalgh Albion, and Jennie Barnes Pope, *A History of England and the British Empire* (New York: Ginn and Company, 1946), 310.

24. *Cambridge*, vol. 13, chapter 14, 822.

25. Max Farrand, *Records of the Federal Convention of 1787* (New Haven: Yale University Press, 1911), 1:465.

26. *The Federalist Papers* (New York: SoHo Books, 2011), 18–21.
27. Richard Bruce Winders, *Mr. Polk's Army* (College Station: Texas A&M University Press, 1997), 33–34, 188–89.
28. Doris Kearns Goodwin, *Team of Rivals* (New York: Simon & Schuster, 2005), 379–83, 514.
29. *Military Situation in the Far East*, 45.
30. Ibid., 289.
31. Alexander, *Korea*, 158; Schnabel and Watson, 191.
32. The Soviet Union had exactly one railroad connecting European Russia with the Pacific, the 5,700-mile Trans-Siberian Railway. Supplying major campaigns by this railroad would have constituted an insurmountable logistical problem, not to speak of the possibility of it being broken by air strikes or clandestine attacks.
33. On June 27, 1950, the U.S. ambassador in Moscow delivered a note to the Soviet government requesting that it use its influence with North Korea to halt its attack on South Korea. On June 29, the Soviet government replied that the matter was an internal Korean affair, and it would not intervene. This assured Secretary of State Acheson that the Soviets did not intend to commit their forces to Korea. See Schnabel and Watson, 96, 107; Truman, 341–42.
34. James, 614–15. The full text of MacArthur's address to the Congress is contained in Rovere and Schlesinger, 270–77, and also in *Military Situation in the Far East*, 3553–58.
35. Schnabel and Watson, 529–30; Alexander, *Korea*, 408–9.
36. *Military Situation in the Far East*, 731–33.
37. Schnabel and Watson, 399–402.
38. Bradley and Blair, 530. The June 14, 1950, memorandum is printed in James, 408–10.

CHAPTER 1 ORIGINS OF THE FAR EAST DILEMMA

1. China had to give up enclaves or concessions to imperial powers where foreign, not Chinese law, applied (extraterritoriality) and to allow Christian missionaries to operate throughout the country. The British and later French and other imperialist penetrations had created in the treaty ports (numbering thirty-three by 1893) a joint Chinese-Western economy that, as China expert John King Fairbank says, stopped colonialism in its tracks. Many Chinese participated in this joint economy and established a highly complex structure that didn't fit the traditional pattern of the imperialist mother country exploiting weak, unsophisticated, and unskilled colonial peoples. Foreign-Chinese cooperation and conflict reached its highest expression in Shanghai, dominated by the international and French concessions there. Shanghai grew into the largest city in China and one of the

largest in the world (3.6 million by 1937), its burgeoning trade and factories drawing people constantly from the hinterland. Many Chinese served as managers for the foreign firms. They and other Chinese quickly learned about foreign markets and technology and a number set up their own factories or shops. Thus, a complex mixed economy developed in which Chinese and foreigners cooperated and competed. With no one country responsible for what went on, an almost inconceivably permissive and exploitative society developed in Shanghai. Entrepreneurs flourished in this unfettered atmosphere, an extreme case of capitalism and laissez-faire, growing rich in part because the labor pool was bottomless and desperate. Coolies pulled rickshas at 5 cents a mile. Peasants came in from the countryside to work at wages barely above starvation. They vied for jobs with children less than ten years old who were sold to factories. The children worked thirteen hours a day, slept under their machines, and were forbidden to leave the factory grounds. Crime flourished. Anyone could arrange to have an enemy murdered, maimed, or disposed of. It was not for nothing that the word "shanghai" passed into the English language as a verb, meaning to kidnap, usually by drugging. There were 668 brothels. Drugs of all kinds could be bought easily, as could women and children. Shanghai, with justification, was known as the wickedest city on the planet. See *Cambridge*, vol. 12, chapter 1, "Introduction: Maritime and Continental China's history," by John King Fairbank, professor of history emeritus, Harvard University, 21, 129, 131, 133, 136. The United States forced Britain to give up its enclaves during World War II. The French also surrendered their rights as a condition of Nationalist Chinese troops evacuating northern French Indochina (Vietnam, Cambodia, and Laos), which they had occupied upon Japan's surrender in 1945.

2. *Cambridge*, vol. 13, 822.

3. Snow, 165–66; Selden, 25–27.

4. The narrative for the long march is drawn from Harrison Salisbury, *The Long March: The Untold Story* (New York: Harper & Row, 1985); James Pinckney Harrison. *The Long March to Power, A History of the Chinese Communist Party, 1921–72* (New York: Praeger Publisher, 1972), 238–59; *Cambridge*, vol. 13, chapter 4, "The Communist Movement 1927–1937," by Jerome Ch'en, 209–16; Alexander, *How Great Generals Win*, 187–208.

5. Schaller, 90–92.

6. Dallek, 328–29. *Time* magazine named Chiang and Madame Chiang "Man and Wife of the Year" in 1937. Henry Luce, publisher of *Time*, was born in China of missionary parents, and he produced an idealized, almost worshipful view of the Chiangs. The missionaries in China rallied to the Chiangs because they were Christians, thus proving to the missionaries, at least, that the missionary effort in China was valid. As Barbara Tuchman writes, "They overpraised Chiang Kai-shek and once committed to his perfection regarded any suggestion of blemish

as inadmissible." The *Missionary Review of the World* proclaimed that "China has now the most enlightened, patriotic and able rulers in her history." See Tuchman, 238.

7. Romanus and Sunderland, *Mission*, 64–65, 75; Feis, 15; Tuchman, 315.

8. Romanus and Sunderland, *Mission*, 25–27, 235–38, 385–86; Feis, 17.

9. Tuchman, 269.

10. Romanus and Sunderland, *Mission*, 76–78, 93; Tuchman, 315–17, 324, 387. Above about seventeen thousand feet, people had to take oxygen, but the C-46s and C-47s were not designed with pressurized interior space. Thus, at fifteen thousand feet, the transports were operating at about the limit of their capability. The Hump air service began on April 5, 1942, when ten DC-3s diverted from Pan American Airlines' trans-African service began flying. Another twenty-five DC-3s (C-47s) were on the way after having been taken over from U.S. domestic airlines. The Curtiss-Wright C-46 could carry twice the payload of the C-47 (up to forty thousand pounds), but it was plagued with high fuel consumption, mechanical problems, and gasoline leaks that led to numerous midair explosions. The United States produced more than ten thousand C-47s during the war, and only thirty-two hundred C-46s. Accordingly, the reliable C-47 was much more heavily used than the C-46 in transport over the Hump.

11. Romanus and Sunderland, *Command*, 254, 261; Tuchman, 433–34, 446–52; Schaller, 119–20; Dallek, 387–88; John M. Blum, *From the Morgenthau Diaries*, three volumes (Boston: Houghton Mifflin, 1959–67), vol. 3, 105.

12. Romanus and Sunderland, *Command*, 258–66; Tuchman, 444.

13. On July 1, 1921, thirteen members of various Communist study groups, including Mao Zedong, began the first Communist "congress" at a girl's school in the French concession of Shanghai. Attending were Gregory Voitinsky, the Russian agent sent out by the Comintern (Communist International), the Kremlin's subversive agency in foreign countries. Because a suspicious character appeared (a spy for the French Sûreté), the delegates fled to Shaoxing in Zhejiang province and concluded their business in a boat on a lake. At these sessions the thirteen delegates inaugurated the Chinese Communist Party. The members defined the party's task in orthodox Marxist terms to "overthrow the capitalistic classes" using the "revolutionary army of the proletariat" in order to abolish classes. Mao Zedong (1893–1976) was a brilliant son of a peasant from Hunan. He became editor of the weekly *Xiang River Review* and quickly established a reputation as a powerful radical thinker. In Russia, a new kind of political party had arisen. Vladimir Lenin, leader of the 1917 Russian Revolution, had concluded that the masses had neither the experience nor the theory necessary to change society themselves and that revolution had to be created by an elite Communist party as a "conscious vanguard" which would operate an authoritarian regime thereafter. Lenin dismissed democracy as "a useless and harmful toy" and centralized dictatorial power

in the hands of the vanguard. This band of disciplined, professional revolutionaries functioned like an army general staff, and Lenin held firmly to the military or command nature of the party. Another essential element was "democratic centralism," which required local and regional committees to obey the policy decisions of the center. When Voitinsky arrived in China, this was the model he was expected to follow. But in the spring of 1921 Lenin added a powerful new element: once the party made a decision, all members were required to support it, outlawing all opposition. Before he died in 1924 Lenin recognized that this rule could be used to eliminate opponents and create a one-man dictatorship. But by then the policy was firm. This policy, of course, led to the dictatorship of Joseph Stalin. See *Cambridge*, vol. 12, 507, 514-16; James Pinckney Harrison. *The Long March to Power, A History of the Chinese Communist Party, 1921–72* (New York: Praeger Publishers, 1972), 27–35. Although the Comintern dominated the Chinese party in its early years, it lost all its prestige in 1934 when it rejected highly successful guerrilla tactics being practiced by Mao Zedong and demanded headlong attacks against Nationalist forces that were driving in on the Communist sanctuary around Ruijin in the Wuyi Mountains of Jiangxi province in southeastern China. These attacks failed miserably, leading to the collapse of the sanctuary and the flight of the survivors in the "long march" to Yan'an in Shaanxi province of northwestern China. See Alexander, *How Great Generals Win,* 187–99.

14. More than one-third of all farmland was rented from rich peasants or landlords. Most landlords lived in cities and got their rents collected by agencies called bursaries. Rents were exorbitant, up to 60 percent of the crop, and bursaries frequently increased the squeeze, often forcing peasants to borrow. Bad years, the costs of marriages and funerals, family crises, or simply the need to buy enough food to last to the next harvest forced many peasants into debt. The landlords were the best source, and they charged interest rates that exploited the peasants' desperation. Small loans in kind often drew interest rates of 100 to 200 percent annual interest. Most loans were less, but nearly a fourth exceeded 40 percent. In some places when a peasant did not keep up with his debt payments, the local police threw him into jail, where he died unless his family brought food and water. Taxation also was unfair. Collusion of landlords and the other elites with the tax collectors was common. The wealthy paid lower taxes than their due, and the burden fell disproportionately on the poor. See Selden, 6–10.

15. Davies, 305–6; Dallek. 489–90; FRUS, *White Paper,* 550.

16. FRUS, *China, 1944,* 253–56; Davies, 327.

17. Dallek, 507–8, 516, 519. Two excellent books on the events at and consequences of Yalta are Diane S. Clemens, *Yalta* (New York: Oxford University Press, 1970), and Daniel Yergin, *The Shattered Peace: The Cold War and the Origins of the*

National Security State (Boston: Houghton Mifflin, 1977). This volume does not attempt to analyze decisions at Yalta other than those related to China and the Far East. The complete record of the conference, however, is available in FRUS, *Yalta*.

18. FRUS, *China, 1945*, 342–44, 346; Davies, 406.

19. *Cambridge*, vol. 13, 768-70. Major General David G. Barr, senior U.S. military adviser in China, described the "wall psychology" of Nationalist generals in FRUS, *White Paper*, 337. Even when the PLA (People's Liberation Army) had artillery and ammunition for the guns, they frequently did not use them because they did not have many prime movers or the fuel to propel them. Also they had no warplanes or trained pilots. Artillery, being mostly confined to roads on the march or in open places when in use, was vulnerable to air attack. Instead of artillery, the PLA relied on mortars, which could be broken down and carried on the backs of men or beasts. For examples of how Reds concentrated on supply lines and Nationalists held to static defense in cities, see FRUS, *China, 1947*, 36–37, 49–50, 88–89, 130–31, 134–47, 157–59, 166–68, 171–73, 178–81, 192–93, 195–96, 198–209.

20. FRUS, *China, 1947*, 83–84, 116, 118–19, 282–83; FRUS, *China, 1948*, vol. 7, 25–26, 36, 43–45, 55–56, 70–71; vol. 8, 479–85. FRUS, *White Paper*, 379–404, 981–87.

21. FRUS, *White Paper*, 319–20, 331–32; FRUS, *China, 1948*, vol. 7, 464–65, 467–78, 470–71, 473–74, 480–86; *Cambridge*, vol. 13, 775.

22. Tucker, 29. A record of Sino-Soviet negotiations regarding Xinjiang is given in FRUS, *China, 1949*, vol. ix, 1037–63. These efforts by Stalin came to naught.

23. FRUS, *China, 1949*, vol. 8, 357–60, 363–64, 368–70, 372–73.

24. Ibid., 405–7.

25. Ibid., 355–57, 369–70, 385, 391; FRUS, *White Paper*, x, xvi–xvii.

26. Dulles, 42–44; Alexander, *Korea*, 19–20.

27. Acheson, 302–3, 306–7. Acheson was preoccupied in his memoirs with justifying his claims that the United States was not at fault for the Communist victory and with complaining about personal attacks he received.

28. FRUS, *China, 1949*, vol. 8, 531–37, 541–47, 551, 552, 556, 565–66; *Cambridge*, vol. 13, 785; vol. 14, 59–60, 77–79.

29. FRUS, *China, 1949*, vol. 8, 540, 547–50, 552–56, 562–65, 569–70, 572, 575–76, 581, 583–84, 586, 593–94, 595–611, 614–20, 622–27; *Cambridge*, vol. 13, 783–84.

30. *Cambridge*, vol. 13, 783.

31. Emile Capouya and Keitha Tompkins, eds., *The Essential Kropotkin* (New York: Liveright Press, 1975), 76.

32. Truman, 317; Appleman, 2–3; Schnabel and Watson, 3, 9; Schnabel, 7–11; Alexander, *Korea*, 10–15.

33. Appleman, 4; Schnabel, 13–28; Bong-youn Choy, *Korea: A History* (Rutland, Vt.: Charles E. Tuttle, Co., 1971), 241–46. Choy (199–302) emphasizes the autocratic practices of Syngman Rhee and his advocacy of reuniting Korea by force.

CHAPTER 2 THE AMERICAN ATTEMPT AT STABILITY

1. On August 4, 1949, Secretary of State Acheson informed the National Security Council (NSC) that preservation of Taiwan from the Communists could not be prevented by economic aid to the Nationalists or by reform of Chiang's government. Acheson wanted the United States to abandon the island, but it was for the NSC to determine whether it was of sufficient importance to commit American forces to its occupation. On August 17, the Joint Chiefs of Staff reaffirmed a previously determined view that "the strategic importance of Formosa [Taiwan] does not justify overt military action." The next month they opposed sending a military mission to Taiwan to examine the state of Nationalist defenses. Secretary of Defense Louis A. Johnson meanwhile had joined the pro-Nationalists and pressed the Joint Chiefs so hard they suggested that the United States send a military fact-finding mission to Taiwan and that Chiang receive military assistance. Secretary Johnson asked President Truman to support the JCS recommendations. But Acheson insisted that nothing short of commitment of U.S. forces could save Taiwan. President Truman sided with Acheson, and on December 29, 1949, the National Security Council endorsed the State Department view rejecting a mission and holding that no American forces should be used to shore up Chiang Kai-shek. See FRUS, *China, 1949*, vol. 9, 369–71 374–78, 392–97, 460–67; FRUS, *China, 1949*, vol. 8, 624–25; vol. 9, 460–61; Acheson, 350; FRUS, *East Asia, 1950*, 257, 264–69.

2. The major opponents of Acheson's Taiwan policy were three Republican senators, William Knowland of California, H. Alexander Smith of New Jersey, and Robert A. Taft of Ohio. These Republicans pressed for an active, interventionist policy in Taiwan. Senator Smith urged that the United States take the position that Taiwan was still officially a part of Japan, since the United States had not signed a peace treaty. Japan had annexed Taiwan in 1895 under terms ending the Sino-Japanese War of 1894–1895. It was returned to China as a result of Japan's defeat in 1945. Under Smith's idea, the United States might assume a sort of protectorate over the island. A few weeks later Smith implied publicly that General Douglas MacArthur, supreme commander in Japan, supported his view. Smith's proposal got nowhere, but it showed the extremes some China lobbyists were willing to go to. See Acheson, 350.

3. Tucker, 25; FRUS, *China, 1949*, vol. 8, 576–79; FRUS, *China, 1949*, vol. 9, 81–85, 615–17, 622–26. On December 16, 1949, Foreign Secretary Ernest Bevin informed Acheson of the British cabinet decision to recognize Red China. For a complete record of negotiations between November 1, 1949, and the end of the year, see

FRUS, *China, 1949,* vol. 9, 149–260. India recognized Red China on December 30, 1949, Pakistan on January 5, 1950, and Britain on January 6, 1950. Between January 6 and 17, 1950, Norway, Ceylon, Denmark, Israel, Afghanistan, Finland, Sweden, and Switzerland recognized the Beijing government. See Tsou, 518.

4. FRUS, *East Asia, 1950,* 264; Acheson, 350-52; Schnabel and Watson, 34-35. For a full text of Truman's statement, see *Public Papers of the Presidents of the United States: Harry S. Truman, 1950* (Washington: Government Printing Office), 11. The key part of Truman's statement was as follows: "The United States has no predatory designs on Formosa, or of any other Chinese territory. The United States has no desire to obtain special rights or privileges, or to establish military bases on Formosa at this time. Nor does it have any intention of utilizing the armed forces to interfere in the present situation. The United States government will not pursue a course which will lead to involvement in the civil conflict in China. Similarly, the United States will not provide military aid or advice to Chinese forces on Formosa. In the view of the United States government, the resources on Formosa are adequate to enable them to obtain the items which they might consider necessary for the defense of the island. The United States government proposes to continue under existing legislative authority the present ECA [Economic Cooperation Administration or Marshall Plan] of economic assistance."

5. FRUS, *East Asia, 1950,* 275; Acheson, 354–57; Schnabel and Watson, 36, 38.

6. In 1949 the Joint Chiefs of Staff had sketched an identical line, and the same year General MacArthur, in an interview with a British journalist, had done the same thing. Few people had noticed this, however, and Acheson's statement was viewed as a wholly new decision by the administration.

7. Schnabel and Watson, 13–16.

8. In June 1949 a JCS study, directed by Chairman Omar Bradley, rejected a possibility that, in the case of war, the United States would apply the Truman Doctrine to protect South Korea. It also rejected the possibility that the United States would intervene unilaterally. Reasons for the rejection were that commitment of U.S. resources would be out of proportion to the low strategic value of Korea. Instead, the study recommended that the United States appeal to the UN Security Council. See ibid., 25–27.

9. Dulles, 57–58.

10. Acheson, 357; Trygve Lie, *In the Cause of Peace* (New York: Macmillan Co., 1954), 258.

11. FRUS, *East Asia, 1950,* 270–77, 286–89, 321–22, 327–29; Tsou, 518–19, 525, 537.

12. FRUS, *East Asia, 1950,* 288, 698–700, 710–15, 730–33; Tsou, 524. The Soviet and Red Chinese moves in Indochina were based on the conviction, also shared by the United States, that the elevation of Vietnam, Laos, and Cambodia to "associated states" within the French Union was a fabrication veiling continued French domination of Indochina.

13. FRUS, *China, 1949*, vol. 8, 632–38, 640, 642–45, 651; FRUS, *East Asia, 1950*, 294–96, 308–12; *Cambridge*, vol. 14, 268–69.
14. FRUS, *East Asia, 1950*, 330, 340–42, 344–46, 347–51.
15. Manchester, 3, 6, 140, 141.
16. Douglas MacArthur (1880–1964) was the son of a well-known Union officer in the Civil War, Arthur MacArthur, but his mother Mary Pinckney Hardy (Pinky) was from Norfolk, Virginia. He grew up on army posts in the Old West. He was first captain at West Point and graduated first in his class of 1903. In the U.S. occupation of Vera Cruz in 1914, MacArthur seized some locomotives but had to fight a running battle with guerrillas to get them back to base. He was chief of staff of the 42nd (Rainbow) Division in World War I and won seven Silver Stars and two Distinguished Service Crosses for valor; he also received the Distinguished Service Medal. He ended the war as a brigadier general, the youngest general in the American Expeditionary Force. He also commanded the Rainbow Division briefly. In 1919 MacArthur became superintendent of West Point because the army chief of staff felt the academy was badly in need of reform. MacArthur moved into the superintendent's house with his mother. In 1922 MacArthur married socialite Louise Cromwell Brooks and the same year became commander of the Military District of Manila, the Philippines. In 1925 MacArthur, age forty-four, became the army's youngest major general. MacArthur and his wife returned to the States, where he commanded the army's 3rd Corps at Fort McHenry, Baltimore. In 1927 Douglas and Louise separated, and in 1929 they divorced. The same year MacArthur received command of the Philippine Department, and in 1930 he returned to Washington as army chief of staff with the rank of general. In 1932 on orders of President Herbert Hoover, he evicted from Washington the "Bonus Army" of veterans seeking federal benefits. In 1935 the Philippine president, Manuel Quezon, asked MacArthur to supervise creation of a Filipino army. In 1937 MacArthur married Jean Marie Faircloth, a thirty-eight-year-old socialite. The marriage produced a son, Arthur MacArthur IV, born February 21, 1938. MacArthur was in command when the Japanese attacked the Philippines on December 8, 1941. American forces were soon driven into the Bataan peninsula and nearby Corregidor, west of Manila, where they were ultimately forced to surrender. In February 1942 President Franklin D. Roosevelt ordered MacArthur transferred to Australia. On the night of March 12, 1942, MacArthur, his wife and son, and a select party of officers left Corregidor in four PT boats. The boats reached the coast of Mindanao near Del Monte Airfield. There U.S. Navy B-17 bombers picked them up and flew them to Australia. MacArthur was named supreme commander of the Southwest Pacific Area and led campaigns through New Guinea to the Philippines. In April 1945 he became commander of U.S. Army Forces Pacific. On August 29, 1945, he was ordered by President Harry S. Truman to become supreme commander of the Allied

Powers to govern Japan. He supervised the surrender of Japan on the deck of the battleship USS *Missouri* on September 2, 1945. MacArthur achieved a splendid record in turning Japan into a democracy during the occupation, which ended in 1951.

17. FRUS, *East Asia, 1950*, 366–67; FRUS, *Korea, 1950*, 161–65.
18. James, 408–10.

CHAPTER 3 WAR AND THE QUARANTINE OF TAIWAN

1. Nikita Khrushchev, *Khrushchev Remembers*, with an introduction, commentary, and notes by Edward Crankshaw (Boston: Little, Brown, 1970), 367–73. Khrushchev says in his memoirs that Stalin consulted Mao Zedong on Kim Il Sung's invasion proposal, and that Mao answered affirmatively and gave the opinion that the United States would not intervene. Khrushchev made a number of factual errors in his memoirs, and it is impossible to know if he was wrong in this instance. However, a North Korean attack was absolutely not in Red China's interests because the attack would almost certainly cause the United States to reappraise its decision to abandon Chiang Kai-shek. This would make it impossible for Red China to occupy Taiwan and end the civil war. Therefore, it is virtually certain that Mao Zedong did not approve the North Korean attack. When it came, Red China made no effort whatsoever to assist the North Koreans. The historian Michael D. Pearlman, who has studied material released from Soviet archives after the fall of the Soviet Union in 1991, writes: "Those recently willing to venture a hypothesis cannot reach agreement. . . . Some support Truman's proposition about a momentum building up behind Communist expansionism, specifically that Stalin used Korea to test 'the prevailing mood' of weakness in Washington. Others, such as Alexandre Mansourov, paint a different picture, wherein Stalin looks a lot like Truman, trying to show determination lest the enemy take advantage of the circumstances. 'The South was determined to launch an attack on the North sooner or later,' the Soviet leader said to Kim [Il Sung] in April 1950, 'and it was apparent to forestall this aggression.'" See Pearlman, 62.
2. Schnabel and Watson, 49–54, 59–65.
3. Ibid., 55. In 1950 there were three to eight Soviet advisers in every North Korean division. However, Moscow withdrew these advisers shortly before the North Koreans attacked, apparently to avoid any of them falling into enemy hands. See Schnabel, 37.
4. Truman, 332–33.
5. Acheson, 405.
6. Schnabel and Watson, 77–80; Truman, 333–36; Paige, 125–41, give a full account of this meeting as well as the decisions leading up to the U.S. intervention.

7. Truman, 337–38; Acheson, 407–8; *Military Situation in the Far East,* 949, 1049–50; 1475, 1643, 2574–75, 2581–82.
8. National Archives, *Public Papers, Truman, 1950,* 492; Schnabel and Watson, 94.
9. Paige, 248.
10. FRUS, *Korea, 1950,* 430. Truman's comment: "In order that there may be no doubt in any quarter about our intentions regarding Formosa, I wish to state that the United States has no territorial ambitions whatever concerning that island, nor do we seek for ourselves any special position or privilege on Formosa. The present military neutralization of Formosa is without prejudice to political questions affecting that island. Our desire is that Formosa not become embroiled in hostilities disturbing to the peace of the Pacific and that all questions affecting Formosa be settled by peaceful means as envisaged in the charter of the United Nations."
11. Schnabel and Watson, 107; Paige, 202–6; Acheson, 408.
12. On June 29, 1950, the Soviet government told the U.S. embassy in Moscow that the conflict in Korea was an internal affair, and it would not intervene. See Schnabel and Watson, 96, 107; Truman, 341–42.
13. By August 4, 1950, North Korean tank numbers had declined to forty, and artillery and mortar pieces were down to about one-third their number at the start of the war. The North Korean 4th Division, for example, had only twelve field artillery pieces when it reached the Naktong River on August 5, 1950. At the time, there were at least forty-four field artillery pieces in an American division (sixty-six at full strength, fifty-four 105mm howitzers and twelve 155mm howitzers). The North Koreans received only one significant weapons addition, when twenty-one new T-34 tanks arrived in early August 1950. See Alexander, *Korea,* 124, 145.
14. Schnabel and Watson, 118.
15. Appleman, 179–80.
16. The full story of the early stages of the Korean War is given in Alexander, *Korea,* 55–147.
17. Napoléon Bonaparte's Italian campaign is explained in Alexander, *How Great Generals Win,* 95–122.
18. Appleman, 488, 493; Collins, 123; Schnabel and Watson, 201–11. A basic problem of the Inchon landing site was that huge mudflats extended westward from the coast for three miles, and landing ships, tank (LSTs) could cross this area only when the tides were at least thirty feet deep, a condition that occurred only a few days a month. Planners were thus severely constrained in choosing a date and hour for an assault. The narrow Flying Fish Channel threaded the flats to reach the port, but it was difficult and tortuous even in daylight. Moreover, the channel was dominated by a small island, Wolmi-do, rugged in terrain and known to be fortified. The need to reduce this island before attacking the mainland would destroy an element of surprise. The city itself was protected by a twelve-foot seawall.

19. Basil H. Liddell Hart, *Strategy* (New York: Frederick A. Praeger, 1954), 341, 348.
20. Bevin Alexander, *Sun Tzu at Gettysburg* (New York: W. W. Norton, 2011), 109.
21. Tides are funneled into the narrow Yellow Sea by the Korean peninsula on the east and the Shandong peninsula of China on the west. Ocean waters rushing in produce extremely high tides, in the same way they do in Canada's Bay of Fundy, closed in by New Brunswick on the north and Nova Scotia on the south. Islands offshore from Inchon slow the flow of waters, causing sluggish tides that produce huge mudflats at Inchon and on either side of Flying Fish Channel leading to the port. These mudflats will not support men on foot.
22. Schnabel and Watson, 191. The implications of the UN resolution of June 27, 1950, were to restore status quo antebellum, not conquer North Korea. The resolution urged UN members to "furnish such assistance to the Republic of Korea as may be necessary to restore international peace and security in the area." See ibid., 95–96.
23. Collins, 83.
24. Bradley and Blair, 544.
25. Ibid., 545.
26. Schnabel, 142.
27. Ibid., 146.
28. Ibid.

CHAPTER 4 MACARTHUR VISITS CHIANG KAI-SHEK

1. Schnabel and Watson, 506–9; Schnabel, 368.
2. Schnabel and Watson, 509.
3. FRUS, *Korea, 1950*, 430.
4. Bradley and Blair, 551–52.
5. McLellan 279; Schnabel, 368–69; the full text of Chiang Kai-shek's statement is given in *Military Situation in the Far East*, 3383–84.
6. Bradley and Blair, 551–52.
7. Schnabel and Watson, 512–13.
8. Bradley and Blair, 549; Schnabel and Watson, 511.
9. Schnabel and Watson, 514.
10. FRUS, *East Asia, 1950*, 415; Schnabel and Watson, 510.
11. Truman, 355–56; FRUS, *Korea, 1950*, 542–44, and FRUS, *East Asia, 1950*, 427–30
12. Schnabel and Watson, 511.
13. Ibid., 512; Schnabel, 369.
14. Truman, 351–52.
15. Ibid., 353
16. Acheson, 450.
17. Truman, 354.

18. Spanier, 72–73; Schnabel and Watson, 510; Acheson, 522; Truman, 354; *New York Times,* August 10, 1950, 1.

19. FRUS, *China, 1950,* 410; Schnabel and Watson, 220. President Truman signed the National Security Act on July 26, 1947. This act unified command of the armed forces, including a now independent air force, within a new Department of Defense, and it established the National Security Council (NSC) and the Central Intelligence Agency (CIA) as secret institutions responsible only to the president. The NSC's task was to refine foreign policy, while the CIA was to gather intelligence information worldwide. The NSC's membership would include the president, vice president, and secretaries of state and defense. The CIA replaced the Office of Strategic Services (OSS), which had operated during World War II.

20. FRUS, *China, 1950,* 410.

21. Ibid., 42–30, 354–55, 373.

22. Ibid., 272, 386–87, 393–95.

23. Ibid., 407–10.

24. Ibid., 395–96, 437–38.

25. Ibid., 469–73, 480–81, 514–16, 567–69, 582–85, 617–23, 635–39, 641–43, 646–52, 660–66.

26. Ibid., 483–87, 502–10, 528–35, 671–79.

27. Ibid., 596; Allen S. Whiting, *China Crosses the Yalu: The Decision to Enter the Korean War* (Stanford, Calif.: Stanford University Press, 1960), 78–79; E. Lloyd Murphy, *The U.S./U.N. Decision to Cross the 38th Parallel, October 1950; A Case Study of Changing Objectives in Limited War,* Air War College Research Report No. 3660, (Maxwell Air Force Base, Ala.: Air War College, 1968), 28.

28. FRUS, *Korea, 1950,* 858.

29. Murphy, *U.S./U.N. Decision,* 29–31; Schnabel and Watson, 260; Whiting, *China Crosses,* 96; FRUS, *Korea and China, 1951,* 1892–93.

CHAPTER 5 MACARTHUR OPENLY DEFIES TRUMAN

1. Truman, 354–55.

2. Ibid.

3. Ibid.

4. Acheson, 423.

5. The controversial MacArthur statement in the VFW speech was as follows: "Nothing could be more fallacious than the threadbare argument by those who advocate appeasement and defeatism in the Pacific that if we defend Formosa we alienate continental Asia. Those who speak thus do not understand the Orient. They do not grant that it is in the pattern of Oriental psychology to respect and follow aggressive, resolute and dynamic leadership—to quickly turn on a leader-

ship characterized by timidity or vacillation—and they underestimate the Oriental mentality. Nothing in the last five years has so inspired the Far East as the American determination to preserve the bulwarks of our Pacific Ocean strategic position from future encroachment, for few of its people fail accurately to appraise the safeguard which determination brings to their free institutions." See Schnabel and Watson, 515. MacArthur's full statement to the VFW is given in *Military Situation in the Far East,* 3477–80.

6. Acheson, 423.
7. Bradley and Blair, 551.
8. Truman, 356.
9. Bradley and Blair, 551; Schnabel and Watson, 517.
10. Schnabel and Watson, 517.
11. Schnabel, 371.
12. Bradley and Blair, 638.
13. McLellan, 283.
14. Schnabel and Watson, 218; Bradley and Blair, 552.
15. Schnabel, 370.

CHAPTER 6 INCHON

1. Collins, 124–25.
2. Ibid., 120.
3. Appleman, 493; Manchester, 575–76.
4. Bradley and Blair, 547; Schnabel and Watson, 211; Truman, 358–59.
5. Schnabel and Watson, 213; Schnabel, 153.
6. Schnabel and Watson, 213; MacArthur, 351.
7. Schnabel and Watson, 213–14; Schnabel, 153–54.
8. Bradley and Blair, 556.
9. For example, when the Inchon landing occurred, the 87th Regiment of the North Korean 9th Division was located at Kumchon, west of the Naktong River line, about 150 miles south of Seoul. Ordered to defend Seoul, the regiment departed Kumchon by rail on September 16, but took four days to get to Seoul. To avoid UN aircraft, the trains had to hide in tunnels during the day. See Appleman, 519.
10. A detailed study of the entire Inchon operation, from invasion to final capture of Seoul, is given in Alexander, *Korea,* 188–227.
11. Truman, 360.
12. Appleman, 537–38.
13. Bradley and Blair, 556.
14. Ibid., 557.
15. Ridgway, 42.

CHAPTER 7 THE ATTEMPT TO CONQUER NORTH KOREA

1. Schnabel and Watson, 226–27.
2. Ibid., 226.
3. Ibid., 258.
4. Ibid., 227.
5. Ibid., 230.
6. Bradley and Blair, 564, 570.
7. Ibid., 570.
8. Ibid., 570.
9. Charles O. Hucker, *China's Imperial Past* (Stanford, Calif.: Stanford University Press, 1975), 125–27.
10. Bong-youn Choy, 67, 88.
11. *New York Times,* September 18, 1950, 22; September 30, 1950, 16; October 1, 1950, 8E; *Time,* September 25, 1950, 35; October 9, 1950, 34–35; *U.S. News and World Report,* October 6, 1950, 52; October 13, 1950, 6, 8; Hanson W. Baldwin, *New York Times,* September 27, 1950, 6.
12. Shortly after Ambassador Warren Austin's first public statement about unifying Korea, on August 10, 1950, the *New York Times* reported from Hong Kong that Mao Zedong and V. M. Molotov, Soviet vice premier, had met and that Red China had agreed to enter the war with Soviet material help if the UN crossed the 38th parallel. See *New York Times,* August 17, 1950, 4. On August 20, Red China premier Zhou Enlai cabled the United Nations: "Since Korea is China's neighbor, the Chinese people cannot but be especially concerned about solution of the Korean question, which must and can be settled peacefully." Zhou's message was broadcast in English and also appeared in the English-language *People's China,* published in Beijing. See Allen S. Whiting, *China Crosses the Yalu: The Decision to Enter the Korean War* (Stanford, Calif.: Stanford University Press, 1960), 79; Murphy, 34; *People's China* 2, no. 5, September 1, 1950. On August 22, Jacob Malik, Soviet representative in the United Nations, stated that any continuation of the war would lead to widening of the conflict, "and the responsibility for this would be fully upon the government of the United States." From the time of Malik's statement, Red Chinese journals and official statements hinted darkly that the People's Republic would defend the Yalu River. See Whiting, 69–70, 92–94. The Military Intelligence Section of the Far East Command estimated that PLA regulars in Manchuria rose to 450,000 by September 21. U.S. intelligence sources also began to get reports that Red Chinese leaders were contemplating intervening or that Chinese troops already had moved into North Korea. See Schnabel and Watson, 258.
13. Schnabel and Watson, 244–45.
14. *Military Situation in the Far East,* 19.

15. Schnabel and Watson, 247. After the failure of the U.S. attempt to conquer North Korea, the administration sought to downplay or even deny its original intent. Dean Acheson, in his memoirs, written nineteen years later, wrote: "No opposing military force remained in the North to frustrate UN efforts, and the chances were believed good that neither Russian nor Chinese troops would intervene if only [South] Korean soldiery attempted to establish whatever degree of order was possible in the rugged country of the extreme north. . . . If the [South] Koreans encountered too heavy resistance, they could fall back to the strong positions across the neck [of North Korea between Pyongyang and Wonsan]. See Acheson, 454. George Marshall, secretary of defense, testified before the Senate committee hearings in May 1951 that the UN resolution of October 7, 1950, authorized in a "somewhat oblique fashion" military operations north of the parallel, but did not require them, and that it set forth unification "as a political, rather than a military objective." See *Military Situation in the Far East*, 361–62. Acheson's and Marshall's comments are also given in Schnabel and Watson, 246–47.

16. Appleman, 608; *New York Times*, October 2, 1950, 3; Harrison E. Salisbury reported in the *New York Times*, October 2, 1950, 3, that Zhou's statement received big headlines in Moscow, something it did not get in the United States.

17. K. M. Panikkar, *In Two Chinas: Memoirs of a Diplomat* (London: Allen and Unwin, 1955), 109–11.

18. Schnabel and Watson, 260–61; Truman, 362; Bradley and Blair, 569; Acheson, 452.

19. MacArthur divided UN forces on both sides of the Nangnim-sanmaek Mountains running from the coast near Wonsan north to the Yalu River. He sent three U.S. divisions (the 3rd and 7th Infantry and the 1st Marines) and two South Korean divisions in 10th Corps east of the mountains and the 8th Army west of them. The mountains, some peaks reaching six thousand feet, were twenty to thirty miles wide and were impassable for any military movements across them. The mountains separated northeastern Korea from western Korea. MacArthur thus failed to concentrate his forces in the face of the enemy. If the three American divisions had been consolidated with the 8th Army west of the mountains, the catastrophe that struck the 8th Army might have been prevented or mitigated. The two South Korean divisions could have advanced in northeastern Korea toward the Soviet border close to the safety of the sea. This is what they did anyway, and they were never in danger of being surrounded.

20. The question naturally occurs: why did the general who conceived the highly imaginative invasion of Inchon order such an inferior, uninspired plan to conquer North Korea only a short time later? There is no easy answer to this problem. MacArthur showed some bold strokes in leading Allied forces across New Guinea to the Philippines in World War II, but nothing comparable to the Inchon land-

ing. The conclusion must be that MacArthur had a stroke of insight that showed him the possibilities available at Inchon, and he insisted on carrying them out. But Inchon was clearly a onetime inspiration. For example, he made no plans to exploit the success of Inchon by driving across Korea after the capture of Seoul, to seal off escape routes of the fleeing North Korean Army. He simply stopped at Seoul. MacArthur thus was not a true military genius on the order of Napoléon or Stonewall Jackson. Both commanders constantly conceived creative solutions, to all military challenges they faced. Stonewall Jackson, for example, solved one strategic or tactical dilemma after another in the Shenandoah Valley campaign of 1862, leaving the Union commanders constantly baffled as to what he would do next. See Bevin Alexander, *Sun Tzu at Gettysburg* (New York: W. W. Norton, 2011), 71–107.

21. Truman, 362–63.

22. Acheson, 456.

23. Truman, 364–65.

24. Ibid., 366. The text of the Truman-MacArthur conference on Wake Island is given in Rovere and Schlesinger, 253–63.

25. Peng Dehuai, *Memoirs of a Chinese Marshal* (Beijing: Foreign Languages Press, 1984), vol. 2, 472. In his account, Peng Dehuai always referred to the troops he commanded as "Chinese People's Volunteers." See also Wu Xuguang, Wang Yan, He Ding, Jiang Baohua, Zhang Xi, *A Single Spark Can Start a Prairie Fire* editorial department, *Biographies of PLA Generals*, vol. 3, *Peng Dehuai* (Beijing: Liberation Army Publishing House, 1986), chapter 6, translated from the Chinese by Ellis L. Melvin, Tamaroa, Illinois 62888.

26. General MacArthur complained bitterly that the Chinese Communists possessed a "privileged sanctuary" in China, especially Manchuria, where they could mass troops and where their aircraft could flee when pursued by American jet fighters. His attitude gained a lot of support among the military, on Capitol Hill, and among the public at large. It was, however, a spurious argument because the very nature of tacit agreement limiting the war to Korea gave *both* sides "privileged sanctuaries." The Chinese made no attempt to contest UN use of Japan and Okinawa for troop supply, reinforcements, and for air combat sorties against the Communists. The Chinese Communists also never challenged UN air supremacy behind UN lines in Korea, although UN aircraft dominated the skies over North Korea and methodically bombed and strafed everything in the north with any conceivable military value. Skies over the front lines and behind them were almost always clear of Communist aircraft. General Omar Bradley in the 1951 Senate committee hearings on the Far East said the Communists "are not bombing our ports and supply installations and are not bombing our troops." See Alexander, *Korea*, 290–91 and 524, endnote 13; *Military Situation in the Far East*, 878–79.

27. George, 127.

28. Montross and Canzona, vol. 3, 92–93.

29. The account on Chinese weapons and tactics is based on First Lieutenant Bevin R. Alexander, "Enemy Materiel," 5th Historical Detachment, 8th Army, National Archives; Montross and Canzona, vol. 3, 91–94; and a study by S. L. A. Marshall, "CCF in the Attack," 8th Army Staff Memorandum, ORS-S-26, January 5, 1951.

30. Appleman, 677.

31. Schnabel, 234.

32. Schnabel and Watson, 281; *Military Situation in the Far East*, 3427.

33. Appleman, 762. See also *New York Times*, November 6, 1950.

34. Schnabel and Watson, 302.

35. Ibid., 300–301.

36. Truman, 378–80; Schnabel and Watson, 305–06.

37. Appleman, 762; Schnabel and Watson, 312; Schnabel, 265.

38. The declaration of the Chinese Communist Party was widely disseminated under the heading "Aid Korea, Protect Our Homes." Here is the statement: "The situation today is very clear. The U.S. imperialists are copying the old trick of the Japanese bandits—first invading Korea and then invading China. Everyone knows that Korea is a small country, but that its strategic position is very important. Just as with the Japanese imperialists in the past, the main objective of the U.S. aggression on Korea is not Korea itself, but China. History shows us that the existence of the Korean People's Republic [North Korea] and its fall and the security or danger of China are closely intertwined. The one cannot be safeguarded without the other. It is not only the moral duty of the people of China to support the Korean people's war against U.S. aggression, but it is also closely related to the necessity of self-defense. To save our neighbor is to save ourselves. To defend our fatherland, we must support the people of Korea. . . . We hold that the Korean question should be solved in a peaceful way and that the aggressive forces of the imperialists should be withdrawn from Korea. But the American imperialists and their accomplices were not only unwilling to withdraw their aggressive forces, halt the war of aggression, and settle the Korean question in a peaceful way, but, on the contrary, frenziedly pushed the aggressive war northward across the 38th parallel toward the Chinese border—the Yalu and the Tumen rivers. Thus we have been forced to realize the fact that if lovers of peace in the world desire to have peace, they must use positive action to resist atrocities and halt aggression." See *People's China (Beijing)* 2, no. 10 (November 16, 1950), 4–5.

39. Acheson, 466.

40. Schnabel and Watson, 282.

41. Schnabel, 272; Schnabel and Watson, 322.

42. Schnabel and Watson, 331.

43. Acheson, 468.

44. Appleman, 606, 768.

45. The narrative on the Chinese counteroffensive against the 8th Army is based on *Report in War Diary*, "The 2nd Infantry Division and the Korean Campaign," vol. 3 (part 1), 1 November 1950–30 November 1950, Historical Section, G-2, Hq 2d Infantry Division; *War Diary*, 1 U.S. Army Corps, 1 November 1950–30 November 1950; *War Diary, Headquarters, IX Corps, U.S. Army*, 1 November 1950–30 November 1950; *Joint Chiefs of Staff Highlights of the Korean Situation*, 24–25 Nov 50, et seq.; *2nd Infantry Division Command Report*, 1 December 1950–31 December 1950, all in the National Archives.

46. The full story of the American attempt to conquer North Korea is told in Alexander, *Korea*, 228–378.

47. *Military Situation in the Far East*, 3536–39; *New York Times*, December, 26, 1950. MacArthur had been explicitly prohibited from sending troops or aircraft over the Chinese and Soviet borders in a directive sent by the Joint Chiefs and approved by President Truman on June 29, 1950. The directive included the following sentence: "Special care will be taken to insure that operations in North Korea stay well clear of the frontiers of Manchuria or the Soviet Union." See Schnabel and Watson, 109, 520.

CHAPTER 8 RETURN TO CONTAINMENT

1. Manchester, 616.

2. Schnabel and Watson, 349, cite National Archives, *Public Papers, Truman, 1950*, 724, 726–27. The president's formal statement also is printed in *Military Situation in the Far East*, 3496–97.

3. Schnabel and Watson, 349.

4. Truman, 396.

5. *New York Times*, December 3, 1950, 1.

6. Schnabel and Watson, 351, cite FRUS, *Korea, 1950*, 1276–82.

7. Both are printed in *Military Situation in the Far East*, 3532–35. See also Manchester, 614; Spanier, 150.

8. Rovere and Schlesinger, 154–55.

9. *Military Situation in the Far East*, 3496.

10. Schnabel and Watson, 363–64; Acheson, 471–72.

11. Schnabel and Watson, 370–78. The official record of the British-American talks is contained in FRUS, *Korea, 1950*. Truman's communiqué regarding his conference with Clement Attlee is given in *Military Situation in the Far East*, 3501–04.

12. Schnabel and Watson, 376.

13. This decision actually occurred at a joint State-Defense conference on December 3, 1950, the day before the British-American talks started. The conferees agreed on the need for a cease-fire, and Dean Rusk, assistant secretary of state, proposed

confining any cease-fire to an agreement to reestablish a line at the 38th parallel. Thus, the United States officially abandoned its resolve to conquer North Korea. The British-American talks confirmed this decision. See Schnabel and Watson, 358–61.

14. A full summary of the British-American talks is given in ibid., 370–78.
15. Schnabel and Watson, 380; *New York Times,* December 8, 1950, 1.
16. Schnabel and Watson, 385, cite *Department of State Bulletin,* January 15, 1951, 115–16.
17. Schnabel and Watson, 399–400.
18. Dodge, Theodore Ayrault, *Hannibal: A History of the Art of War among the Carthaginians and Romans,* (Breinigsville, Penn.: Nabu Public Domain Reprints, 2011), 96.

CHAPTER 9 THE SEARCH FOR A WAY OUT

1. Manchester, 612–13.
2. Schnabel and Watson, 359–60.
3. Ibid., 336–37.
4. Ibid., 346.
5. Ibid., 397–99.
6. In the first week of April 1951, U.S. intelligence identified nine Chinese armies totaling twenty-seven divisions and tentatively identified ten more armies with thirty divisions. They also identified eighteen North Korean divisions. Casualties had reduced these forces, but at full strength the Chinese armies amounted to 570,000 men, and the North Koreans to about 150,000. See Alexander, *Korea,* 402.
7. Ridgway, 93–96.
8. Schnabel, 317.
9. Schnabel and Watson, 408–10.
10. MacArthur's full statement is contained in Schnabel and Watson, 410–12.
11. Acheson, 515.
12. Schnabel and Watson, 415–16.
13. Ibid., 416–19. In case open war developed between the United States and China, the Joint Chiefs said the United States should do the following: (1) preserve the combat effectiveness of U.S. forces and stabilize the situation in Korea or evacuate to Japan if forced out of Korea; (2) limit ground forces in the Far East to those already committed, if possible; (3) expedite the buildup of Japanese defense forces; (4) move troops from Korea, if necessary, to defend Japan; (5) intensify an economic blockade of China; (6) impose a naval blockade of China if conditions so dictate; (7) remove restrictions on air reconnaissance of China coastal areas and of Manchuria; (8) remove restrictions on Chinese Nationalist troops and give assistance to help their operations; (9) continue to bomb military targets in Korea; (10) press for UN action branding China as an aggressor; (11) send a military training mis-

sion to Taiwan and increase aid to the Nationalists; (12) furnish covert aid to Nationalist guerrilla forces in China; (13) initiate naval and air attacks on China when Chinese Reds attack any U.S. forces outside of Korea.

14. Ibid., 428–29; the text is also given in *Department of State Bulletin,* January 29, 1951, 164.
15. Ibid., 429; Acheson, 513.
16. Acheson, 513; *New York Times,* January 13, 1951, 9; January 16, 1951, 9; January 17, 1951, 1.
17. Acheson, 513; Schnabel and Watson, 431, 433; *Department of State Bulletin,* January 29, 1951, 166–69, 192–93; February 5, 1951, 235–36.
18. Schnabel and Watson, 432–39.
19. Collins, 255; Schnabel and Watson, 438.
20. Schnabel and Watson, 436.
21. Ibid., 437–39.
22. Ibid., 439–40.
23. Manchester, 618; Acheson, 474–75.
24. Ridgway, 105–23.
25. Ibid., 109.

CHAPTER 10 MACARTHUR STOPS A CEASE-FIRE

1. Schnabel and Watson, 468–69.
2. Schnabel, 357–58.
3. Schnabel and Watson, 525.
4. Truman, 439–40.
5. Ibid., 440–41; *Military Situation in the Far East,* 3541–42; *New York Times,* March 24, 1951.
6. Spanier, 201–02.
7. Bradley and Blair, 626.
8. Manchester, 617.
9. *Military Situation in the Far East,* 3365.
10. Truman, 441–42.
11. Spanier, 206; *Military Situation in the Far East,* 1774–75.
12. Manchester, 638.
13. *Military Situation in the Far East,* 3543–44.
14. Bradley and Blair, 629.
15. Manchester, 639–40.
16. These sources are the basis for the following narrative regarding the decision on MacArthur: Truman, 445–48; Collins, 271–87; Acheson, 521–24; Schnabel, 364–77; Schnabel and Watson, 536–46; Bradley and Blair, 624–39; Manchester, 635–44.
17. Truman, 444.

18. Schnabel and Watson, 545–46. The full statement is also printed in *Military Situation in the Far East*, 3546–47.
19. *Military Situation in the Far East*, 26.
20. Matthew B. Ridgway as told to Harold H. Martin in *Soldier* (New York: Harper and Brothers, 1956), 223.

CHAPTER 11 RETURN OF THE HERO

1. The full text of Truman's address to the nation on April 11, 1951, is given in Rovere and Schlesinger, 264–69, and also in *Military Situation in the Far East*, 3547–52.
2. Spanier, 211–12.
3. Ibid.
4. Ibid., 213–14.
5. Rovere and Schlesinger, 179–82.
6. Ibid., 179.
7. Spanier, 216.
8. The full text of MacArthur's address before Congress is given in Rovere and Schlesinger, 270–77, and also in *Military Situation in the Far East*, 3553–58.
9. This sentence has come to be closely identified with MacArthur. On January 9, 2012, the University of Alabama defeated Louisiana State University 21–0 in the football national title game. In doing so, it claimed its sixth MacArthur Bowl, breaking the tie it held with the University of Notre Dame. The MacArthur Bowl, established in 1959 by the National Football Foundation, is made of four hundred ounces of silver and named after Douglas MacArthur, a founding member of the National Football Foundation. Engraved on the bowl is General MacArthur's quote, "There is no substitute for victory." See *On Point: The Journal of Army History* 17, no. 4 (spring 2012), 64.

CHAPTER 12 NO VINDICATION IN CONGRESS

1. *Military Situation in the Far East*, 38–40.
2. Ibid., 21.
3. Ibid.
4. Schnabel and Watson, 334; Schnabel, 273; Appleman, 751, 758. MacArthur had also estimated that he was facing about eighty-three thousand North Koreans. This figure was too high, but irrespective of size, the North Korean Army was very weak because it possessed few weapons. The Soviet Union and the Chinese Communists as yet had provided North Korea few new weapons. In the event, the North Koreans played a minuscule role in the counteroffensive of November and December, 1950.

5. Schnabel and Watson, 322.

6. Ibid., 329; MacArthur, 372–73.

7. Alexander, *Korea*, 312; *New York Times*, November 24, 1950, 1.

8. MacArthur, 372–73.

9. Schnabel and Watson, 329–30.

10. *Military Situation in the Far East*, 3495.

11. Schnabel and Watson, 337.

12. Alexander, *Korea*, 318, 356–57, 366–67; 2nd Infantry Division Command Report, 1 December 1950–31 December 1950, in the National Archives; Montross and Canzona, vol. 3, 277–359; November War Diary summaries, Headquarters X Corps, 1 November–30 November 1950; Headquarters, X Corps, Special Report on Hungnam Evacuation, 9–24 December 1950; Headquarters X Corps, Command Report for December 1950, in the National Archives. Manchester, 580, gives final casualty figures for Inchon as 536 dead, 2,550 wounded, and 65 missing. These figures refer to the entire operation, from the Inchon landing through the capture of Seoul. Most U.S. casualties occurred in the assault on Seoul, not in the Inchon landing. Official Defense Department figures for the period September 15, 1950, through October 6, 1950, (Seoul had been captured by September 28) show 10,250 total casualties. For the period from November 24, 1950, to January 5, 1951, which encompasses the Chinese counteroffensive, total casualties were 11,685. These figures include both 10th Corps and 8th Army. See *Military Situation in the Far East*, 3279–87. While losses in these two periods were roughly comparable, a large part of the casualties during the Inchon campaign period were suffered by the 8th Army, whose operations along the Naktong and in the advance northward after the North Korean collapse were entirely separate from the Inchon invasion and capture of Seoul.

13. *Military Situation in the Far East*, 39–40.

14. Ibid., 13–14, 40, 42; Spanier, 223.

15. *Military Situation in the Far East*, 13–14, 26–28, 69–71, 3556–57.

16. Ibid., 735–36, 738. In their conference with MacArthur on January 15, 1951, in Tokyo, Collins and Vandenberg, army and air force chiefs of staff, told MacArthur specifically that the January 12 memo was tentative and was still under study. See Schnabel and Watson, 433; *Military Situation in the Far East*, 1189, 1210–11 (Collins testimony); 1408–09 (Vandenberg testimony).

17. *Military Situation in the Far East*, 324, 329–41.

18. Ibid., 323.

19. Ibid., 324–25, 329–41.

20. Ibid., 1378–79.

21. McLellan, 168–69.

22. Spanier, 259.

23. *Military Situation in the Far East*, 733.

24. Ibid., 325.
25. Ibid., 730–31.
26. Ibid., 731–32.
27. Ibid., 733.
28. Ibid., 878–79.
29. Ibid., 3119–33, 3135–64, 3561–605.
30. Acheson, 524.

EPILOGUE THE TRIUMPH OF CIVILIAN CONTROL

1. Manchester, 6.
2. *Military Situation in the Far East,* 45.
3. Ibid., 289.
4. *Military Situation in the Far East,* 3556–57.
5. James, 616–17; Manchester, 639–40, 661.
6. Truman, 441–42.
7. Ibid., 444.
8. *Military Situation in the Far East,* 878–79.

SELECTED BIBLIOGRAPHY

Acheson, Dean. *Present at the Creation.* New York: W. W. Norton, 1969.

Alexander, Bevin. *Korea: The First War We Lost.* New York: Hippocrene, 1986, 2000.

_____. *How America Got It Right.* New York: Crown, 2005.

_____. *How Great Generals Win.* New York: W. W. Norton, 1993, 2002.

Appleman, Roy E. *South to the Naktong, North to the Yalu, The United States in the Korean War.* Office of the Chief of Military History. Washington: U.S. Government Printing Office, 1961, 1975.

Barnett, A. Doak. *China and the Major Powers in East Asia.* Washington: Brookings Institution, 1977.

Bong-youn Choy. *Korea: A History.* Rutland, Vt.: Charles E. Tuttle, Co., 1971.

Bradley, Omar N., and Clay Blair. *A General's Life, an Autobiography.* New York: Simon & Schuster, 1983.

Cambridge History of China. Denis Twitchett and John K. Fairbank, general eds. Cambridge: Cambridge University Press. Vol. 12, *Republican China 1912–1949, Part 1,* 1983. Vol. 13, *Republican China 1912–1949, Part 2,* 1986. Vol. 14, *The People's Republic, Part 1: The Emergence of Revolutionary China 1949–1965,* 1987.

Collins, J. Lawton. *War in Peacetime: The History and Lessons of Korea.* Boston: Houghton Mifflin, 1969.

Dallek, Robert. *Franklin D. Roosevelt and American Foreign Policy, 1932–45.* New York: Oxford University Press, 1979.

Davies, John Paton Jr. *Dragon by the Tail.* New York: W. W. Norton, 1972.

Dulles, Foster Rhea. *American Policy Toward Communist China, 1949–1969.* New York: Thomas Y. Crowell Company, 1972.

Feis, Herbert. *The China Tangle*. Princeton, N.J.: Princeton University Press, 1953.

Foreign Relations of the United States (FRUS) (Department of State). *United States Relations with China, with Special Reference to the Period 1944–1949*. Washington: Government Printing Office:

White Paper. Published 1949

China, 1944. Vol. VI. Published 1967.

China, 1945. Vol. VII, The Far East China, 1945. Published 1969.

Yalta. The Conferences at Malta and Yalta, 1945. Published 1955.

Potsdam. Conference of Berlin (Potsdam), 1945, 2 vols. Published 1960.

China, 1946. Vols. IX, X, The Far East: China, 1946. Published 1972.

China, 1947. Vol. VII, The Far East: China, 1947. Published 1972.

China, 1948. Vols. VII, VIII, The Far East: China, 1948. Published 1973.

China, 1949. Vols. VIII, IX, The Far East: China, 1949. Published 1978 (Vol. VIII), 1974 (Vol. IX).

East Asia, 1950. Vol. VI, East Asia and the Pacific, 1950. Published 1976.

Korea, 1950. Vol. VII, Korea, 1950. Published 1976.

Korea and China, 1951. Vol. VII, Korea and China, 1951 (in two parts). Published 1983.

China and Japan, 1952–54. Vol. XIV, China and Japan, 1952–54 (in two parts). Published 1985.

Gaddis, John Lewis. *George F. Kennan: An American Life*. New York: The Penguin Press, 2011.

George, Alexander L. *The Chinese Communist Army in Action: The Korean War and Its Aftermath*. New York: Columbia University Press, 1967.

Halberstam, David. *The Fifties*. New York: Villard Books, 1993.

James, D. Clayton. *The Years of MacArthur*. Vol. 3, *Triumph and Disaster: 1945–1964*. Boston: Houghton Mifflin, 1985.

MacArthur, General of the Army Douglas. *Reminiscences*. New York: McGraw-Hill Book Company, 1964.

Manchester, William. *American Caesar: Douglas MacArthur 1880–1964*. New York: Back Bay Books, 2008.

McLellan, David S. *Dean Acheson: The State Department Years.* New York: Dodd, Mead and Co., 1976.

Military Situation in the Far East. U.S. 82nd Congress, Senate, Committees on Armed Services and Foreign Relations. *Hearings, Military Situation in the Far East, 1951.* Found on the Web at Hathi Trust Digital Library—Holdings, catalog.hathitrust.org/Record/001606736.

Montross, Lynn, and Capt. Nicholas A. Canzona (USMC). *U.S. Marine Operations in Korea, 1950–1953,* 5 vols. Washington: Historical Branch, G-3, Headquarters, U.S. Marines Corps, 1954.

Murphy, Lt. Col. E. Lloyd, U.S. Army. *The U.S./U.N. Decision to Cross the 38th Parallel, October 1950. A Case Study of Changing Objectives in Limited War.* Air War College Research Report No. 3660. Maxwell Air Base, Ala.: Air War College, 1968.

National Archives. *Public Papers of the President of the United States of America, Harry S. Truman, 1950.* Washington: U.S. Government Printing Office, 1965.

Paige, Glenn D. *The Korean Decision* (June 24–30, 1950). New York: Free Press, 1968.

Pearlman, Michael D. *Truman & MacArthur: Policy, Politics, and the Hunger for Honor and Renown.* Bloomington: Indiana University Press, 2008.

Ridgway, General Matthew B. *The Korean War.* Garden City, N.Y.: Doubleday & Co., 1967.

Romanus, Charles F. and Riley Sunderland. *United States Army in World War II. China-Burma-India Theater.* Center of Military History, U.S. Army. Washington: U.S. Government Printing Office. *Stilwell's Mission to China,* 1987 (first published 1953). *Stilwell's Command Problems,* 1985 (first published 1956).

Rovere, Richard H., and Arthur Schlesinger Jr. *General MacArthur and President Truman: The Struggle for Control of American Foreign Policy.* New Brunswick, N.J.: Transaction Publishers, 1992. Originally published as *The General and the President.* New York: Farrar, Straus, and Giroux, 1951.

Schaller, Michael. *The U.S. Crusade in China, 1938–1945.* New York: Columbia University Press, 1979.

Schnabel, James F. *Policy and Direction: The First Year, United States Army in the Korean War.* Office of the Chief of Military History. Washington: U.S. Government Printing Office, 1972, 1978.

Schnabel, James F., and Robert J. Watson. *The History of the Joint Chiefs of Staff, The Joint Chiefs of Staff and National Policy.* Vol. 3, *The Korean War, Part 1* (1978) and *Part 2* (1979). Produced in softcover and by duplicator by the Historical Division, Joint Secretariat, Joint Chiefs of Staff, and available at Modern Military History, National Archives.

Selden, Mark. *The Yenan Way in Revolutionary China.* Cambridge, Mass.: Harvard University Press, 1971.

Snow, Edgar. *Red Star over China.* New York: Grove Press, Inc., 1973.

Spanier, John W. *The Truman-MacArthur Controversy and the Korean War.* New York: W. W. Norton, 1965.

Tierney, Dominic. *How We Fight: Crusades, Quagmires, and the American Way of War.* New York: Little, Brown, 2010.

Truman, Harry S. *Memoirs.* Vol. 2, *Years of Trial and Hope.* Garden City, N.Y.: Doubleday, 1956.

Tsou, Tang. *America's Failure in China 1941–50.* Chicago: University of Chicago Press, 1963.

Tuchman, Barbara W. *Stilwell and the American Experience in China 1911–45.* New York: Bantam Books, 1980.

Tucker, Nancy Bernkopf. *Patterns in the Dust: Chinese-American Relations and the Recognition Controversy, 1949–1950.* New York: Columbia University Press, 1983.

Wainstock, Dennis. *Truman, MacArthur, and the Korean War.* Westport, Conn.: Greenwood, 1999; New York: Enigma, 2011.

INDEX

Page numbers in *italic* indicate maps.